Index to English

Index
to
English

Eighth Edition

Wilma R. Ebbitt
David R. Ebbitt

New York   Oxford
Oxford University Press
1990

Oxford University Press

Oxford   New York   Toronto
Delhi   Bombay   Calcutta   Madras   Karachi
Petaling Jaya   Singapore   Hong Kong   Tokyo
Nairobi   Dar es Salaam   Cape Town
Melbourne   Auckland

and associated companies in
Berlin   Ibadan

Published by Oxford University Press, Inc.,
198 Madison Avenue, New York, New York 10016-4314

Oxford is a registered trademark of Oxford University Press

Library of Congress Cataloging-in-Publication Data
Ebbitt, Wilma R.
Index to English / Wilma R. Ebbitt and David R. Ebbitt.—8th ed.
p.   cm.   ISBN 0-19-505960-3 (paper)
1. English language—Rhetoric.   2. English language—Grammar—1950–
I. Ebbitt, David R., 1919–   . II. Title.
PE1411.E22   1990   808'.042—dc20   89-37564   CIP

Printing 9

Printed in the United States of America
on acid-free paper

PREFACE

In preparing this fiftieth-anniversary edition of the *Index to English,* we have
rethought and reconsidered, added and deleted, rewritten and revised, all with
the aim of offering writers sound, up-to-date information and practical advice
in a readily accessible form.

All writers face problems—choices in punctuation and mechanics, in syntax
and vocabulary, in structure and style. To say what they want to say in a
manner that earns the attention of an audience they want to reach, they must
continue making decisions as they plan and write and rewrite. They are more
likely to make wise decisions if they have on their desks a resource book that
indicates what choices are available and which choice is appropriate in the
particular context.

So that users of this handbook can find what they want quickly and easily,
we have retained from previous editions an alphabetical arrangement of articles
and an extensive system of cross-references. So that the treatment of usage will
be immediately helpful, we have kept the simple division of standard English
into formal, informal, and general. The Introduction describes the book, explains its rationale, and tells how it can be used—for course work, for individual reference, for browsing.

To help students write so that what they have to say will be understood,
respected, even enjoyed by their readers, we provide them with some rules,
remind them of certain conventions, and suggest some of the uses that can be
made of the three stylistic varieties. Recognizing that for most writers the practical functions of informal English are sharply limited and that the occasions
when strictly formal English is required are few, we recommend that they set
out to master general American English, the variety of English that all educated
Americans read and that all need to be able to write. Because general English
is the English that we read in school, at work, and for relaxation, its rules and
conventions make sense to us: we are accustomed to seeing them applied. The
great majority of the illustrative passages in the *Index*—many of them new ones
drawn from books, learned journals, popular magazines, and newspapers for
this edition—represent this most useful and versatile variety of our language.

On the issue of standards, we endorse neither anarchy nor absolutism. We don't believe that writers should be encouraged to think that just any rush, or gush, of words on paper necessarily has value. Nor do we believe that they should be misled into thinking that there is only one Good English—the Good English that demands observance of all the rules embalmed in prescriptive handbooks and guides to linguistic etiquette.

On certain specific matters, we offer unequivocal advice. In the articles keyed to the correction chart, we have made the *Index* as prescriptive as honesty and realism permit. But we refuse to condemn as "wrong" failure to observe a rule that has never been observed consistently by gifted writers, and we think it a waste of time to keep deploring practices that (though anyone may choose *not* to adopt them) have long been accepted in widely esteemed periodicals. When a locution is considered wrong, or illiterate, or merely distasteful by a sizable number of educated readers, we say so, even if the locution is firmly established as majority usage—but we also report that it *is* majority usage. When the same locution appears regularly in publications edited by men and women of skill, taste, and intelligence, we offer an example. The writer can then decide whether or not to use it in a particular rhetorical situation.

The correction entries answer directly and explicitly such questions as "What mark of punctuation do I need here?" "Should this verb be singular or plural?" "What can I do to improve the continuity of this paragraph?" But they, too, take into account appropriateness to the writer's subject and purpose and audience, and to the writer's self. And in most of the entries relating to usage, style, and rhetorical strategies, appropriateness is the primary criterion writers are urged to apply.

In usage entries, after identifying the current status of a locution—standard or nonstandard; if standard, formal, informal, or general—we often include the alternatives: the *"pretty* good time" of informal and the *"fairly* good time" of general; the formal *arising* and the general *getting up*. The Introduction makes clear that the varieties overlap and that on occasion good writers deliberately shift from one variety to another. In a paper that is predominantly in general English, then, the informal *about* may be used instead of *almost* ("I was about done") as a tactic for moving a bit closer to the reader. Here and elsewhere, we neither deny writers a choice nor simply list alternatives and invite them to take their pick. What we try to do is guide them toward making intelligent choices, choices that reflect their awareness of the rhetorical context in which they are writing, including the biases of readers they may not want to offend.

Index to English does not limit application of the labels "general," "formal," "informal" to words and phrases. It applies them as well to punctuation, to sentence patterns, to transitions, and to the styles that are the end result of the countless choices that every writer makes, deliberately or intuitively. For writing—certainly good writing—is all of a piece, and even worse than the categorical separation of words into "right" words and "wrong" is the separation of usage from style and of style from rhetoric.

Nor does the *Index* limit discussion to small writing problems that can be safely detached from the context in which they occur. Many of the entries bear on the composing of whole essays—on prewriting and getting started, on choosing details, on ways to achieve logical sequence, on organizing and developing different kinds of papers, on how to stop. And many entries, like those on grammar, usage, and the origin of words, introduce readers to broad areas of scholarship and open the door to further study.

A word about editorial procedure: In order to keep the topic of each entry in sharp focus, unnecessary words and phrases have been deleted from illustrative quotations; and when what remains is grammatically a complete sentence, it is presented without opening or closing ellipsis. To protect against the frustration of blind references, or dummy entries—like *"effect, affect*. See *affect, effect"*—every entry title is followed by at least a sentence of information. If that tells readers what they want to know, well and good. If not, they can turn to the main entry.

Our primary purpose is to offer a guide to good writing, and we believe that we can best achieve that purpose if we stick to our last. In order to maintain the focus of the *Index* and prevent the book from becoming too bulky and too costly, we have reduced coverage of documentation to some general remarks and have referred readers to specialized works on note form and bibliographical form.

Although the *Index to English* is addressed to college students in writing courses, we believe that it can serve as a ready-reference manual for all writers—experienced or inexperienced, in school or out of school—who look for information and advice as they pursue the craft.

Newport, R.I.   W.R.E.
September 1989   D.R.E.

INTRODUCTION

The big questions in writing are the ones you have to face up to first, when you set about planning and drafting a paper, and the ones you need to keep steadily in mind as you write and rewrite. Essentially they are questions of rhetoric—how to find, organize, and present your ideas so as to achieve a specific purpose as you address a specific audience on a specific topic. Questions like these:

What do I want to say on this subject?

What am I trying to accomplish in writing about it?

Who are my readers? What sort of people are they? What are their tastes and interests, their values and prejudices? What are their preconceptions about my subject? How can I persuade them to share what I think and feel about it?

What relationship do I want to establish with them? Shall I write as if I'm addressing them from a lecture platform, or shall I try for the style and tone of good talk with old friends?

But though settling on the major strategies that are the concern of rhetoric is certainly the most important job in writing, it's not always the one that gives the most trouble. Many writers find themselves puzzling longest over what words to use, how to spell them, where to place them, and how to punctuate them:

If I begin my paper with *I*, will it sound egotistical? Can I use *you* without making the reader think I'm putting words in his mouth? If I use *he* as the pronoun after *any student,* will I be accused of being sexist? Would it be better to use *he or she,* or should I avoid the issue by changing everything into the plural or by rewriting the sentence in the passive voice?

Can I open a paragraph with *and?*

Do these two ideas belong in one sentence, or should they be in two? If in one, how should they be connected? Is the relationship between them most accurately expressed by *and* or *because* or *therefore?*

What punctuation do I need here—a comma, a semicolon, or a colon?

Should I write *among* or *between, different from* or *different than, if I was going* or *if I were going, the girl I knew* or *the girl whom I knew?*

Shall I say *request* or *ask, cannot* or *can't?* Is it *flushed with anger* or *blushed with anger?*

And spelling! *It's* or *its? There* or *their? Traveled* or *travelled?*

Questions like these, especially if they are considered in isolation, can cause headaches. True, some of them have clear-cut answers, to be found in almost any dictionary. *It's,* the contraction for *it is,* is wrong when used as the possessive (*its,* not *it's,* color). *Their* and *there* have separate meanings, which should not be confused. *Traveled* and *travelled* are both correct; American dictionaries give *traveled* as first choice.

As any handbook of English would point out, the comma has certain functions that it does not share with other marks of punctuation; the semicolon has separate functions; so has the colon. But in some sentences either the comma or the semicolon is satisfactory, and in other sentences either the semicolon or the colon would do. There are conventions to be learned, habits to be established, alternatives to be noted, so that the right punctuation comes automatically or so that, when there is a choice, it will be made on sensible grounds—because it fits with other choices that were made earlier.

What is true of punctuation is often true of diction: there may be no one "right" answer to the question of which word to use. *Request* and *ask* are both correct; which word is preferable depends on the style of the paper, which in turn depends upon purpose and audience. Both *can't* and *cannot* appear regularly in print; in a specific context, one is likely to be better—because more appropriate—than the other.

In these cases and a great many more, rhetoric and style and usage intersect; for rhetoric includes style (*how* we say *what* we say), and style is the sum of many individual choices in syntax and usage and even punctuation. It is when all these choices come together to create one prevailing manner of expression that a piece of writing can be said to have a particular style.

If good writing depends upon skill in solving rhetorical problems, why do we spend so much time fussing about small, individual points of usage? Perhaps the situation is less paradoxical than it appears. Viewed in proper perspective—not as a series of *do*s and *don't*s—many questions of usage turn out to be broader questions of rhetorical strategy.

Initially, questions about usage arise because there are different varieties of English and because these varieties don't fit equally well into every social and rhetorical situation. What is appropriate in casual talk is not always appropriate on paper. What sounds natural to an audience of teenagers baffles an audience of an older generation. What amuses readers in one context alienates them in another. Knowing what kinds of English there are and recognizing how and why the alternatives differ puts you in a position to suit your style to your subject and to your audience and to the occasion. When you write English that is appropriate to the rhetorical situation, you're using the language skillfully. Good English is not just arbitrarily "good." It's good because it's right for the job.

The Varieties of English

There are many ways of classifying the English we use, both the spoken and the written. *Index to English* is concerned primarily with *written* varieties of the language in their edited form—that is, with writing that has been gone over with some care. Its purpose is to help you increase your skill and confidence in writing standard English.

Standard and nonstandard English. Standard American English is the dialect generally accepted by educated speakers and writers. Nonstandard English, the other cultural variety of the language, includes usages from numerous regional and social dialects. In speech the distinction between standard and nonstandard hinges on a number of pronunciations, words, word forms, and grammatical constructions habitually used by people of noticeably different educational backgrounds and social standings. In writing, the distinction is chiefly based on a carryover of those speech habits, with spellings taking the place of pronunciations. He et a apple; They ain't wrote us in months; She seen them kittens drownded. Nonstandard English appears in published writing chiefly in dialog and in other prose that attempts to reproduce nonstandard speech patterns. It is inappropriate in the writing that most of us are ever called on to do.

In this *Index* we divide standard English into general, formal, and informal. The labels "general," "formal," and "informal" broadly correspond to the social and rhetorical situations in which the varieties commonly occur. Since they shade into each other, with large areas of overlap, the categories should not be rigidly interpreted nor the labels rigidly applied. While some words are clearly more formal than others—*disputatious,* for example—and some more informal—like *hassle*—many can be labeled only in context. A word that stands out as inappropriately formal in one paper might, in a different one, pass as general. To say that a passage is formal, then, doesn't mean that the vocabulary and sentence structure are exclusively formal. It means that there are enough traits usually associated with that variety of the written language to give the passage a formal feel or tone even though much of it—perhaps most of it—may be general in style.

The boundaries between the varieties continue to shift, as they have been doing for hundreds of years. Today's good formal English is close to what would have been considered general English in the essays of a half century ago, while what might be called the High Formal of the 1800s has almost disappeared. General English, meanwhile, has become increasingly relaxed, taking in more and more words, phrases, and constructions from informal. Even short periods of time bring changes in the status of individual usages. A word or phrase that's looked on as informal one year may appear often enough

in well-edited publications to be considered general a year later, as the verb *bug* (to plant a secret listening device) did in the early 1970s. A formal word may catch on in general English (as *charisma* and *ambience* did), enjoy a vogue, and then either return to its source or become a permanent part of the general vocabulary. Given such short-term change, the best way to keep in touch with what's going on in the language is not by relying on dictionaries and guides to usage, which are inevitably out of date, but by reading current books and newspapers and magazines and by listening to all the voices that reach your ear, directly and by way of radio and television. As you do, you'll become increasingly aware that the language is a living, changing thing; you'll expand your range of choices; and if you read and listen intelligently and critically, you'll also increase your ability to choose well.

Formal English. Old-fashioned formal English—what we have referred to as High Formal—survives today chiefly in oratory—in some political speeches, some sermons, some eulogies and other ceremonial addresses, as at graduation time. At its best, old-fashioned formal demonstrates that the English language is a magnificent instrument that can disseminate information with clarity and precision and can spark the imagination, stir the emotions, lift up the heart. At its worst, it is empty verbal posturing, or arid, sleep-inducing pedantry, or a stiff parade of big words and stock phrasings.

   Formal written English is found today in some textbooks—particularly those for advanced courses—and in some learned journals. Outside academic circles it appears in books and articles addressed to well-educated audiences willing to make a greater intellectual effort than is called for by a good read. Formal is appropriate for writing on philosophy, religion, aesthetics, literature, theoretical science, and so forth. But though its subject matter may be intellectual and complex, its tone need not be solemn. Wit and formal English have a long history of collaboration.

   The vocabulary of formal English smacks of the literary, the scholarly, the philosophical. It includes words seldom used in ordinary conversation *(desultory, ubiquitous, importunate)* and a high proportion of nouns like *hiatus, resurgence, synthesis,* which generalize about experience rather than present it directly. For those familiar with them, the words—many from Latin—are often rich in suggestion *(omen, luminous, transcend)* or have some special appeal of sound or rhythm *(immemorial, quintessence),* while the scholarly nouns and technical terms permit the exact and concise statement of ideas.

   Though formal English uses short, compact sentences for emphasis, its typical sentence is fairly long, and the elements in it are carefully ordered. Here is a sample of current formal English on a topic that is not at all complex but that lends itself to some complexity of style:

   Persons who address letters to the editor of a newspaper or other journal are usually angry at something that has appeared there and write to express their outrage or dissent, whereas those who write to the author of a book or article generally want to tell the writer of their enjoyment and approval. This is a happy difference, for it is gratifying how often the written word generates a strong emotion in the reader and moves him to express his or her satisfaction, or the reverse, to the unknown and unseen individual behind the pen. Although authors too receive their portion of hate mail, the receipt of letters is encouraging evidence that what they have written has reached into a reader's mind and caused it to take notice and consider the matter at hand or simply enjoy the unfolding of a tale—in short, evidence that the writer's business is performing its function and the product is not left to wither in sterility on a dead page.—Barbara W. Tuchman, *American Scholar*

The three sentences, all of substantial length, move at a deliberate pace, in part the result of carefully considered pairs ("outrage or dissent," "unknown and unseen"). Other marks of formality appear in the word choice—the special meaning of *happy* in "happy difference" and the metaphorical use of "reached into." Another metaphor rounds out the paragraph with an impact quite different from that of more casual styles.

When modifiers and qualifications are placed with care, as in the following passage, the writer creates the opportunity for a climactic (and comical) effect, underlined in this case by the decidedly emphatic words in the final phrase:

But the Navy had, during the war, one characteristic that set it off from the mass of civilians: it was not, so far as I came into contact with it, manned by hysterical and demented people.—Lewis Mumford, *Findings and Keepings*

In the next sentence the prose requires more concentrated attention from the reader, combining as it does a technical vocabulary with several interruptions in syntax, all made in the interest of precision:

The attempt to establish a unilinear classification of mental deficiency, a rising scale from idiots to imbeciles to morons, embodies two common fallacies discussed in this book: the reification of intelligence as a single, measurable entity; and the assumption, extending back to Morton's skulls . . . and forward to Jensen's universal scaling of general intelligence . . . , that evolution is a tale of unilinear progress, and that a single scale ascending from primitive to advanced represents the best way of ordering variation.—Stephen Jay Gould, *The Mismeasure of Man*

Throughout this *Index* formal preferences in grammar and syntax, in usage, and in punctuation are regularly identified, not because formal English is called for in most writing but because, in school and out, some of your readers may insist that the conventions of formal English be followed. Knowing what the conventions are puts a writer in control of the rhetorical situation.

When you set out to write a paper in a formal style, you run some risks. The bad imitations of formal English called "officialese" are prize exhibits of unreadable prose, and unsuccessful literary efforts are often plagued by words selected more to impress than to inform and by styles so self-conscious that they divert attention from the content. Beyond that is the problem of sustaining a formal style—not writing just one or two neatly balanced sentences but continuing to show control of phrases and clauses, mastery of the rules of close punctuation, conservative taste in usage, and a vocabulary adequate to the demands of the subject and the style. In short, writing a successful essay in formal English is a challenging undertaking. Meeting the challenge when the occasion arises is one measure of your sophistication as a writer.

Informal English. Informal written English is the variety of standard English that most of us use naturally in letters to close friends, in diaries and journals, and in other kinds of personal, intimate expression. Writers who share no intimacy with the readers they are addressing may try to reduce the distance between themselves and their audiences by using elements of informal. Sometimes the effort succeeds; sometimes it flops.

Although actually differing a good deal from the English we use in casual, spontaneous conversation, informal written English suggests speech in several of its characteristics. It swings over a wide range, sometimes mixing vocabulary from formal English with verb forms from nonstandard. It makes free use of slang and draws on the shoptalk that develops in every occupation and the in-group vocabulary that attaches to every sport. The writer takes many syntactic shortcuts, regularly using contractions and usually skipping optional relative pronouns ("I hear he's in town" instead of "I hear that he is in town"). Some of the sentences of informal are short and elliptical ("Bet I won more than you" instead of "I'll bet that I won more than you won"); others are unusually long, with asides and afterthoughts keeping the structure loose and rambling.

In published nonfiction the extended use of informal English is mostly limited to some periodicals addressed to special audiences (rock fans, surfers, motorcyclists), to the work of determinedly personal columnists in more general publications, and to letters from readers. But when used skillfully, it can achieve remarkable effects. With vocabulary ranging from *splif* to *apocalypse* and syntax controlled more by rhythm than by convention, the reporter in the following passage captures the exhilaration of reggae in its Jamaican homeland:

> But as soon as the cricket winds down, Bulldog the Rude Boy lights up a splif the size of a sno-cone and the music comes on again, the reggae, something by Bang High and the Lionaires called "Rasta No Born Yah," Number Ten this week, and everybody all over the island's plugged into the same shuffle, the same stutter guitar and choppy drums and, most of all, the bass. All over the island windows are shifting in their sills and cups are rattling in their saucers and the gold fillings are humming in Bulldog's teeth, and one way or another everybody from the two-year-olds crawling in the garbage in Ghost Town to the 135-year-old Rasta out at the beach awaiting the imminent apocalypse, everybody's got the beat, the upbeat, everybody's all hooked up to the common throb.—Michael Thomas, *Rolling Stone*

Informal English appears in small doses in a great variety of newspapers, magazines, and books, where writers of general English use informal words and phrases to move closer to their readers. The following excerpts, from a range of sources, share the feel of informal and the personal note that is one of its chief characteristics:

When I was 10, gangs of hoods would stone us Jewish kids.—Audrey Gelis, *Ms.*

Zelda's occasional accusations that Fitzgerald was homosexual have usually been put down to the fact that she was either off her rocker or, mounted on that rocker, she was eager to wound Fitzgerald. . . . In any case, Zelda managed to so bug her husband on the subject that one day in Paris . . . he suddenly let go.—Gore Vidal, *New York Review of Books*

Meese showed no hard feelings that North gave him the swerve on such major items as the diversion of arms sales money to the Contras. . . . Miss Marple on an off-day would have done a better job.—Mary McGrory, syndicated columnist

If you have occasion—and the urge—to use informal English in your writing, you face the task of capturing the easy, casual, entertaining quality of good talk without falling into the sloppiness and vagueness that even good talk often reveals when it's fixed on paper. That calls for care and restraint.

General English. Occupying the great middle ground between formal and informal is general written English. It's the variety of standard English that educated people most often read and that they themselves most often write. The words in its vocabulary include *spacious* as well as *roomy, spacey* as well as *strange, precipitation* as well as *rainfall, nutty* as well as *eccentric, rip off* as well as *steal;* but unless there's a special reason for using the formal or informal words, *roomy, strange, rainfall, eccentric,* and *steal* will be its choices. Writers of general English are likely to use words that are concrete, close to experience, referring to things, people, actions, and events more than to abstractions. The turns of phrase reflect those of speech *(look into, give up, take over);* coordinating conjunctions like *and* and *so* are much more common than conjunctive adverbs like *furthermore* and *consequently.* Typical sentences are moderate in length, with few interrupting phrases or elaborate constructions.

General written English is much less conservative than formal, more controlled than informal. Though it's more likely than informal to follow strict conventions of subject-verb agreement, it doesn't do so as consistently as formal does. It often ignores formal distinctions, as between *can* and *may, raise* and *rear.* Yet it's slower than informal to accept slang. And while writers of general English are less conservative than writers of formal English, they may be quite as careful. Indeed, because the style is not so restricted by convention, the writer of general English has more choices to make than the formal writer does.

General English is the most versatile and the most serviceable of the three varieties of standard written English this *Index* deals with. It is the variety we use in this book, because it can reach more people than formal or informal can. For the same reason, it's the variety you will use in most of your writing while you're in college and after you've graduated. But keep alert to the opportunities informal and formal English offer you. Mixing the varieties of English is common practice in current writing. In many magazine articles, you'll find an informal phrase dropped into passages whose predominant tone is general or formal—possibly to shock readers to attention, possibly to mock them or to amuse them, possibly because the writer wants to project a new persona. Or an essay that has been light and casual may move to a thoughtful, measured, formal conclusion. The example that follows is from an essay published in *The American Scholar,* the periodical in which our first sample of formal English appeared. The dominant style of the essay is general-to-formal; but the piece is neither solemn nor weighty, and the mixed usage contributes to its lighthearted tone:

> In bringing up boyhood with regard to gambling, I am, I fear, playing into the strong hand of the Freudians. This is a dangerous thing to do, for those guys will sandbag you and whipsaw you.—Joseph Epstein, *American Scholar*

Sudden shifts in style that have no discernible motive are distracting and suggest that the writer has lost control. Sometimes writers do. But good writers know what they're doing: by calling attention to *what* they're saying by the *way* they say it, they make shifts in style perform double duty. Even though most of your writing may be general, then, the more you acquaint yourself with the alternatives that formal and informal English offer, the better you will be able to use them when you want to achieve rhetorical effects that rely on contrasts in style.

Using *Index to English*

Index to English applies the principles of usage described in this Introduction. Because it deals with English as it exists—in publications addressed to educated audiences, as well as in writing by students—many of its articles don't offer a simple Right and Wrong, Do and Don't. Often they give both the formal choice and the general choice, sometimes the informal choice as well. When you have a particular job of writing to do, with a particular audience in mind, the relevance of the choices will come clear.

The articles in the *Index* are alphabetically arranged. They fall roughly into six categories, with some overlapping:

1. Entries on particular words and constructions like *among, between; definitely; like, as; who, whom; not about to.* Information about the standing of a locution in current usage is often supported by examples quoted from newspapers, popular magazines, scholarly journals, and books. (The fact that something is printed doesn't mean that it's recommended; bad writing may appear in respectable publications.) Read the article to see where the locution is placed among the varieties of English, and then decide whether it fits your style in the particular rhetorical situation. The titles for entries on words and phrases are the only ones that are not capitalized.

2. Entries on grammar, offering definitions and discussions of standard grammatical terms and concepts—Collective nouns, for example, and Restrictive and nonrestrictive modifiers, Relative clauses, Subjunctive mood, and the parts of speech.

3. Entries on composition, rhetoric, and style. (Many of the entries in the sixth category also belong in this group.) Prewriting, Beginning, Thesis statement, Organization, Outline form, Paragraphs, Coherence, Transition, Emphasis, Unity, and Ending—these and other entries carry you through the stages of writing a paper. Some entries deal with specific topics in rhetoric—Argument, Cause and effect, Classification and division, Comparison and contrast, Definition, Deduction, Description, Fallacies, Induction, Logical thinking, Narration. Style is treated more directly in such entries as Abstract language, Adjectives and style, Adverbs and style, Conjunctions and style, Diction, Figures of speech, Infinitives and style, Nominalization, Parallelism and style, Periodic sentence, Phrases and style, and Prepositions and style.

4. Entries offering information and advice on a range of topics that are useful in special writing situations—Business letters, Research papers, Technical writing, and so on.

5. Entries about language and language study, such as British English, Origin of words, Sexist language, and Usage.

6. Entries to be used in correcting and revising papers. Signaled by abbreviations in longhand, these entries are listed in the correction charts on the inside front and back covers of this book. They offer straightforward advice—practical *dos* and *don't*s. Go to them when your corrected papers have been returned to you, but also get in the habit of consulting them *before* you submit your essays, while you're in the process of revising your first drafts. Checking what you've written against their instructions and illustrations will help you decide whether you've punctuated a sentence correctly, used the expected case of a pronoun, made clear what a modifier relates to.

Refer to the *Index* when you're faced with a writing assignment (see Prewriting), as you write, as you revise what you've written, and when your corrected essay is returned to you for further revision. Besides following up the cross-references that most entries contain, look up any term you come upon that is new or unclear to you—*modal auxiliaries,* for example, or *deep structure*. Most such terms are explained in entries of their own.

Index to English is intended to be more than a reference work for students. It's meant to be browsed in and annotated. By updating the slang and vogue words and by noting changes in usage, fresh figures of speech, allusions, and turns of phrase, you can keep the *Index* alive at the same time that you keep yourself in touch with your language.

Index to English

a, an

Use *a* before all words beginning with a consonant sound: a business, a D, a European trip, a usage. Use *an* before all words beginning with a vowel sound, including words that begin with an *h* that's not pronounced: an apple, an F, an uncle, an honor, an hour.

In words beginning with *h* that are not accented on the first syllable, like *histo'rian, hyster'ical,* the *h* used to be silent, so *an* preceded such words. Today, though Americans often pronounce the *h,* some still say and write "an historian," "an hysterical witness," "an habitual set of choices" (Josephine Miles, *College Composition and Communication*). Even if you don't sound the *h* when you speak, *a* is preferred to *an* by guides to good writing: The Jews had a historic task. But usage is divided.

When you use a series of singular nouns, you may want to repeat *a* or *an* before each one in order to give emphasis to each—"All of the village was of a piece, a time, and a style" (Shirley Jackson, *We Have Always Lived in the Castle*)—or you may run them together with *a* or *an* before only the first noun: Soon she had bought a skirt, shirt, and scarf.

See *half; kind, sort 2.*

ab Abbreviations

Write in full the word or words inappropriately abbreviated. Or use the correct form of the abbreviation marked.

1. Appropriateness. Abbreviations are used to save space in manuals, reference books, business and legal documents, scholarly footnotes, and some other kinds of writing. You can also use them in informal writing—notes for your own use, letters to friends. In general and formal writing, use only those abbreviations that are fully established in standard usage (see **2**) or that regularly occur in discussions of a particular subject.

2. Standard abbreviations. Always use the abbreviations *Dr., Mr., Mrs.* with names. (A comparable term, *Ms.,* is technically not an abbreviation but a com-

3

bination of *Miss* and *Mrs.*) A number of abbreviations, such as *St.* (see **saint**), B.C. and A.D., A.M. and P.M., *Jr.* for Junior, and initial letters for government agencies like CIA and SEC, are standard. In formal writing, titles like Professor, President, Senator, and the Reverend are not abbreviated, nor are naval and military ranks. In general writing they may be abbreviated when initials or given names are used: Professor Hylander *or* Prof. G. W. Hylander (*but not* Prof. Hylander).

3. Period with abbreviations. Where standard practice requires a period after an abbreviation, omitting it (*p* instead of *p.* for *page* in a footnote) is a careless slip. Use only one period at the end of a sentence: The abbreviation for both *saint* and *street* is *St.*

Increasingly, periods are omitted from abbreviations that are used in place of the words they stand for *(FBI, AFL-CIO, CBS, GNP, ID, IQ, CD, VCR, hp, kwh, rpm).* In addressing letters, don't use periods with the two-letter abbreviations for states adopted by the Postal Service *(PA, TX).*

For abbreviations of dates, see **Months.** Compare **Acronyms, Contractions, Numbers.**

ability to

The idiom is *ability* plus a *to* infinitive (ability *to* do): He has the ability to design (*not* of designing) beautiful buildings. You can often express the idea better with an adjective or a verb: He is able to (*or* He can) design beautiful buildings; He designs beautiful buildings. See **Idiom.**

able to

Avoid using a passive infinitive (like *to be done* or *to be ended*) after *able:* This was not able to be done because of lack of time. Instead write: This could not be done because of lack of time. Or: They were not able to do this because of lack of time (*or* because they didn't have time).

about

About has a variety of uses. Check the following for trouble spots:

1. about–around. In describing physical position, *about* and *around* are nearly interchangeable, though *around* is more common: They wandered about (*or* around) the town. In the sense of "nearly" or "approximately," *about* is more common (about 70°), but both are standard American usage. In telling time, *around* (around two o'clock) is considered more informal.

2. about–almost. In the sense of "almost" (about finished), *about* is standard but somewhat informal.

3. at about. Some writers avoid *at about* on the grounds that something must be either *at* or *about*. But *about* in *at about* is being used as an adverb, and the preposition-adverb pattern is well established: at approximately noon; in about ten minutes.

4. about to. *About to* is a convenient idiom for "on the point of": She was about to make a third try. The negative *not about to* (an emphatic "not going to") is more informal: I'm not about to sign up for a class at that hour.

above

Using *above* as an adverb in such phrases as "the evidence cited above" and using it as an adjective (the above prices) and as a noun (the above is confirmed) are fully established as standard; and though some writers of formal English avoid using *above* as an adjective, others use it freely: "for a comment on the above use of the word 'claims' . . ." (Theodore Bernstein, *Watch Your Language*). In many business, legal, and other technical contexts, all three uses of *above*—as adverb, adjective, and noun—would be entirely acceptable. In general and formal writing they would bother some readers.

absent

As a substitute for "in the absence of" or "without," *absent* (Absent an economic miracle, taxes will rise) offers no obvious advantage and, to some, suggests bureaucratic jargon.

Absolute phrases

An absolute phrase modifies all the rest of the sentence it appears in, not just a word or group of words: *The battle lost,* the army surrendered.

Absolute phrases are economical, offering a compact way of singling out details of a scene or relating parts to a whole: He came downstairs looking much the worse for wear, *eyes bloodshot, shirt rumpled, tie askew*. But their somewhat formal quality makes them seem out of place in casual writing: *The long day finally at an end,* the kids went to bed. And absolute phrases that contain auxiliaries *(being, having, having been)* may be cumbersome: *The description of the scene having been completed,* the stage is set for the crucial action. A dependent clause is often smoother and sometimes more precise: After the scene has been described . . .

Some absolute phrases have been used so often that they've become fixed formulas, or idioms: all things considered, this being the case, God willing.

See **Dangling modifiers, Idiom.**

Absolutes, comparison of

Logically, absolutes like *perfect* and *final* can't be more or most, less or least. But see **Comparison of adjectives and adverbs 4.**

abst Abstract language

Make this word or passage more concrete or more specific.

Abstract words refer to emotions, qualities, concepts, relationships: *love, courage, square root, symmetry.* They contrast with concrete words like *kiss, lion, computer, hoop,* which refer to things we can see or touch or otherwise perceive with our senses.

Abstract terms are essential in communicating ideas, and abstract language can be just as precise as concrete language. But if you rely too much on abstract vocabulary, your papers may seem to lose contact with human experience. To keep your rhetorical feet on the ground, follow these suggestions:

1. Provide concrete examples. If you're writing about courage, describe a brave act, or contrast a brave act with a cowardly one. The shift from the concept to the example will make it natural to use concrete terms. Or follow an abstract statement with a concrete expression of the same idea:

> The survey's assumption that the bodily symptoms in question are indicators of psychological distress leads to the conclusion that the working class tends to somatize its emotional troubles, whereas the middle class experiences them more directly. In other words, clammy hands and upset stomach are apt to be the poor man's substitute for angst.—Charles J. Rolo, *Atlantic*

2. Replace general terms with specific ones. *General* and *abstract* are sometimes used interchangeably, and so are *specific* and *concrete.* But the matchups are not exact. Though we can easily classify a word as concrete or abstract, we can say that a term is specific or general only if we compare it with a related term. In the series *Volvo, car, vehicle,* all the words are concrete, but judged in relation to each other, *car* is more general than *Volvo* and more specific than *vehicle.* In the series *emotion, love, lust,* all the words are abstract, but *love* is more specific than *emotion* and more general than *lust.* So a concrete term is not always specific, and an abstract term is not always general.

Prose that strikes the reader as abstract often contains a high proportion of general terms, both abstract and concrete. Instead of using the general, abstract term *immorality,* specify the kind of immoral act you have in mind *(adultery, bribery, robbery).* Instead of the general, concrete term *lawbreakers,* use *speeders, vandals, muggers, burglars, rapists*—naming the kind of lawbreakers you're writing about.

3. Choose your abstract terms with care. What often causes trouble isn't the use of abstract terms but the particular terms chosen. If every sixth or seventh word you write is a noun ending in *-ence, -ity, -ment,* or *-tion (permanence, responsibility, management, utilization),* your style will be abstract and heavy. Many abstract nouns are related to verbs: *intention (intend), refusal* *(refuse), response (respond).* Given a choice between representing an action in an abstract noun or in a full verb, you'll generally write a livelier, clearer sentence if you choose the verb:

> The achievement of clarity of thought has a definite dependence on the correctness of the formulation of the problem.

> **Better:** To think clearly, you need to formulate your problem correctly.

Though neither sentence contains any concrete words, the second is more direct and easier to read than the first. Its style, we say, is more concrete.

See **Description, Details, Nominalization.**

accept, except

Accept means "receive" or "say yes to." *Except,* as a verb, means "leave out," "exclude." See **except, accept.**

Accusative case

The object of a verb or a preposition is said to be in the accusative (or objective) case. Six distinctive pronoun forms are often called accusative (or objective) forms: *me, her, him, us, them, whom.* (*You* is both accusative and nominative.) See **Case 2; Gerunds 2; Infinitives and style 2; it's me; Objects; who, whom.**

acquiesce

If you have reason to use the formal verb *acquiesce,* be sure to follow it with the right preposition. You can agree *to* or *with* a decision, but you acquiesce *in* a decision (when you simply go along with it).

Acronyms

An acronym is a word made up of the initial letters, or bits and pieces, of the word sequence it names: NATO = *N*orth *A*tlantic *T*reaty *O*rganization; NOW = *N*ational *O*rganization for *W*omen; sonar = *so*und *na*vigation *r*anging; Amex = *Am*erican Stock *Ex*change. Originating in military bureaucratese, acronyms multiplied in World War II (Nazi, Gestapo, radar, Wac), and thousands have been created since (SALT, OPEC, NASA, laser, AIDS).

Trade names—especially those ending in *-co* like *Sunoco, Amoco,* and *Nabisco*—are often acronyms of the names of corporations. Names of organizations are sometimes devised to guarantee attention-getting acronyms. But whether their purpose is efficiency, profit, publicity, or just wordplay, acronyms are an important recent source of new words.

Active voice

All verbs are in the active voice except those consisting of a form of the verb *be* and a past participle (is cooked). See **Voice.** Compare **Passive voice.**

actually

Like *basically, definitely,* and *really, actually* is seldom necessary in writing, even when it's meant literally: "My nomination for the 'most neglected book' is actually a trilogy" (Carlos Baker, *American Scholar*). All four words are overused in conversation as fillers or as attempts to provide emphasis. In revising your papers, delete every *actually, basically, definitely,* and *really* that isn't serving a useful purpose, particularly if it appears at the beginning of a sentence: [Actually] I prefer Chicago to New York.

ad

Ad, the clipped form of *advertisement,* is appropriate in all but formal writing. It's not an abbreviation, so it shouldn't be followed by a period.

A.D.

A.D. stands for *anno Domini,* "in the year of the Lord," and logically, therefore, should precede a year (A.D. 107) and should not label a century. But there's a strong tendency to treat A.D. as if it meant "after Christ" (as B.C. means "before Christ"), and phrases like "in the second century A.D." have appeared regularly in the works of respected writers for many years. Consider your audience.

adapt, adopt

To *adapt* is to adjust so as to fit or conform: Immigrants often have difficulty adapting to American customs and values. To *adopt* is to accept, to choose, to make your own: The motion was finally adopted; The engineers adopted the third alternative; They adopted three children in two years.

ad hominem

The Latin term *ad hominem,* meaning *"to* the man," refers to the practice of bypassing arguments that bear on the issue under debate and instead appealing exclusively to the emotions, beliefs, and special situation of the specific audience addressed. The term is now commonly used in the quite different sense of *"against* the man"—an attack on the opponent instead of on the opposing point of view. This is the sense John Ciardi intended when he protested that the public's response to a review of his was "the ever-present *ad hominem,*" summed up in "You are a mean low horrid person" ("The Reviewer's Duty to Damn"). See **Fallacies.**

Adjectivals

Phrases, clauses, and words that are not adjectives may function like adjectives. That is, they may restrict or limit a subject, object, or indirect object. When they do, they can be called *adjectivals.*

1. Phrases and clauses used in adjectival function.

The man *with the hat on* is Harry.

I like the one *on the end* best.

Everyone *who agrees* should raise her right hand.

That was the summer *we went to Bermuda.*

He asked the first woman *he met.*

2. Other parts of speech in adjectival function. Participles, which are derived from verbs, function as adjectivals: a *coming* attraction, a *deserved* penalty. And one of the most characteristic traits of English is the use of nouns in the adjectival function: a *glass* jar, the *Roosevelt* administration, *adjective* modifiers, *high-school mathematics* test. Like adjectives that precede the words they modify, adjectival nouns are said to be attributive. See **Adjectives and style 2.**

Adjectives

An adjective modifies—that is, restricts or limits—a subject, object, or indirect object. *Good* performs this function in the sentence "A good dancer isn't just any dancer but a dancer who's better than others."

1. Forms. Many adjectives don't have a form that sets them off from other parts of speech *(high, civil).* Other adjectives consist of a noun or verb plus a suffix such as *-able (bearable)* or *-ible (reversible), -al (critical), -ed (chilled), -ful (playful), -ish (childish), -less (harmless), -ous (joyous),* or *-y (dreamy).*

Many adjectives are compared by adding *-er* or *-est* to the positive, or base, form or by putting *more* or *most* before it: *warm, warmer* or *more warm; warmest* or *most warm.* See **Comparison of adjectives and adverbs.**

Proper adjectives are capitalized, like the proper nouns they're derived from: *French* restaurants, *Italian* wines, *Elizabethan* drama, *Victorian* furniture. When used frequently in a merely descriptive sense, a proper adjective becomes an ordinary adjective, written without a capital: *diesel* fuel, *india* ink.

2. Functions. The main function of adjectives is to modify a subject or object, but when preceded by *a, an,* or *the,* some adjectives serve as subjects or objects: the *just*, the *rich*, a new *high*. When so used, words that are ordinarily adjectives function as nouns and can be called *nominals*. See **Adjectivals, Nominals.**

adj Adjectives and style

Reconsider your choice of the adjective marked.

The adjectives you use should make your statements more precise or more forceful.

1. Adjectives that fail. Some adjectives are redundant. In "briny ocean," *briny* adds nothing because all salt water is briny. (Adjectivals can be similarly redundant, as in "wandering nomads.") Very general adjectives like *good, bad, beautiful, wonderful, terrible, terrific, fantastic, incredible, awful,* and so on communicate attitudes rather than specify characteristics. The reader who finds someone described as "good" wants to know the particular kind of goodness. Is the person agreeable? kind? virtuous? talented? generous? Many adjectives that are specific enough have been teamed so often with particular nouns (*beady* eyes, *fond* farewell) that the combinations have become trite. In writing, think twice before using any combination of adjective and noun that comes to mind automatically. See **Triteness.**

2. Adjectives that clutter. Sometimes in reading over what you've written, you'll find that you've piled up adjectives. Deleting most of the adjectives and adjectivals from the following passage would improve it considerably.

> My blurred, aching, stinging eyes focused not on the shiny, slippery, polished, golden oak floors that reflected the frilly-white sparkle of the neat, spandy-clean room of my long-gone childhood but on the ugly lumps of dirty, worn-out jeans, decrepit, sagging jogging shorts, and gray, smelly, mud-caked sweat socks that littered the dingy, dusty, ragged old rug.

The stylistic effect is particularly bad when the words in adjectival position are nouns. Piling nouns in front of nouns produces prose that's heavy and hard to understand. "The chairman selection committee progress report date has been changed" needs to be translated into "The date for the progress report of the committee on selecting a chairman has been changed." A string of prepositional phrases isn't very graceful, but it's better than the rear-end collisions in a string of nouns.

3. Adjectives that work. Used sensibly and sensitively, adjectives reinforce meaning and improve style. If your material is technical and your audience is familiar with the technical vocabulary, you need only be careful to use the right term—*biaxial*, perhaps, or *extravascular,* or *granular*. But if you're writing on a technical subject for readers who lack the technical vocabulary, or if you're dealing with a subject that has no special vocabulary of its own, then you have to make choices. Choose your adjectives with the needs of your subject matter and your audience, as well as your purpose, in mind. Chosen well, they'll seem to fit, to belong, as in this account:

> His face was a study in basset melancholy. He had a high, narrow forehead and thin, dark hair. A single, ironbound furrow ran across the lower part of his forehead, and it seemed to weigh on his eyes, which were heavily lidded and slanted down at their outer corners. Two deep furrows bracketed his generous nose and his mouth, and he had a cleft chin. His cheeks were heavy but firm. His smile was surprising; it easily lifted and lit the mass around it.—Whitney Balliett, *American Musicians*

According to E. B. White, "The adjective hasn't been built that can pull a weak or inaccurate verb out of a tight place." True enough. And Carl Sandburg is said to have warned a writer, "Think twice before you use an adjective." This is probably sound advice for anyone who automatically attaches an adjective to every noun and so produces what has been called adjective-benumbed prose. But adjectives can help you describe your subject as you see it, and if you choose the right ones, they'll make the reader see it too.

See **Description.** Compare **Adverbs and style.**

Adverbials

Phrases and clauses that function like adverbs can be classed as *adverbials:* He came *in the morning; After the exam* he quit; *When it was time to go,* she didn't know what to do. Words like *home* in "He went home" and *days* in "She works days" are nouns in form but adverbials in function.

Adverbs

The grammatical category "adverbs" is a ragbag containing a variety of words that modify verbs, adjectives, other adverbs, and whole clauses and sentences.

1. Forms. Most adverbs are formed by adding *-ly* to adjectives or participles: *badly, deservedly, laughingly, surely.* Some have no special adverbial sign: *now, then, here, there.* A number of adverbs have the same form as adjectives, including these:

bad	doubtless	hard	much	slow
better	early	high	near	smooth
bright	even	late	new	straight
cheap	fair	loose	right	tight
close	fast	loud	rough	well
deep	first	low	sharp	wrong

Most of these unchanged adverbs are matched by forms in *-ly*, with which they may or may not be interchangeable. See **Adverbs and style.**

Most adverbs are compared either by adding *-er* and *-est* to the positive, or base, form or by preceding it with *more* and *most*. See **Comparison of adjectives and adverbs.**

2. Functions. Adverbs are typically used in two functions:

  a. To modify single words, phrases, and clauses: He left early *(early* modifies *left); * They were practically in the street *(practically* modifies *in the street); * Fortunately no one was home *(fortunately* modifies *no one was home).* In direct and indirect questions, *when, where, why,* and *how* perform adverbial functions: *When* did he leave? Do you know *why* he left?

  b. To connect separate sentences or the independent clauses of a compound sentence (see **Conjunctive adverbs**):

  We found the dormitories empty, the classrooms silent and deserted. *Nevertheless,* we continued the search.

  They agreed to call the matter closed; *however,* they were by no means convinced.

See **Adverbials.**

adv Adverbs and style

Correct the form of the adverb marked, change its position, or reconsider your choice.

1. Use the standard form of the adverb. You can say "He sang loud" or "He sang loudly"; both are standard. The short form is often preferred in general and informal English, the *-ly* form in formal English. (Cookbook compilers, who ordinarily use general English, are nevertheless addicted to chopping finely and slicing thinly.) The choice is a matter of style. But in some situations standard English doesn't permit a choice:

  a. Omitting the *-ly* ending. When adverbs are formed by adding *-ly* to the adjective *(considerably, regularly, suddenly),* the form without *-ly* is nonstandard: It hurt *considerable;* He did it *regular.* Use the *-ly* ending unless your dictionary also treats the form without *-ly* as standard.

  b. Adding an unnecessary *-ly.* Even when an adverb has two forms, they're not always interchangeable. Though you can say "Drive slow" or "Drive slowly," you can't replace *close* with *closely* in "That shot hit too close." It's *deep* (not *deeply*) in the heart of Texas, and *deep* is the way still waters run. Adverbial *important* and *doubtless* can stand on their own feet; and *first, second, third* do very well without *-ly.* If you're tempted to add *-ly* to every adverb you use in your writing, think twice. Often the *-ly* is not only unnecessary but undesirable and contrary to idiom.

After a linking verb, use a predicate adjective, not an adverb: The breeze smelled sweet (*not* sweetly). And don't use an adverb-adjective combination when the adjective alone can do the job: Like many of that breed, her dogs were high-strung (*not* highly strung). Compare **bad, badly.**

Don't add *-ly* to a word that already ends in *-ly (kindlily* for *kindly).* To make an adverbial from an adjective ending in *-ly (leisurely, orderly, worldly),* put the adjective in a prepositional phrase ending with a noun like *way* or *manner:* He approached us *in a friendly way;* She handled the problem *in a scholarly manner.* Words ending in *-ly* that indicate time may function either as adjectives (an hourly schedule) or as adverbs (the bus departed hourly).

2. Place adverbs for clarity and style. Many adverbs can occupy different positions in a sentence:

Tom had *never* liked pizza. Tom *never* had liked pizza.

Patiently she explained. She *patiently* explained. She explained *patiently*.

When you have a choice, first of all place the adverb so that it makes your meaning clear: not "She answered the questions that the students asked patiently" but "She patiently answered the questions that the students asked"— if it was the answering and not the questioning that was patient. Other considerations are rhythm and emphasis. Some writers hesitate to insert an adverb between the parts of a verb: instead of "have easily seen," they write "have seen easily." But "have easily seen" is smoother and more idiomatic. See **only, Split infinitive.**

3. Making adverbs count. The use of adverbs should at least be precise and, if possible, should contribute to the impact of the sentence. Adverbs hurt rather than help when they're used unnecessarily and redundantly (truck horns blast *threateningly;* automobiles careen *wildly;* buses lumber along *heavily),* when they qualify excessively (the *seemingly* difficult problem of controlling inflation), and when they set up a flutter of *-lys* (as in this sentence). Sometimes writers use an adverb to shore up an imprecise adjective or verb when more compact expression would do the job better:

Scholarships should be kept for *those who are academically energetic* (the studious).

When no one was looking, I took the goggles and *swiftly made my way* (hurried) out of the store.

adverse, averse

Be careful not to confuse these two adjectives. *Adverse* means "unfavorable" or "hostile" (adverse conditions). *Averse* means "opposed" (We would not be averse to such legislation). Both have a formal tone.

advise

Besides meaning "to give advice," *to advise* is used to mean "to inform, to give information." In this sense the verb is commonly used for informing that's somewhat formal: Reporters were advised by an administration spokesman that . . . In all other situations simple *tell* is more appropriate: Peter tells (*not* advises) us that he won't be back next term.

affect, effect

Affect is used most often as a transitive verb meaning "influence" (This will affect the lives of thousands) or, rather formally, "put on" (He affected a stern manner). The noun *affect* is a technical term in psychology. *Effect* is most common as a noun meaning "result": The effects will be felt by thousands. But it's also a formal verb meaning "bring about": The change was effected hurriedly.

aggravate

In general and informal usage *aggravate* ordinarily means "annoy" or "irritate": The higher he turned the volume, the more aggravated I got. Many writers of formal English still limit *aggravate* to the meaning "make worse," as to aggravate a wound or a situation: Friction between faculty and administration was aggravated by cuts in the budget.

 ## Agreement

Make the verb or pronoun marked agree in form with the word to which it is related—its subject if it is a verb, its antecedent if it is a pronoun.

When used together, certain parts of speech should agree, or correspond in form in such a way as to express relationships of number, person, or gender. This pair of sentences illustrates several instances of agreement:

> *This* habit, which in *itself is* harmless, *is* likely to lead to *others* that *are* decidedly harmful. *(This, itself, is,* and *is* agree with the singular *habit. Are* agrees with the plural *others.)*

> *These* habits, which in *themselves are* harmless, *are* likely to lead to *another* that *is* decidedly harmful. *(These, themselves, are,* and *are* agree with the plural *habits. Is* agrees with the singular *another.)*

In English, agreement is largely a matter of linguistic etiquette. If you used *is* after *habits* in the sentence above, your readers would have no trouble figuring out your meaning, but they'd frown at your carelessness. Understanding the causes of mistakes in agreement will alert you to what to look for when you proofread your writing and help you avoid lapses in grammatical good manners.

1. Subject and verb agree in number (Those *birds were* seen; That *bird was* seen). There are four main causes for problems in subject-verb agreement: (a) phrases or clauses between subject and verb, (b) collective nouns as subjects, (c) compound subjects, and (d) dialect differences in verb forms.

a. Most mistakes in agreement occur when a writer makes the verb agree with a word that's not the subject and that differs from the subject in number. Often the word is the noun at the end of a clause or phrase that comes between the true subject and the verb: An *analysis* of the extent to which audiovisual aids are used in schools *make* me conclude that books are no longer the chief tools of education. The singular subject *analysis* calls for the corresponding verb form *makes,* but the plural noun *schools* immediately before the verb, and perhaps also the plural *aids are,* led the writer to use the plural *make.* The same trouble may occur in a very short sentence: "But only one in 100 patients die" *(Newsweek).* In such situations take the time to make sure what the subject of your verb is.

b. The first question with collective nouns as subjects is whether to treat them as singular or plural. If you're thinking of what the noun names as a unit, make the verb singular: The last *couple* on the floor *was* Janet and Tom. If you're thinking instead of the individuals that make up what the noun names, use a plural verb: The *couple* next door *were* disagreeing noisily, as usual.

Once you've made this decision, be sure you use the verb and any related pronoun consistently: If the team *was* very much on edge, the reason was that *its* (not *their*) big game was only a week away. Sometimes the pronoun will determine the verb form: When we found ourselves near where the old couple *were* living, we dropped in to see *them.* "We dropped in to see *it*" would be impossible, even after "was living." So the sentence demands the *were-them* combination. See **Collective nouns.**

c. Problems with compound subjects sometimes arise because the writer is uncertain whether to treat the subjects as plural or singular. Some compound subjects name a unit that calls for a singular verb: Bacon and eggs *is* my favorite breakfast. Other compound subjects represent a unit to one writer, separate things to another:

> Her loyalty and patriotism *was* unparalleled in the history of her people.
>
> Her loyalty and [her] patriotism *were* unparalleled in the history of her people.

Before deciding to use a singular verb with a compound subject, be sure your readers will not only recognize your intention but accept the logic behind it. Only subjects that are closely allied *(loyalty* and *patriotism)* can reasonably be thought of as a unit. This principle rules out "Her beauty and tolerance *was* apparent even to me," which readers would see as an error in agreement.

When both elements of a compound subject connected by the correlative conjunctions *either . . . or* or *neither . . . nor* are plural, the verb is naturally plural; and when both elements are singular, the verb is usually singular. When one subject is singular and the other plural, the traditional rule is that the verb should agree with the nearer subject:

Neither the ideas nor the style *is* satisfactory.

Neither the style nor the ideas *are* satisfactory.

Although usage varies, this is a sensible rule to follow. See **Compound subject, Correlative conjunctions.**

d. Some American dialects, notably in Black English, lack an ending in the third-person singular, so that *do* and *see,* for example, are treated like standard English *can:* he can, he do, he see. Writers for whom this is the natural grammatical pattern have a double problem when they use a variety of standard English: they must add the ending to most present-tense, third-person-singular verbs *(starts, stops, sees)* and not add it elsewhere, as in plural verbs (they *stop*) and past-tense forms (I, you, she, we, they *stopped*). See **Principal parts of verbs 2.**

2. A third-person pronoun agrees with its antecedent in number and gender. If the antecedent—the noun it refers to—is plural, the pronoun is *they, their(s),* or *them,* depending on its use in the sentence. If the antecedent is singular, the choice of pronoun is more complicated because gender enters in. Generally, if the noun refers to a male, we use *he, his,* or *him;* if to a female, *she, hers,* or *her.* Otherwise, including situations where the sex is unknown or irrelevant, we use *it(s):* The baby dropped *its* rattle; The dog was looking for *its* master.

Problems sometimes arise when the antecedent is a noun referring to one of a group that includes both sexes (each member of the class) or when it's one of the indefinite pronouns, like *one, anyone, everyone, no one, anybody, everybody,* or *nobody.* The question of which possessive pronoun to use with an indefinite may be solved by the context: No one in the Girl Scout troop looked forward to *her* test. But when both sexes are referred to (No one at the dance . . .), the problem is whether to use *he, he or she,* or *they.* Some grammarians assert that *they,* like *you,* has both singular and plural functions and that in indefinite reference it is usually a singular pronoun. But conservatives reject *they* as a singular. Though the use of a form of *they* to refer to words like *everyone* (Everyone in the class turned in their paper) is firmly established in speech and is increasingly common in writing, it is resisted in formal English, where a form of *he* (his paper) would be expected. Using a subject that's clearly plural avoids the problem of sexist language: All the students handed in their papers. See **Sexist language, they.**

3. The demonstrative adjectives (or determiners) *this, that, these, those* usually agree in number with the nouns they modify: *That coat* is expensive; *These shoes* cost more than my old pair did. See **kind, sort.**

agree to, agree with

One person agrees *to* a plan and agrees *with* another person. One thing agrees *with* another. Other idioms: I agree *in* principle; We agreed *on* a plan of attack; He agreed *to* fly or *on* flying or *that he would fly.*

ain't

Though in speech millions of Americans use *ain't* regularly as a contraction for *am not, is not, are not, has not,* and *have not,* it never appears in formal writing and rarely in expository prose except when a speaker is being quoted. In general writing, use of *ain't* is almost always a deliberate attempt to suggest informality or humor or down-to-earth common sense:

> It will never reach the audience Welles might have and should have reached, because there just ain't no way.—Pauline Kael, *New Republic*

> Those tiresome people with their tiresome quotes from Socrates about the fact that youth is going to the dogs are just trying to reassure themselves that it's all just a little bit more of the same. It ain't.—John M. Culkin, *New York Times*

See **Divided usage.**

albeit

Albeit, meaning "even though," occurs occasionally in academic and bureaucratic prose: "Those familiar with the U.S. Army tactical doctrine will note that Iraq's mobile defensive tactics have all the elements of 'combined arms' operations, albeit in a well-rehearsed, 'set-piece battle' atmosphere" (David Segal, *Foreign Affairs*). It also crops up in the general English of popular journalism, where it strikes some readers as out of place.

all, al-

Note the spelling of these words and phrases:

1. all ready (adjective phrase): At last they were all ready to begin.
   already (adverb of time): They had already begun.

2. all together (adjective phrase): We found them all together in an old trunk.
   altogether (adverb, equivalent to *wholly*): That's another matter altogether.

3. all right (adjective phrase): The seats seemed all right to me.

Alright now appears frequently enough to be accepted as a variant spelling in some dictionaries. Others specifically label it a misspelling.

Alliteration

Alliteration is repetition of the same sound, usually at the beginning of several words in a series. Besides possibly appealing to the reader's or listener's ear, alliteration binds the phrase, or sometimes a series of phrases, into a unit: "Individual cells in a tissue are mindless machines, perfect in performance, as absolutely inhuman as bees" (Lewis Thomas, *The Medusa and the Snail*). Alliteration is appropriate in some formal prose but distracting in ordinary exposition unless it helps reinforce meaning. Check your first drafts to break up any string of words that begin with the same sound for no purpose. Compare **Assonance.**

all of

In many constructions with *all of, of* can be omitted: All [of] the milk was spilled; They passed all [of] the candidates; You can't fool all [of] the people all [of] the time. Usage is divided. With personal pronouns and the relatives *who* and *which, all* may follow the pronoun (we all), or *all of* may precede it (all of us). *All of whom* and *all of which,* as subjects of relative clauses (four attempts, all of which failed), are more formal than *who all* and *which all* (four attempts, which all failed).

all that

"It wasn't all that bad" and similar uses of *all that* are informal. See **not all that, not too.**

all the farther

In some parts of the country *all the farther* is common in informal and general speech (This is all the farther I'm going), but standard written English uses an *as . . . as* construction: This is as far as I'm going.

Allusion

Loosely, an allusion is a brief reference to something that's not a part of the subject under discussion. Strictly, an allusion differs from a reference in that it doesn't name the event, person, or place but mentions it indirectly. "This latter-day Paul Revere calls us to arms against home-grown revolutionaries" is a reference to Paul Revere. In the same context, "His signal is always a single lantern in the church steeple" is a literary allusion that leaves it to the reader to make the connection through knowledge of Longfellow's poem about Revere's ride ("One if by land, and two if by sea"). Like other aspects of style, allusions should fit the rhetorical situation.

allusion, illusion

Allusion, discussed in the preceding entry, should not be confused with *illusion,* a misapprehension or a misleading appearance: Smoking a pipe can create an illusion of wisdom.

almost

Most for *almost* is informal. See **most, almost.**

also

Also as an adverb ordinarily stands within a sentence, not at its beginning: "They also serve who only stand and wait" (John Milton). But inversion may shift an *also* to initial position: Also defeated was the party's candidate for mayor. As a loose conjunction mcaning "and," *also* is a weak sentence opener:

> He subscribed to eight magazines. Also he belonged to the Book-of-the-Month Club.

In many cases the information introduced with initial *also* should be included in the preceding sentence: He subscribed to eight magazines and belonged to the Book-of-the-Month Club. If you do use an initial *also,* don't separate it with a comma from the clause it introduces. See **but 4, Conjunctive adverbs, Inversion, plus.**

alternative

Alternative comes from the Latin *alter,* "the second of two." For that reason some formal writers restrict its meaning to "one of two possibilities," but the word is regularly used to mean one of several possibilities: Another alternative would be to . . . Dictionaries record this broader meaning.

As an adjective, *alternative* also refers to two or more choices: an alternative route. The adjective *alternate* is often used in the same sense but shares with the verb *alternate* the primary sense of turn and turn about: on alternate Thursdays.

although, though

Although and *though* introduce adverbial clauses that qualify the main statement:

> Although (*or* Though) the rain kept up for almost three weeks, we managed to have a good time.

> We managed to have a good time, though (*or* although) the rain kept up for almost three weeks.

In these examples there is no distinction in meaning. The choice between the two words may be based on sentence rhythm. *Although* is slightly more formal.

Often one of two clauses connected by *but* can be turned into an *(al)though* clause for a slight change of emphasis or for sentence variety:

> We had rehearsed time and again, but we all missed our cues the first night.

> Although (*or* Though) we had rehearsed time after time, we all missed our cues the first night.

> *Though* is also used as a less formal *however:* She did it, though.

> See **but.**

alumnus, alumna

A male graduate is an *alumnus*, a female graduate an *alumna*. Two or more male graduates are *alumni*, two or more female graduates *alumnae*. The graduates of coeducational schools—males and females together—have traditionally been called *alumni*, but *graduates* itself is a satisfactory, and sexless, alternative. Another sexless alternative is *alums*, the plural of the clipped word *alum*. See **Sexist language.**

A.M. and P.M.

These abbreviations for *ante meridiem* ("before noon") and *post meridiem* ("after noon") are most useful in tables and lists of times. They may be written in capitals or small letters and are frequently printed as small capitals: A.M. They are also used in general writing for specific hours, usually with figures: from 2 to 4 P.M. (*not* I went there in the P.M.). Though *m.* is the abbreviation for noon (12 m.), *12 noon* is more common. Midnight is *12 P.M.* The twenty-four-hour system used in Europe and by the U.S. military makes A.M. and P.M. redundant: 9 A.M. = 0900, 9 P.M. = 2100. See **Hours.**

amb Ambiguity

Make your meaning unmistakable.

An ambiguous word or phrase or sentence is one that can be interpreted in two or more ways. Though the context usually shows which of the possible meanings was intended, the reader may be confused at least momentarily. The most common sources of confusion are these:

1. Inexact reference of pronouns, especially in indirect discourse: He told his father he had been talking too much. Who is the second *he*, the father or the son? Rewrite as: He admitted to his father that he had been talking too much. Or: He criticized his father for talking too much. Or recast as direct speech. See **Indirect discourse, Reference of pronouns 1.**

2. Modifiers that can be misinterpreted.
a. Modifiers should not be so placed that they can seem to refer to either of two words or constructions: The governor dismissed those officeholders who had opposed him ruthlessly. Does *ruthlessly* refer to the dismissal or the opposition? Rewrite as: The governor ruthlessly dismissed those officeholders who had opposed him. Or: The governor dismissed those officeholders who had ruthlessly opposed him. See **Squinting modifier.**
b. Modifiers should be clearly identified as restrictive or nonrestrictive. Setting off a restrictive modifier with commas or failing to set off a nonrestrictive modifier changes your meaning: Out-of-state students[,] who were delayed by the blizzard[,] will not be penalized for late registration. With commas, the

sentence means that no out-of-state students were penalized, because all were delayed by the storm; without commas, it means that only some out-of-staters were delayed, and only those were excused. See **Restrictive and nonrestrictive modifiers.**

c. Modifiers shouldn't mislead even momentarily. In revising a first draft, be on the lookout for puzzlers like the headline "Police Repair Man Killed by Car." See **Hyphen 5.**

3. Incomplete idioms, especially in comparisons: I liked Alice as well as Will" might mean "I liked Alice as well as Will did," "I liked Alice as well as I liked Will," or "I liked both Alice and Will."

4. Confusing coordination, as in: The movie deals with student protests against war and sexual experimentation. Repeating *with* after *and* would limit the target of the protests, as would placing *sexual experimentation* first.

5. Ambiguous words. When a writer uses the wrong word—say, *incredible* for *incredulous*—the result is confusion but usually not ambiguity. Ambiguity occurs when a writer uses a word that has the meaning he intends but another meaning as well—for example, the dialect word *cookie* for *doughnut,* or the word *rhetoric,* which has unfavorable connotations for some but favorable connotations for others. Instances of divided usage are particularly troublesome. Readers who find *disinterested* where they expect *uninterested* are likely to be not so much confused as irritated. See **censor, censure; Connotation; convince, persuade; disinterested, uninterested; Divided usage; imply, infer; incredible, incredulous; rhetoric; Wrong word.**

See also **Comma 6.**

American

Because there's no simple adjective that corresponds to the United States of America (as *Italian,* for example, corresponds to Italy), *American* is ordinarily used. It's obviously inexact, in that all the other inhabitants of the Americas have as much right to the term as we do. Many Latin Americans refer to themselves as Americans and to us as North Americans. But the use of *American* as the adjective ("the American economy" for "the economy of the United States") and as the noun for a citizen of the United States is standard.

U.S. is a general-to-informal substitute for *American,* common in journalism: The U.S. economy stumbled last month.

Americanism

An Americanism is a word or construction in English that originated in the United States *(hydrant, zipper, peanut butter)* or was first borrowed here, as from an African language *(goober, juke, okra)* or an Indian language *(hominy, caucus, mugwump)* or from Spanish *(canyon, rodeo, lariat). Americanism* also refers to a sense of a word that was added in the United States *(campus, carpetbagger, creek)*. And it may be extended to include words that have continued to be used in the United States after becoming obsolete in England *(loan* as a verb, *gotten)* or any item of usage characteristic of the United States and not of other areas of the English-speaking world. The label *American* or *chiefly U.S.* in dictionaries identifies Americanisms.

among, between

Between is used with two, *among* with more than two. But see **between, among.**

amount, number

Number is used of countable things: a number of mistakes, a number of apples. *Amount* is preferred with mass nouns—a small amount of snow, a certain amount of humor—but is sometimes used with countables: Thieves took an unknown amount of tickets. Writers of formal English keep the distinction. See **Mass nouns.** Compare **fewer, less.**

Ampersand

An ampersand is the & sign. Because its primary use is to save space, the ampersand belongs only where it has become established: AT&T, Arm & Hammer, R & D (research and development), r & b (rhythm and blues). Otherwise, write out *and*.

Analogy

Analogies may be either figurative or literal. A figurative analogy suggests a resemblance between things or situations that on the surface are totally unlike— a mathematical equation and a musical composition, for example, or a football team and an epidemic. There are no literal resemblances between an undefeated team and the Black Death, but both can be said to mow down what stands in their paths. The team figuratively slaughters its opponents as the plague literally killed its victims in the fourteenth century.

Literal analogies uncover relationships between two members of the same class of things or situations. Often they reveal surprising similarities between widely separated events or individuals. The attitude of young people toward marijuana laws in the 1960s was analogized to the attitude of their grandparents toward liquor laws in the 1920s.

Whether it's compressed into a phrase (the Peter Pan of American politics) or elaborated through a long essay, an apt analogy throws new light on the subject. Presenting something unfamiliar in terms of something familiar (the earth's strata in terms of the layers of an onion) is a common method of exposition. Here a writer uses analogy to soothe readers fearful of the computer's effect on our culture:

Just as those historians made a major mistake who maintained that the printing press was necessary to have the Western mind moulded by the "linear thought," so it would be a mistake to believe that the computer itself threatens the survival of the literate mind.—Ivan Illich, *North American Review*

Analogy becomes the basis for argument when a writer tries to persuade an audience that because two situations are alike in some respects (proposals for gun registration in the United States and gun registration in Nazi Germany), they're alike in still another (if enacted into law, the proposals will result in government seizure of all guns owned by civilians). Though analogies can't carry the full burden of logical proof, they can be powerful persuaders. If the likenesses they cite have real bearing on the point at issue and the differences aren't fundamental, analogies have logical force as well.

Whether used to explain or to persuade, an analogy can stir the imagination and stimulate ideas. For both writer and reader, a good analogy offers a fresh way of looking at things.

See **Comparison and contrast, Figurative language.**

Analysis

The term *analysis* is applied to a wide range of intellectual undertakings— attempts to grasp the nature of a thing or a concept, to separate a whole into its parts, to discover the similarities and differences between two or more things, to investigate causes, to attribute effects. The aim of analysis is to increase understanding of the subject. Writers may also use analysis as a guide to action, analyzing an assignment in order to decide how to organize the paper it calls for, or what details to include, or what arguments to use. See **Cause and effect, Classification and division, Comparison and contrast, Definition, Logical thinking, Rhetorical situation.**

and

1. Appropriate uses. *And,* the conjunction we use most frequently, should join two or more elements of equal grammatical rank:

> *Adjectives:* a *pink* and *white* dress; a *blue, green,* and *white* flag
> *Adverbs:* He drove *very fast* and *rather carelessly.*
> *Nouns: trees* and *flowers; trees, shrubs,* and *flowers*
> *Verbs:* I *picked up* the book and *opened* it.
> *Phrases: in one ear* and *out the other*
> *Dependent clauses: While the children were swimming* and *[while] the old folks were resting,* we took a walk.
> *Independent clauses: The first generation makes the money,* and *the second spends it.*

2. Inappropriate uses. In careless writing, elements that are not grammatically equivalent are sometimes connected by an unnecessary *and:*

Main verbs and participles: The men *sat* on the edge of the lake with their backs to the road, [and] apparently *watching* the ducks.

Independent and dependent clauses: A contract has been let to install new copper work on the post office [and] which will give it the facelifting it needs.

Besides being used where no connective is needed, *and* sometimes appears where some other connective would show the logical relationship more clearly: "Shah was a founding member of the Club of Rome and [but?] while he retains his membership, he did not attend last fall's gathering in Berlin" (Elizabeth Hall, *Psychology Today*). See **Coordination 2, Shifted constructions.**

3. To begin sentences. In current writing of all varieties, *and* can be used to begin a sentence, signaling a link with the preceding sentence or paragraph. Used sparingly, it will also contribute to the movement and emphasis. Over-used, it will damage both.

4. Omitted or repeated. *And* can be omitted in a series (Cousins, uncles, [and] aunts—all the relatives were there), but if it's omitted again and again, the result is a telegraphic style that's inappropriate in most writing. *And* may also be repeated to separate the items in a series, as an effective way of giving emphasis to each: "I do not mean to imply that the South is simple and homogeneous and monolithic" (Robert Penn Warren, *Southern Review*).

5. Punctuation. *And* should not be separated by a comma from the clause it introduces: And[,] both of those estimates turned out to be too high. Nor should a comma before *and* separate the two parts of a compound predicate: She switched from music to history[,] and was elected to Phi Beta Kappa in her junior year.

and etc.

Etc. is the abbreviation for Latin *et cetera*, in which *et* means "and." So *and* before *etc.* is redundant. See **etc.**

and/or

And/or is used primarily in business writing. In most legal writing it is no longer welcome, and elsewhere it is objected to by some readers because *and/or* looks odd and because *and* or *or* alone is often all that's needed. But it's sometimes useful when there are three alternatives—*both* the items mentioned or *either* one of them: inflation and/or depression; "Gorbachev's willingness and/or ability to make any troop withdrawals" (F. Stephen Larrabee, *Foreign Affairs*). For other uses of the diagonal slash, or virgule, see **Slash.**

angle

Angle means "point of view" or "aspect" (from an economic angle) in standard general English, but it carries a strong suggestion of jargon. In the sense of "scheme" or "plan" (What's his angle?), *angle* is informal. See **Jargon.**

ante-, anti-

Don't confuse *ante-* ("before," antedate) with *anti-* ("against," antipollution).

Antecedent

An antecedent is the word, clause, or sentence that a pronoun refers to. It usually stands before the word that refers to it, but not always: We did not hear their call again, and when we found the Thompsons, they were almost exhausted. *(The Thompsons* is the antecedent of the possessive pronoun *their* and of *they.)* For relations between antecedents and pronouns, see **Agreement 2, Reference of pronouns.**

Anticipatory subject

In sentences like "It was Ann who found the food stamps" and "There are more important things than graduating," *it* and *there* are anticipatory subjects. See **it; there is, there are.**

any

1. Uses. *Any* is used primarily as an adjective (Any job will do) but also as a pronoun (Any will do). The pronoun *any* takes either a singular verb (Any of them *has* a chance of winning first prize) or a plural verb (Any of them *have* a chance of ending up in the top ten), depending on the sense of the statement.

In comparisons of things in the same class, use *any other:* He shaped the university more than any other president in its history. *Any* alone should always be used when different classes are compared: I like a pickup truck better than any car.

2. Compounds with *any.* *Anybody, anyhow, anything,* and *anywhere* are always written as single words. *Any rate* is always two words: at any rate. *Anyone* is written as one word when the stress is on the *any* (Anyone would know that) and as two when the stress is on the *one* (I'd like any one of them). *Anyway* is one word when the *any* is stressed (I couldn't go anyway) and two when the stress is about equal (Any way I try, it comes out wrong). If the word *whatever* can be substituted for the *any* (Whatever way I try, it comes out wrong), *any way* should be written as two words.

3. Pronouns referring to *anybody, anyone.* *Anybody* and *anyone* are singular in form and take singular verbs: Anybody (or anyone) feels bad at times. They are referred to by *he, his, him* (Anybody knows what he deserves) or, since they often apply to a person of either sex, by *he or she, his or her, him or her,* or a form of *they* with the same meaning: "It is not usually possible to achieve intimacy with anybody in the back seat of a car; you have to live with them in every sense of the phrase" (Edgar Z. Friedenberg, *New York Review of Books*). Most writers of formal English insist on a singular pronoun. See **Agreement 2, he or she, Sexist language, they.** Compare **every.**

4. Other forms. *Anymore* as an adverb meaning "now" commonly appears in print as one word, usually in negative statements (We don't go there anymore) or in clauses with a negative feel: "whether or not they mean something anymore" (Herbert Warren Wind, *New Yorker*). Though established in speech in some parts of the United States, *anymore* in a strictly affirmative context (Anymore they do as they please) would be inappropriate in most writing.

Referring to quantity (she didn't want any more; he refused any more green chilies), *any more* is two words.

Anyplace (now usually written as one word) has become a general synonym for "anywhere": "You will hear bitter attacks on the United States for subverting Chile, but not a word about Soviet subversion in Afghanistan or anyplace else" (Jane Rosen, *New York Times Magazine*).

Anytime, short for "at any time" (They invited us to drop in anytime), now is printed as a single word in some well-edited periodicals.

Anyways is regional for the generally used *anyway,* and *anywheres* is nonstandard for *anywhere.*

apos Apostrophe

Insert an apostrophe where it belongs in the word marked. Or take out an apostrophe that is incorrectly used.

Typical mistakes in the use of the apostrophe are *mans* for *man's, mens'* for *men's, it's* for the possessive *its, their's* for *theirs, dont* for *don't,* and *doesnt* for *doesn't.* Apostrophes are often added to simple plurals (as in "the Smith[']s"), to the possessive forms of personal pronouns like *hers, theirs, ours,* and *yours,* and to words where they don't belong: it's *till,* not *'till* or *'til.* Review the following uses:

1. In possessives. The most common use of the apostrophe is in spelling the possessive case of nouns and indefinite pronouns *(anyone, nobody, someone . . .):* Dorothy's first picture, the companies' original charters, everybody's business is nobody's business, the boys' dogs. An apostrophe should be used in singular possessives (or genitives) of time and value even though they carry no idea of possession: a day's hike, this month's quota, a dollar's worth. In formal writing, an apostrophe is also preferred in plural possessives of this kind (two weeks' work), but in some instances the omission of the apostrophe has become established: teachers college, menswear, *Publishers Weekly* (but *Reader's Digest*). For special examples of possessive form, see **Possessive case.**

2. In contractions. The apostrophe shows the omission of one or more letters in contractions: *can't, I'm, I'll, it's* (for *it is*).

3. In plurals. An apostrophe sometimes but not always precedes the -s in plurals of figures and letters (three *4*'s, two *e*'s) and in plurals of words being discussed as words (the first of several *that*'s). Decades in figures are regularly written without an apostrophe (the mid-80s). When an abbreviation includes periods, an apostrophe is used in the plural (M.D.'s); when it does not, the apostrophe is usually omitted (IOUs, VIPs).

4. In representing speech. An apostrophe may be used to indicate that the speaker omits certain sounds represented in the conventional spelling: " 'Lily,' he pleaded, 'I swear t'God, you'll get it back on pay-day. You c'n meet me up at the barn if you wanna' " (I. J. Kapstein, *Something of a Hero*). Because too many apostrophes are distracting for the reader, it's better to indicate pronunciations of this sort occasionally than to try to represent all of them.

Apposition, appositives

Beside a noun or noun equivalent in a sentence, you can put another nominal expression called an appositive: My aunts, *Mary and Agnes,* moved to Boulder in 1969. The noun and its appositive refer to the same person(s) or thing(s). Typically, the appositive is set off by commas, but sometimes no punctuation is needed: He caught so many fish that we called him Jim[ ] *the fisherman.* See **Nominals.**

Don't use appositives unnecessarily. In writing about the current chief executive by name, there's no need to identify him as the president, and if you refer to "the President," there's no need to tell the reader what his name is.

arguably

Arguably expresses a tentative opinion: arguably the best candidate.

Argument

Aside from its everyday meaning of "disagreement" or "dispute," *argument* is used in three ways. It refers to a speech or essay designed to convince an audience (a newspaper editorial, for example). Or it refers to the line of thought, the string of key propositions, that runs through a piece of writing—the argument of a book or essay or poem. Or it specifies a reason for believing what might otherwise seem doubtful; an argument in this sense might be a single sentence. Thus, in presenting his argument (first sense) to Congress, a legislator may use as his argument (second sense) the thesis that tax shelters should be eliminated, and he may offer as one of his arguments (third sense) the proposition that tax shelters favor the rich at the expense of the poor.

Argument in the first sense may make appeals that are primarily intellectual or primarily emotional. Either kind of appeal can be used well or badly, for good purposes or evil ones.

Sometimes argument is distinguished from persuasion on the basis of purpose: argument is designed to change the mind of an audience; persuasion is designed to make an audience act. But when argument is classed with description, narration, and exposition as one of the four forms of discourse, it normally includes both purposes.

See **Analogy, Deduction, Fallacies, Forms of discourse, Induction, Logical thinking, Rhetorical situation, Syllogisms.**

arise, rise, get up

In referring to standing up or getting out of bed, *arise* is formal and poetic, *rise* is slightly less formal, and *get up* is the general idiom.

around

Around, like *about,* can be used to mean "approximately." See **about 1; round, around.**

Articles

Traditionally *a* and *an* are known as indefinite articles, *the* as the definite article. See **a, an; Nouns 3c.**

as

Among the meanings of *as* are "while" (As we walked along, she told us stories) and "because" (His speed is amazing, as he weighs 260 pounds). *While* is preferable to *as* if the emphasis is on the time of the action (While we were walking along, she told us stories). Though some readers object, *as* is used to mean "because" (or "since") in all varieties of English. It can be ambiguous. In the sentence "As we have continued responding to erratic changes in Asia, our position has inevitably become more complex," *as* can mean either "because" or "while." See **while.**

For the growing tendency to use *as* where *like* would be expected, see **like, as.**

as, like

As is the conjunction (He voted as he was expected to). *Like* is the preposition (He voted like the rest). See **like, as.**

as . . . as

1. *As I* or *as me.* In a sentence like "He admires her as much as I/me," meaning determines whether the nominative *I* or the accusative *me* is used. If you mean "as much as I admire her," use *I*. If you mean "as much as he admires me," use *me*.

In a sentence like "They sent for somebody as big as I/me," the choice doesn't affect the meaning. Both nominative *I* and accusative *me* are good English.

For a third type of sentence—"He is as big as I/me"—in which there's no preceding noun or pronoun in the accusative position, usage has always been divided. The nominative *I* is preferred in formal contexts and is insisted upon by many word watchers. See **Accusative case, Nominative case.**

2. Omitted *as*. In a first draft, you may carelessly omit the second *as* in a comparison of equality (as large as) when it's joined by *or* or *if not* to a comparison of inequality (larger than): It was as large or larger than last year's crowd. But in revising, expand to the complete form: It was as large as, or larger than, last year's crowd. To avoid making the mistake, whenever possible move the second comparison to the end of the sentence: It was as large as last year's crowd, if not larger.

3. *As . . . as* and *so . . . as*. *As . . . as* is much more common than *so . . . as* in simple comparisons of degree (as small as that, as late as you like). Both *as* and *so* are used to begin the phrases "– far as I know" and "– far as that's concerned." Attempts have been made to restrict *as . . . as* to affirmative statements (She's as clever as any of them) and *so . . . as* to negative statements (She's not so clever as she thinks), but the distinction has never become established in practice.

as far as

The phrase *as* (or *so*) *far as . . . is concerned* (As far as tuition is concerned, I don't think we're getting any bargain) is now regularly shortened in speech: As far as tuition, I don't think we're getting any bargain. The reduced phrase makes no sense and, at least in writing, should be replaced by the shorter and more sensible *as for:* As for tuition, I don't think we're getting any bargain.

as if, as though

In formal English the subjunctive mood of the verb is commonly used after *as if* and *as though:* He acted as if (*or* as though) he *were* losing his temper. In general English the indicative mood is usual: He acted as if (*or* as though) he *was* losing his temper. See **Subjunctive mood.**

Assonance

Assonance is the repetition of vowel sounds in words having different consonant sounds, as in *brave–vain* and *lone–show*. Assonance is characteristic of verse and also occurs in prose, especially in poetic styles: "that ideal country of green, deep lanes and high green banks" (Osbert Sitwell). Like unintentional alliteration, unintentional assonance can be distracting.

as though

As though is commonly followed by a verb in the subjunctive mood in formal English. See **as if, as though.**

as to

As to is often a clumsy substitute for a single preposition, usually *of* or *about:* Practice is the best teacher as to (*better:* in, for, of) the use of organ stops. In some locutions it should simply be omitted: [As to] whether college is worth-while is a question we all must try to answer. But for introducing subjects, *as to* is better than more cumbersome expressions like *as regards, as concerns, in respect to:* As to the economic value of going to college, the effect on earning power is clearly established.

as well as

When an *as well as* phrase between subject and verb gives a strong impression of adding to the subject, some writers treat it as part of the subject and let it influence the number of the verb: The singer as well as four members of the outstandingly successful band were arrested in Moose Jaw. In such cases the phrase is seldom set off by commas. But according to traditional rules the phrase is parenthetical, should be enclosed in commas, and has no bearing on the verb: "This volume, as well as others, consists of a collection of basic articles" (Robert R. Wilson, *ISIS*).

at

In writing of any formality, avoid the phrase "where it's at." People and things are where they *are:* When she called home from the airport, her father wanted to know where she was (*not* where she was at).

at about

At about can be reduced to either *at* or *about*. But see **about 3.**

athletics

When the collective noun *athletics* refers to sports and games, it usually takes a plural verb and pronoun: Our athletics *include* football, basketball, and base-ball. When *athletics* refers to a skill or activity, it usually takes a singular verb and pronoun: Athletics *is* recommended because *it* contributes to good health.

author

An author writes books. But does a writer author books? *Author* as a verb is widely used (by publishers, among others) but also widely disapproved. It may be most defensible when it's used to refer to publication by a group (the report was authored by a presidential commission) or to a compilation that required little if any original writing or to the participation of a celebrity in producing an autobiography "as told to" a professional writer.

Auxiliary verbs

A verb used with other verbs to form tenses or, in the case of *be*, to change the active voice to the passive is called an auxiliary verb or helping verb. The most common auxiliaries, *be* and *have*, are used in forming the progressive and perfect tenses and the passive voice: I *am* going; He *has* gone; They *were* shot. *Do* is used in questions (Do they care?) and contradictions (They do not care) and for emphasis (Yes, they *do* care). The modal auxiliaries—*can, may, shall, will, must, ought to, could, should, would,* and *might*—are used to refer to future time *(shall* and *will)* and to suggest obligation, necessity, or possibility: You *should* reply; She *must* leave; He *could* break the record. See **Modal auxiliaries, Tenses of verbs,** and entries on individual verbs.

awful

In formal English *awful* means "inspiring awe." In informal English it's a convenient word of disapproval meaning "ugly," "shocking," "ridiculous," "very poor" (an awful movie). In informal and sometimes in general writing, the word is also used to intensify meaning: ". . . delusions that are being chosen by an awful lot [that is, a very large number] of people in preference to standard, orthodox explanations" (Elizabeth Janeway, *Atlantic*). This use of either *awful* or *awfully* (an awfully long wait) is deplored by word worriers.

The formal meaning of *awful* is retained in serious writing by *awesome:* the awesome dangers of nuclear weapons in space. But *awesome* has also become a popular intensifier, applied to everything from rock CDs to frozen yogurt, and as a result has lost much of its force.

awhile, a while

Awhile is an adverb meaning "for a short time": They talked awhile. Prepositional phrases with the noun *while* should consist of three or more words: in a while, in a little while. See **while.**

bad, badly

Bad is ordinarily used as the adjective (a bad apple) and *badly* as the adverb (They sing badly). But though the grammatical rule calls for a predicate adjective after a linking verb, the linking verb *feel* is frequently followed by *badly* instead of *bad:* I feel badly about it. Both *feel bad* and *feel badly* are generally accepted as standard. Usage is divided. Formal stylists prefer *bad.*

Badly meaning "very much" (He wanted it badly) is standard. As a group adjective, *badly off* is general: "But we are not Satan. Fallen though we are, we are not that badly off" (John Morris, *American Scholar*).

Bad as an adverb (I played bad all through the game) is inappropriate in writing.

See **Hypercorrectness.**

Bad grammar

Bad grammar is applied as an expression of disapproval to all sorts of locutions, from "I ain't got none" to supposed confusions in the use of *shall* and *will*. As criticism, the label is too vague to be helpful. Often it refers to matters having nothing to do with grammar in a scholarly sense. See **Grammar; grammatical, ungrammatical.**

Balanced sentence

When parallelism in a sentence produces structures that are noticeably alike in length and movement, the sentence is said to be balanced:

> During the last few years, my concern about the state of the higher learning in America has reached the panic stage, and my hopes for the reform of the American college and university have dwindled to the verge of despair.—Mortimer J. Adler, *Newsweek*

basically

Basically is one of many words we use in conversation without meaning much of anything: Basically it was a good course. Don't use it in writing unless you're making a contrast, either expressed or implied: [On the surface they seem carefree and irresponsible, but] basically they're very concerned about getting established in jobs with a future.

be

Be is the most common linking verb, joining a subject and a predicate noun (Jerome was the secretary) or predicate adjective (She is energetic). When it joins a subject and a pronoun, the pronoun is in the nominative case in formal written English (It was *he*), in the accusative in informal (It was *him*). "It's I" is formal for the general "It's me." See **it's me.**

When the infinitive *be* has a subject and complement, both are in the accusative case: I wanted *him* to be *me*. When the infinitive has no subject, formal usage has a nominative as the complement (I wanted to be *he*). General usage more often has an accusative (I wanted to be *him).*

Be has more forms and a greater variety of forms than any other verb in English:

Present: I am, you are, he is; we, you, they are
Past: I was, you were, he was; we, you, they were
Infinitive: be
Present participle: being
Past participle: been

See **ain't, Subjunctive mood.**

because

Because introduces an adverbial clause that gives the reason for the statement in the independent clause that follows or precedes it: *Because we were getting hungry,* we began to look for a restaurant. Or: We began to look for a restaurant *because we were getting hungry. Since* and *as,* which are sometimes used to introduce such clauses, are less definite and less explicitly causal. In some contexts, *for* is a rather formal substitute for *because.* See **as, for, reason is because.** For *because of,* see **due to.**

begging the question

Begging the question is the logical fallacy of assuming something to be true that, in fact, needs to be proved. The debater who bases his argument for reform on the assertion "This unfair method of voting must be changed" begs the question of the method's fairness. In a broad sense we all beg questions all the time—"Use enough evidence to prove your point" begs the question of how much is enough—but as a deliberate tactic in argument, begging the question is notably unfair. See **Fallacies.**

beg # Beginning

Revise the opening of your paper so that it will lead more directly and smoothly into your subject or so that it will do more to stir your reader's interest.

The best advice for beginning a short paper is "Get on with it." An opening that indulges in philosophizing (Since the days of Plato's Academy, violence and learning have been alien entities) or announces a grand strategy (In the paragraphs that follow, I shall attempt, first by analyzing and then by synthesizing, . . .) is much too pretentious for a two-page paper on a local controversy.

Ordinarily, the first step is to let your readers know what you're writing about—not by telling them what you're going to discuss but by discussing it: "We think of the drug addict as unwilling or unable to work, but he works harder to get his dope than most of us do to get our daily bread" *(Psychology Today).* This doesn't rule out a personal approach. There may be good reason for you to tell why you've chosen your topic or how you're qualified to discuss it: "I want to focus on this dietary idiosyncrasy, for the questions of when, why, and how the human diet came to include so much meat have been the source of paleontological controversy over the years'' (Pat Shipman, *Discover*). It does rule out beginnings that fail to begin.

Besides getting the paper under way, the opening paragraph or two should make a reader want to continue reading. But straining for humor or excitement or cuteness or sentiment is no way to arouse interest. As imitations of the techniques used by professional journalists, such attempts are likely to fail. The humor doesn't amuse, the excitement doesn't stir, and so on. Instead of trying out gimmicks, move into the subject and treat it with the interest *you* feel. If it doesn't interest you, your chances of making it interest your readers are slim. If it does interest you, and if you write about it as honestly and directly as you know how, your readers will keep on reading.

For long papers—from five to ten pages, say—somewhat more elaborate beginnings are sometimes necessary. But getting on with the discussion remains fundamental. If you provide the historical background of the problem you're dealing with, make sure that this material contributes to the solution you propose. If you announce what you're going to do in your paper, be sure you do it.

beside, besides

Beside is used chiefly as a preposition meaning ''by the side of,'' as in ''beside the road,'' ''beside her.'' It's used figuratively in a few rather formal idioms like ''beside the point,'' ''beside himself with rage.'' *Besides* is used as a preposition meaning ''in addition to'' (Besides ourselves, about a dozen students came to the meeting) and as an adverb and a conjunctive adverb meaning ''in addition'' (He didn't think he ought to get into the quarrel; besides, he had come to enjoy himself).

between, among

Among implies more than two objects: They distributed the provisions among the survivors. *Between* is used of two: They divided the prize between Kincaid and Thomas. But attempts to limit *between* to use only with two items have failed. When the relationship is between individual items—participants in discussions or negotiations, for example—*between* is the word to use no matter how many items there are: ''This is so . . . of some part of the debate between Einstein, Bohr, Wolfgang Pauli, and Max Born'' (George Steiner, *Atlantic*).

When treating a group as a collective unit, use *among*: Divide the books among the poor.

between you and me

Though *you and I* as the object of a preposition or a verb is frequently heard and has a long history in written English, some of those who know better regard anyone who says or writes "between you and I" as only half-educated. *Between you and me* is always correct. See **Hypercorrectness.**

bi-

Some words related to time that begin with *bi-* can cause confusion. *Bimonthly* and *biweekly,* for example, are sometimes used to mean "every two . . . ," sometimes "twice a . . . ." *Biennial* means "every two years," but *biannual* means "twice a year." When the context doesn't make the meaning clear, it's safest to use phrases such as "every two months," "twice a week," "twice a year."

Bible, bible

When it refers to the Christian Scriptures, the word is capitalized but not italicized: You'll find all that in the Bible; The New English Bible. In the sense of an authoritative book, the word is not capitalized: *Gray's Manual* is the botanist's bible. The adjective *biblical* is seldom capitalized.

Bibliographical form

The details of bibliographical form in a research paper may differ from author to author, from publication to publication, and especially from discipline to discipline. For the form you should use, consult the manual or style sheet published by the authority for your discipline—the Modern Language Association, for instance, or the American Psychological Association, or the Council of Biology Editors. *The Chicago Manual of Style* offers comprehensive coverage of forms. Whatever style you adopt, remember that the first rule for bibliographical form, as for note form, is consistency. Follow one style of documentation throughout. See **Research papers.**

"Big" words

A word is "big" if it's pretentious or excessively formal for the subject. See **Diction 2.**

black

Since the 1960s the term *Negro* has been replaced by *black,* usually not capitalized. *African-American* is also used.

bloc, block

Leave off the *k* only when you're writing about a common-interest group—of senators, for example—whose members can be expected to vote the same way

on legislation affecting the interest they share: The amendment was defeated by the farm bloc.

born, borne

In most senses of *bear,* the past participle is spelled with a final *e,* but the spelling *born* is used in the sense "brought into being" in the passive voice. Thus, "She has borne three children," but "Three children were born to her." *Born* is also used in the sense "determined by birth," as in "He was born to be hanged."

both

Both is used to emphasize two-ness: The twins were both there; Both Harry and his sister went. Though neither of these *both*s is necessary, each gives a legitimate emphasis. In "They both dressed alike," on the other hand, *both* adds nothing but awkwardness. "The two sides reached an agreement" makes better sense than "Both sides reached an agreement." "The both of them," a fairly common spoken idiom, should be avoided in writing.

both . . . and

When used as a pair (both the tire and the tube), the coordinating conjunctions *both* and *and* are called correlative conjunctions. See **Correlative conjunctions.**

Brackets

Brackets have specific uses in scholarly writing. Their main function is to enclose alterations and additions within quoted material:

> The story answers precisely . . . to that told in the third paragraph of Curll's *Key:* "But when he [Thomas Swift] had not yet gone half way, his Companion [Jonathan Swift] borrowed the Manuscript to peruse."—Robert Martin Adams, *Modern Philology*

In brackets Adams has identified for the reader the "he" and the "Companion" referred to by Curll.

Sic in brackets indicates that an error in the quoted material is being reproduced exactly: New Haven, Connecicut [*sic*]. Brackets may also be used to insert a correction: Cramer writes, "In April 1943 [the month was July], Jones published his first novel." And brackets function as parentheses within parentheses, particularly in legal documents and scholarly footnotes.

bring, take

Bring implies motion toward the speaker or writer (Bring it with you when you come). *Take* implies motion away from (Take it with you when you go). When the speaker or writer is doing the moving, he's glad he *brought* his camera along. When he has returned, he's glad he *took* his camera and *brought* it back. When the point of view doesn't matter, either term can be used: Potatoes were brought (*or* taken) from Ireland to France.

bring up

Bring up, like *raise,* is general usage for the more formal *rear* or *nurture* (That's the way I was brought up). It also means "to introduce" a subject: Having brought it up, he couldn't stop talking about it. See **raise, rear.**

British English

British English and American English differ noticeably in spelling. The British prefer *-re* to *-er* in ending words like *center* and *theater,* though they use both forms. They keep *-our* in a number of words (*honour, colour*) where Americans use *-or.* They use *x* in a few words like *inflexion* where Americans use *ct.* They double more consonants, as in *traveller* and *waggon.* And they spell some individual words differently, including automobile *tyre* for U.S. *tire.* They use more hyphens than we do and the opposite order of double and single quotation marks. They omit the periods we use after some abbreviations, including *Dr., Mr., Mrs., Ms.* Differences like these occur just often enough to show that a book is of British rather than American origin—certainly not enough to interfere with comprehension.

   The grammar of the popular levels of British and American English differs somewhat, though less than the vocabulary. Collective nouns referring to institutions are more likely to be plural in British usage (the government intend). British practice differs in small matters like the position of *only,* the proper preposition with *different,* the use of *shall,* and various idioms. It would be possible to assemble a fairly long list of such minor differences, but their importance shouldn't be exaggerated nor their occurrence allowed to obscure the fact that the resemblances far outnumber the differences and that the speech habits of the two countries represent two strands of the same language.

   Usages that originate in Great Britain frequently become vogue expressions in the United States. *Early on* and *a good read* are now established, but many popular imports soon become tiresome, as home-grown vogue words and phrases do. Hostility to Briticisms represents an attitude almost as old as the Republic. So does its opposite—an eagerness to embrace all things British, including Briticisms. British attitudes toward Americanisms are similarly divided.

Broad reference

A pronoun referring to the idea of a preceding clause rather than to a particular antecedent is said to have broad reference. See **Reference of pronouns 2.**

bunch

In formal English *bunch* is limited to objects that grow together like grapes or can be fastened together like carrots or keys. Used of people, *bunch* is moving into the general vocabulary: ". . . another monumental American myth—that Washington is run by a bunch of cynical, untrustworthy fools" (Nona B. Brown, *New York Times Book Review*).

burglar, robber, thief

All three take what isn't theirs, but the robber uses violence or threats, and the burglar breaks into a building. See **rob.**

Business letters

Business letters include not only the correspondence sent out by companies and corporations but also the letters of individuals to business firms, colleges, government agencies, newspapers, civic organizations, and so forth. When you write a letter to apply for a job or a scholarship, to obtain information, to request assistance, or to register a complaint, the recipient is more likely to give it serious attention if you have done your best with the packaging as well as the content.

1. Materials and appearance. Use good-quality white paper measuring 8½″ × 11″. If at all possible, type your final draft. Keep a copy of every business letter you write.

Most business letters are now written in block style without indentions, as shown in the sample. Convention calls for two lines of space between inside address and salutation, between salutation and body, and between body and close. Four lines of space are usually left for the signature. Other spacing depends on the length of your letter. In your drafts—and you may need to write several—work for an attractive, balanced page, with generous margins and plenty of space at top and bottom.

If you can sensibly do so, limit your letter to a single page. When you write more than one page, number the additional pages.

2. Heading. Give your full address and the date. Unless you use the abbreviations adopted by the Postal Service (which are not followed by periods), write out the names of states. Note that there's no comma between state and ZIP code and no punctuation at the ends of lines. If you use stationery with a letterhead that provides the address, type the date beneath it.

3. Inside address. Give the name and full address of the person you're writing to, just as it will appear on the envelope, beginning each line at the left margin. How far down the page you start the inside address depends on the length of your letter. For good balance, begin a short letter lower than a longer one.

Whenever possible, direct your letter to an individual or at least to an office (Personnel Director) or a department (Personnel Department).

4. Salutation. When you're writing to a person you can name, the best greeting is the simplest:

> Dear Ms. Nash:
> Dear Mr. Mahoney:

Note that a colon follows the name. When the circumstances call for special formality, "Dear Sir" or "Dear Madam" is the right choice. If you're addressing an organization, the traditional greeting is "Dear Sirs" (or "Gentlemen") or "Dear Sir" or, if there is reason for a feminine title, "Dear Mesdames" or "Dear Madam." But now the organization is frequently addressed by its name alone.

5. Body. Let the reader know immediately why you're writing. If you're replying to a letter, answering an advertisement, or writing at the suggestion of someone known to your reader, say so. By making your purpose clear from the outset, you help your reader concentrate immediately on what you have to say.

Your paragraphs will usually be much shorter than in a college paper—often no more than two or three sentences. Use a new paragraph for each item or each subdivision in your message, so that your reader can quickly identify the specific requests you're making or the facts you're providing and can refer to them in his response.

The style of a business letter should be clear and direct, and the letter itself should be as brief as clarity and completeness permit. The tone should be brisk without being brusque. You don't want to waste your reader's time, but neither do you want to insult him. And while being concise, be careful not to confuse or mystify him. Provide all relevant information, especially if you're complaining about defective merchandise, outlining a proposal, or seeking a job.

Finding just the right tone to use in your letter may require some effort, since you'll often have little notion what sort of person your reader is. Under such conditions, trying to make your writing seem personal may instead make it sound insincere. On the other hand, if you make no attempt to speak to the reader as an individual, your writing is likely to sound cold and aloof. The best technique is to address the reader as a stranger who is intelligent, respected, and probably short of time.

Don't make the mistake of trying to write in what you may think of as business style. The good business writer of today uses general English, avoiding both the clichés of commerce *(contact, finalize, angle, and/or)* and pretentious words like *ameliorate* for *improve, terminate* for *end.*

6. Close and signature. Begin the close at the left margin, in the middle of the page, or aligned with the heading, depending on overall balance. Follow it with a comma. For most business letters "Sincerely" or "Sincerely yours" is appropriate. If you're writing as an official—as purchasing agent for a campus co-op, for example—give your title under your typed name:

```
Leslie Archer
Purchasing Agent
```

In typing her name, a woman may or may not choose to indicate her marital status:

```
Dorothy Olson          (Mrs.) Dorothy Olson

(Ms.) Dorothy Olson     Dorothy Olson
                        (Mrs. Henry Olson)
(Miss) Dorothy Olson
```

7. Mailing. An envelope measuring 4″ × 9½″ is best for business letters, but an envelope measuring 3½″ × 6½″ can be used. Repeat the inside address on the envelope, and give your own name and address in the upper left corner.

Heading

```
                                    431 University Place
                                    Madison, Wisconsin 53706
                                    November 12, 1989
```

Inside
address

```
Mr. Dwight Morrison
Program Director
WSTR Television
546 Main Street
Madison, Wisconsin 53703
```

Salutation

```
Dear Mr. Morrison:
```

Body

```
Members of the Sociology Club at the University of Wisconsin have been
examining the influence of the university on the surrounding community,
and we believe that some of our findings may be of interest to your
viewers.

In order to assess the importance of the university to local business,
we have talked with many shop owners about the products they carry to
attract student customers. We have looked into the way political opin-
ions in some Madison neighborhoods have changed since students began
taking an active role in local elections. And we have found that a tu-
torial project started by students has begun to change some people's
attitudes toward the university.

Members of the Sociology Club would like very much to discuss with you
the possibility of using our study as the basis of a special program.
Two or three of us could arrange to meet with you at your convenience.
```

Close

```
                                    Sincerely yours,
```

Signature

```
                                    Marilyn Thompson
```

```
                                    Marilyn Thompson
                                    President
                                    Sociology Club
                                    University of Wisconsin
```

bust, burst, break

Bust, with *bust* or *busted* as past tense and past participle, is a slang variant of *burst* in its literal meanings: in general and formal writing, dams and balloons burst, *not* bust, and people burst out laughing. In contexts where the meaning is figurative, *bust*—frequently with the adverb *up* or *out*—is an informal substitute for *break,* as in this description of Dan Rather: "It was the up-from-poverty ardor of one who believed himself always a step from going bust, long past the time when his going bust was even a remote possibility" (Peter Boyer, *Vanity Fair*).

Broncos and trusts and noncommissioned officers are busted. So are hands in poker and blackjack, often causing their holders to go bust, or broke. Ball games can be busted wide open. After being busted (arrested), prison inmates may attempt to bust out.

Covered wagons heading west wore signs saying "California or bust," and in referring to the economy, *bust* as the opposite of *boom* is standard.

but

But is the natural coordinating conjunction to connect two contrasted statements: He left, but she stayed. *But* is lighter than *however,* less formal than *yet,* and, unlike *(al)though,* doesn't subordinate the clause that follows it.

1. Connecting equals. The locutions connected by *but* should be of equal grammatical rank:

> *Adjectives:* not *blue* but *green*
> *Adverbs:* He worked *quickly* but *accurately.*
> *Phrases:* She finally arrived, not *at lunch time* but *in the early evening.*
> *Clauses: The first day we rested,* but *on the second we got down to work.*
> *Sentences: The Rio Grande defied the best engineering minds of two countries for a century. But $10 million in flood-control work harnessed the treacherous stream.*

2. Connecting statements in opposition. The statements connected by *but* should be clearly opposed:

> He knows vaguely that the nation is not much good any more; he has read that the crust of the earth is shrinking rapidly and that the universe is growing steadily colder; but he does not believe that any of the three is in half as bad shape as he is.—James Thurber, *My Life and Hard Times*

In "The blisters on my feet were killing me, but the road seemed to go on forever," there's no real opposition. What's needed is a second clause like "but somehow I hobbled the last long mile."

3. Beginning sentences. *But,* like *and,* is often used to begin a sentence. Separation emphasizes the contrast with the preceding sentence. Be careful, though, not to follow a *but* clause with another *but* (or *however*) clause, or both the contrast and a measure of sense will be lost:

> The magazine they founded lasted only four years and was a financial failure, *but* its influence was enormous. *But* that was not the only contribution they made to literary history.

4. Punctuation. Two independent clauses connected by *but* should ordinarily be separated by a comma. The contrast in ideas makes punctuation desirable even when the clauses are relatively short: I couldn't get the whole license number, but I know it began with AOK. Though writers frequently use a comma after an initial *but* (But[,] it was too late for the aging man to regain his lost skill), no punctuation should separate *but* from the clause it introduces.

but that, but what

But that as a subordinating conjunction after a negative is avoided in formal styles but appears often in general and informal styles: I don't doubt but that she will come. *But what* is sometimes used in the same construction. *That* alone can be substituted for either *but that* or *but what:* I don't doubt that she will come.

but which

If you write a clause that begins with "but which," be sure it's preceded in the sentence by a *which* clause. See **which 3.**

can, may (could, might)

1. To express possibility, both *can* and *may* are used. *Can* is the only choice for simple ability: "I can swim" = "I'm able to swim." For feasibility ("I can swim today" = "There's nothing to prevent me from swimming today") *can* is less formal than *may:* "The Introduction only hints at the many paths the reader may follow" (Anna Benjamin, *Classical Philology*). Repeated use of *may* in this sense sounds excessively tentative or uncertain.

Could and might are used chiefly to convey a smaller degree of possibility than *can* and *may* or a shadow of doubt: She could be here by Saturday; I might have left it in my room. But *might* is also commonly substituted for *may,* with no difference in meaning. (*Might could* for *might be able to* is regional.) See **Tense 3.**

2. In requesting permission, *may* has a cool politeness appropriate to formal occasions: May I add one further point? Informally, *can* requests permission: Can I borrow the car next Sunday? *May* is also the formal choice in granting or denying permission. Except when the sense of institutional authority is central (Students may not attend class barefoot), *can* is more common: "After forbidding the Colonel to speak of love to her, she . . . tells him he can" (Henry Hewes, *Saturday Review*).

See **Divided usage.**

cannot, can not

Usage is divided. *Cannot* is usual.

can't hardly

Can't (or *cannot*) *hardly* should be changed to *can hardly,* since *hardly* means "probably not." See **Double negative.**

can't help but, can't seem to

Can't (or *cannot*) *help but* and *can't* (or *cannot*) *seem to* are established general idioms:

> The reader cannot help but question whether they, indeed, were so universally excellent.—Peter Walls, *Annals*

> What they can't seem to tolerate is unemployment, the feeling of being useless.—Alfred Kazin, *Saturday Review*

Even so, *cannot help but* is avoided by some conservative stylists, who prefer *cannot help* followed by a gerund: cannot help saying. In formal usage *seem unable to* is the alternative to *can't seem to.*

cap Capital letters

Capitalize the word marked.

Almost everyone uses capital letters at the beginning of sentences and proper names and for the pronoun *I*. Some other uses of capitals are matters of taste. Formal English uses more capitals than general English, and newspaper style cuts them to a minimum. The best policy is to capitalize in accordance with well-established convention and otherwise not to capitalize without good reason.

1. Sentence capitals. Capitalize the first word of a sentence.
a. Capitalize the first word of a sentence unless the sentence is set off by a dash or dashes or by parentheses within another sentence.
b. Capitalize the first word in a sentence following a colon if you want to emphasize the sentence (He promised this: The moment agreement was reached, the trucks would roll). Capitalize the first word of a question following a colon: "These findings raise an additional question: What effect does the structural organization of the lens have on accommodation?" (Jane F. Koretz and George H. Handelman, *Scientific American*).
c. In dialog, capitalize the first word of what the speaker says but not the second part of an interrupted quoted sentence: "Well," he said, "it [*not* It] was nice to see you again." Except in dialog, don't capitalize parts of sentences that are quoted: "First, what does it mean to 'compose as a woman'?" (Elizabeth A. Flynn, *College Composition and Communication*).

2. Proper names. Capitalize proper names and abbreviations of proper names: names of people and places, months, days of the week, historical events (the Civil War, the Council of Trent, the New Deal), documents (the Emancipation Proclamation), organizations, companies and their trade names, religious denominations, holidays, races and ethnic groups (but see **black**), languages, ships, named planes and trains, and nicknames. See **Course names.**

a. Capitalize *north, south,* and so on when they denote particular regions (the Southwest, the East) but not when they indicate direction (They started west in 1849).

b. Capitalize *army, navy,* and so on when they appear in full titles (the United States Army) and when they stand for the teams of the service academies. In other cases usage is divided: the American army (*or* Army), their navy (*or* Navy).

c. Capitalize *college* as part of a full title (He went to Beloit College) but not as a level of schooling (Neither of them went to college).

d. Don't capitalize proper nouns that have become common nouns: *tweed, sandwich, bohemian, plaster of paris,* and so on. Many proper adjectives in senses that no longer suggest their origins are not capitalized *(india ink, diesel engine),* but others usually are *(French cuffs, Spanish onion, Bibb lettuce).* Follow your dictionary.

e. Don't capitalize the names of the seasons except in *Fall term, Spring semester,* and so on, or for stylistic reasons.

3. Titles of books, articles, etc. Capitalize the first word, the last word (and the first word after a colon), and all other words except the articles *(a, an,* and *the)* and prepositions: *With Malice toward Some; Social Humanism: An International Symposium; Now Don't Try to Reason with Me;* "Biological Clocks of the Tidal Zone." See **Titles 2b.**

4. Titles, positions, relatives.
a. Capitalize personal titles before proper names: President Taft, Ambassador Clark, Senator Lodge, Sergeant York. Usage is divided when an individual is referred to by title alone: The President was there; The senator spoke at length. Official titles, including that of president of the United States, are seldom capitalized when they refer to no specific officeholder: "The president must be candid; the Senate must restrain itself" (Louis Henkin, *Foreign Affairs).* The trend is toward eliminating capitals.

b. Capitalize the names for family members when used as proper nouns: We had to get Father's consent. Don't capitalize when they are used as common nouns: My mother is a better dancer than I am.

5. Deity. Capitalize the name of the Supreme Being *(God, Jehovah, Allah), Jesus,* and nouns such as *Savior.* With pronouns referring to God and Jesus, practice is divided: *He, Him, His* or *he, him, his.*

6. *Street, river, park*, etc. Capitalize such words as *street, river, park, hotel,* and *church* when they follow a proper name (Fifth Avenue, Missouri River). Abgreviations of these words should also be capitalized: 2319 E. 100th St.

7. Abstractions. Usage is divided. Abstract nouns are likely to be capitalized in formal writing (less often in general) when the concepts they refer to are personified or when they refer to ideals or institutions: The State has nothing to do with the Church, nor the Church with the State.

8. Quoted lines of verse. Follow the poet's capitalization exactly.

Writers once used capitals as a form of emphasis, to stress certain words or call attention to them. Now when such initial capitals appear, the purpose is usually to amuse. If what you have to say isn't funny to begin with, capitals won't help.

X Careless mistakes

Correct the obvious mistake marked.

Careless lapses are inevitable in writing that's rushed. All writing that matters should be carefully edited and proofread. Comma splices and fragments, mistakes in the forms of verbs and pronouns *(broke* for *broken, it's* for *its),* missing words, and similar slips are likely to occur if you give too little time or too little attention to the final stages of preparing a paper.

Train yourself to proofread carefully. Check your manuscript for such elementary mistakes as these:

Letters omitted (the *n* of *an,* the *d* of *used to,* a final *y*)

End punctuation omitted (including the closing quotation marks after a quoted passage)

Words run together (a/lot, dining/room)

Words confused (accept, except; affect, effect; break, brake; capital, capitol; diffuse, defuse; loose, lose; principal, principle; quiet, quite; than, then; there, their; to, too; whether, weather; whose, who's)

Check also for the unnecessary repetition of a preposition or a conjunction: It is only natural *that* with the sudden change in the administration *that* people are worrying about what new policies may be introduced.

If you're uncertain about the spelling of a word, consult your dictionary. If you're unsure what word, word form, construction, or punctuation to use, consult this *Index.*

Caret

The caret, an inverted V, points to the place in a line of manuscript where something written above the line or in the margin should be inserted:

> because
> There was no reason for them not to get good grades, ∧ all they did was study.

This is an acceptable way to revise papers as long as the revisions are few and completely clear.

A caret used by an instructor as a correction mark indicates that something has been omitted.

Case Case

Correct the mistake in case.

The case of a noun or pronoun is one indication of its relationship to other elements in the sentence. (Another indication is word order.) The subject of a verb and the complement of a linking verb are in the nominative, or subjective, case *(Who is she?)*. The object of a verb or a preposition is in the accusative, or objective, case (I introduced *them;* He walked behind *her*). Certain modifiers of a noun are in the possessive, or genitive, case *(his* hat, the *dog's* bone).

Except for the spelling differences in the possessive singular *(dog's),* the possessive plural *(dogs'),* and the regular plural *(dogs),* the case of nouns presents no problems. The same form, called the common form or common case, is used in both subject and object positions: Your *dog* chased my *dog.* Pronouns have more forms—especially the pronouns we use most often. And when we're in the habit of using a few nonstandard forms in speech, the case of these pronouns may cause some problems in writing.

Most of the problems involve the six pronouns that change form to indicate all three cases: *I, he, she, we, they, who* (and its variant *whoever*). Thus: *She* sings (nominative); The song pleases *her* (accusative); It's *his* song, not *hers* (possessive). Four of the pronouns have a second form of the possessive, used when the pronoun doesn't precede a noun: *mine, hers, ours, theirs.* The pronouns *it* and *you* change their form only in the possessive: *its; your, yours.* These pronouns, as well as the indefinites (like *some/one, any/thing, each*), have the same form whether they are subjects or objects.

Here are the basic conventions to observe in standard written English:

1. Use the forms *I, he, she, we, they, who(ever)*
a. In subject position: *She* and *I* played on the same team; *He* asked *who* wrote the play *(who* is the subject of *wrote,* not the object of *asked); Whoever* wrote it had a good ear for dialog.
b. In apposition to a noun or pronoun in subject position: The winning couple, Phil and *I,* got a trip to Disneyland; We, Phil and *I,* got a trip. . . .
c. After a linking verb: It is *he* who should pay the bill. (But see **it's me.**)

2. Use the forms *me, him, her, us, them*
a. In object position: The song reminded Jack and *me* (object of verb) of our high-school graduation; College is harder for *him* than for *me* (object of preposition); He wanted to meet *her* (object of infinitive).

b. In apposition to a noun or pronoun in object position: Prizes went to the top students, Mary and *me;* The prizes went to us, Mary and *me.*

3. The special problem of *whom(ever)*. The object form *whom(ever)* is regularly used after a preposition: To *whom* was the remark addressed? But speakers and writers sometimes deliberately shift the preposition to the end of the sentence and use *who* for its object: *Who* was the remark addressed to? In general English, *who* at the beginning of a sentence is also increasingly common for the object of a verb: *Who* do we ask for advice? Even among formal stylists, usage is divided. See **who, whom.**

4. Use the possessive case of nouns and pronouns to indicate possession and the other relationships discussed in **Possessive case 2,** except when the *of* phrase is customary (the end *of the street,* the roof *of the house):* It was the other *man's* hat, not *his;* the mixup resulted from *their* putting them on the same hook. *"Their* putting" illustrates the standard form for a pronoun that's the subject of a gerund. When a noun is the subject of a gerund, the common case is usual in informal and general English and is the choice of some formal writers: He complained about the *book* (more formal: *book's*) going out of print. See **Gerunds 2.**

    Avoid the nonstandard *hisself* for *himself* and *theirself* or *theirselves* for *themselves.*

    See **Pronouns 1, 4; Possessive case.**

catholic, Catholic

Written with a small *c, catholic* is a rather formal synonym for "universal or broad in sympathies or interests." In general American usage, *Catholic* written with a capital *c* is taken as equivalent to *Roman Catholic,* both as a noun (She's a Catholic) and as an adjective (Catholic labor unions).

Cause and effect

Why something occurred (cause) or what will result from it (effect) often interests us as much as what happened.

1. Signals of cause-effect relations. Causal connections are conveyed by explicit statements *(A caused B; B is the effect of A),* by many familiar transitional words and phrases *(because* or *since, so that* or *in order that, thus* or *as a result),* and sometimes by simply placing one statement immediately after another (In March, he became the target of an investigation; three months later he disappeared).

2. Discovering causes. Papers that investigate cause range from discussions of historical events and scientific experiments to arguments that assign responsibility or predict the consequences of a course of action. Almost all causal analysis has an argumentative edge to it. To win acceptance for a *probable* interpretation of the facts, the writer must not simply state a conclusion but must justify and support it by demonstrating, offering specific information, tying probable cause to known effect or probable results to an existing situation.

Because we all have a habit of jumping to the most obvious conclusion, in analyzing causes and effects you must discipline yourself to keep an open mind until you've collected enough evidence to make a convincing case, and you must avoid oversimplifying: most events have a number of causes, not just one. At the same time, resist the temptation to search out more and more remote causes. There's no need to go back to Genesis to explain the genesis of an event of current local interest. Finally, be sure you end up showing that something happened *because* of something else—the whole purpose of causal analysis—not merely that something happened *after* something else. Confusing temporal sequence with cause is a logical fallacy called *post hoc, ergo propter hoc,* "after this, therefore because of this." See **Fallacies, Logical thinking.**

censor, censure

When we *censor,* we delete or suppress. When we *censure,* we condemn or express serious disapproval. To complicate matters, the adjective *censorious* refers to censuring.

center around

Precisionists condemn it as illogical, but *center around* (The story centers around the theft of a necklace) is standard idiom: "accompanied by a propaganda war centered around her rightness and fitness for the throne" (Kerby Neil, *Modern Philology*). In some formal styles *on* or *upon* may be substituted for *around,* or *revolve* may be used instead of *center.* See **Logic and language.**

Centuries

The first century A.D. ran from the beginning of the year 1 to the end of the year 100. The twentieth century began on January 1, 1901, and will end on December 31, 2000. To name the century correctly, add one to the number of its hundred except in the last year, when the number of the hundred is the number of the century, too.

For clarity, the hundred can be named, even in formal writing: Dr. Johnson lived in the seventeen-hundreds. Similar practice—with and without the centuries—is standard in naming decades: the Sixties, the nineteen-twenties. (Except when the date begins a sentence, use figures for century plus decade: the 1920s.)

chauvinist

Originally *chauvinist* was used almost exclusively to mean "super-patriot" or "jingoist." Then feminists began to use the label *male chauvinist* to describe a man who considered women inferior to men; and *chauvinist* alone was often used with this second meaning. *Chauvinist* may also be applied to anyone who is devoted to a particular group, place, or cause. In using the term, the surest way to make your meaning clear is to specify what sort of chauvinist you're writing about. The surest way to use the term fairly is to keep in mind that a point of view that conflicts with yours is not proof of chauvinism.

Circumlocution

A circumlocution is a roundabout way of saying what could—and usually should—be expressed directly. See **Wordiness.**

Cities

If you refer to a city in your writing, locate it by state or by country only if it's a city your readers aren't familiar with or if it's not the city they might assume it is: Paris, Texas, but not Paris, France; Athens, Georgia, or Athens, Ohio, but not Athens, Greece.

claim

Used in the sense of "say" or "declare," *claim* suggests to many readers that the assertion should be regarded skeptically: He claims to be opposed to gun control. Using it as a mere variant of *say* (He claimed he was taking Chemistry 301) can therefore be misleading. See **say.**

Classification and division

Classification and division are related methods of analyzing and writing about a subject. Division is the process of separating a single object (a car) or institution (a college) or concept (communism) into its parts or constituent elements. Classification is the process of bringing together objects, institutions, or concepts that have something in common: cars, colleges, political philosophies can be sorted into groups on the basis of their resemblances. Division reveals internal structure; classification identifies family likenesses. In writing a paper on college life, you might draw on both methods, dividing the curriculum into its subject areas or campus social life into its various organizations and activities and classifying students on the basis of their attitudes toward their courses or the ways they use their leisure time or some other principle.

As the example suggests, one group can be classified in many different ways, and the same object can be divided into different collections of parts, depending on the writer's purpose or interest. That interest will determine whether the division or classification should meet strict requirements of completeness (all parts or items accounted for) and consistency (no overlapping of parts or of groups). In some informal groupings there is no attempt to be either complete or consistent. But a writer interested in trying to organize her experience—the real purpose of classifying or dividing—will work hard to make her analysis reasonably complete and consistent. And if she uses an original basis for dividing or classifying, she may offer her readers a new way of looking at things.

See **Logical thinking.**

Clauses

Each combination of a complete subject, like *he,* and a complete predicate, like *came home,* is traditionally called a clause. "He came home" is an independent clause. Grammatically it can stand alone. "When he came home" is a dependent clause. In ordinary prose a dependent clause does not stand alone as a sentence but is preceded or followed by an independent clause: When he came home, he looked for the cat.

1. The clause structure of sentences. The sentences that follow in **a, b, c,** and **d** both define and illustrate. Simple subjects and simple predicates are italicized. *IC* in brackets introduces an independent clause, *DC* a dependent one.

a. [IC] A simple *sentence* (like this one) *consists* of a single independent subject-predicate combination.

b. [IC] A compound *sentence has* two or more clauses of equal grammatical value; [IC] these *clauses are joined* by a coordinating conjunction, by a conjunctive adverb, or (as in this sentence) by a semicolon. [IC] *A writer may decide,* for reasons of emphasis or rhythm, to break a compound sentence into two separate simple sentences, [IC] and in such cases the only *difference* between the compound sentence and the separate sentences *is* punctuation.

c. [IC begun] A complex *sentence,* like the one [DC] that *you are* now *reading,* [IC continued] *has* at least one independent clause and one or more dependent, or subordinate, clauses, [DC] *which function* as nominals, adjectivals, or adverbials.

d. [DC] As the hyphenated *term indicates,* [IC] a compound-complex *sentence* (again illustrated by the sentence [DC] *you are reading*) *combines* the features of both compound and complex sentences: [IC] *it contains* two or more independent clauses and one or more dependent clauses.

See **Adjectivals 1, Adverbials, Noun clauses, Relative clauses.**

2. Reduced clauses. Though the typical clause as traditionally defined has an expressed subject and a predicate with a full verb, many constructions lack one or the other of these elements and yet function in sentences like typical clauses. Reduced clauses are of two types:

a. Elliptical clauses, in which a full verb can be reconstructed because it occurs earlier in the sentence:

> I don't *believe it* any more than you [*believe it*].
> They can *speak Russian,* and so can Bill [*speak Russian*].

b. Abridged clauses, in which the reader must rely on sense to fill in the missing subject and a form of *be:*

> While [*I* was] waiting, *I* read the newspaper.
> When [*he* had] fully recovered, *he* went back to work.
> Though [*she* was] a rapid reader, *she* disliked books.
> After [*they* had been] standing in line for an hour, *they* left.
> Though [*we* were] tired, *we* kept on working.

When the omitted subject isn't the same as the subject of the main clause, the result is often a dangling modifier.

See **Complex sentence, Compound-complex sentence, Compound sentence, Dangling modifiers, Elliptical constructions, Restrictive and nonrestrictive modifiers.**

Cliché

A cliché is a worn-out word or phrase like "tragic death," "bright and early." See **Triteness.**

Clipped words

Ad[*vertisement*], [*news*]*paper, photo*[*graph*], and [*tele*]*phone* are clipped words. See **Origin of words 3c.**

clone

As noun and verb, *clone* has moved from biology, where it refers to asexual reproduction and a result thereof, into the general vocabulary, where it is often used to mean no more than "copy" or "imitation": still another sitcom clone. For that meaning, *copy* or *imitation* is the better choice.

coh Coherence

Make clear the relation between the parts of this sentence or between these sentences or these paragraphs.

Coherence—the traditional name for relationship, connection, consecutiveness—is essential in expository writing. It's essential because you can't count on the minds of others working the same way your mind works. You must guide your readers from one idea, from one sentence, to another. To make a coherent presentation, you have to arrange your ideas so that others can understand them.

Though careful planning in the prewriting stage will help you make clear the relationship of your ideas, testing for coherence must come after you've written a draft of your paper. To see if it hangs together, try to read it as your readers will—as if the content is new to you. Ask yourself if the relationship between statements is clear, if it's possible to move easily from one clause or sentence or paragraph to the next without losing the thread. For a passage like the following, all the logical connectives were probably in the writer's head, but that didn't help readers who tried to make sense of what was on paper:

> Disco isn't usually written to express a deep emotional meaning. All over the world people like a rhythm they can dance to. Sometimes they get such crowds that they have to turn people away.

There are many words and phrases that signal the relationship between sentence parts, sentences, and paragraphs. These signs, and suggestions for establishing coherence, are discussed in **Conjunctions and style, Prepositions, Reference of pronouns, and Transition.**

cohort

Even though formal stylists may have given up demanding that any use of *cohort* reflect the origin of the term—a Roman military unit of several hundred—many continue to reject *cohort* as a substitute for singular *admirer, supporter, companion, pal.* In general styles *cohort* gets by but smacks of newspaper jargon.

Collective nouns

A collective noun is a noun whose singular form names a group of objects or persons or acts. Here are some familiar examples:

army	crowd	group	offspring
audience	dozen	herd	orchestra
class	faculty	jury	public
committee	family	majority	remainder
couple	gang	number	team

Some collectives have regular plural forms *(army, armies).* Some do not *(offspring).* The plural of a collective noun signifies different groups: The *audiences* of New York and Seattle differed in their reception of the movie.

Some collectives are typically used in the singular *(committee is)* and some typically in the plural *(police are).* Most are singular in one context, plural in a different one, depending on the way the writer thinks about the group. When it's the group as a whole, the collective noun takes a singular verb and a singular pronoun: "A *group* of the . . . stories *features* characters whose lives have become misshapen through means other than self-assertion" (Welford Dunaway Taylor, *Sherwood Anderson*).

When it's the individual units of the group that the writer has in mind, the noun takes a plural verb and plural pronoun: "Psychologists asked a *group* of young men and women what sex *they* wanted *their* first child to be" *(Psychology Today).* With this example, compare "Now that John is back, the *group has its* old solidarity."

Trouble occurs when a writer treats a collective noun inconsistently. He begins by treating the word as a singular, and as long as the verb follows it closely, he makes the verb singular: The inner *circle has* great influence. But if a plural modifier comes between the collective noun and the verb, he thinks of the members of the group rather than of the group as a unit, and he shifts to a plural verb: This inner *circle* of ambitious men *pose* a serious threat.

A writer is also likely to be inconsistent when his way of thinking about the collective comes into conflict with the meaning of a sentence he's writing. He may want to keep a collective noun singular, but if the meaning calls for a plural construction, he'll often make the shift unconsciously, sometimes in midsentence:

> The entire *congregation troops* into the church, *seats itself,* and *remains* for a good two hours, while an aged curé berates *them* [consistency demands *it*] for *their* [*its*] sins.

In making your constructions consistent, you may find that it's the collective subject that needs to be changed, rather than the pronouns. In the example just given, beginning the sentence with "All members of the congregation troop into the church, seat themselves . . ." would avoid the problem.

Casual shifts in number are common in speech, but they're likely to attract unfavorable attention in general writing, and they're almost certain to in formal writing. When you read over your papers, be sure you haven't treated the same collective nouns as both singular and plural.

See **Agreement 1b, each, every.**

Colloquial English

Usage that's characteristic of the way we talk is called colloquial. Though the division between spoken English and written English isn't nearly as sharp as it once was, some spoken usages may be inappropriate in all but the most informal writing *(You know? Terrific! Awesome!),* just as some features of written English are inappropriate in all but the most formal speech.

Dictionaries sometimes mark words *Colloq.* to indicate that they're more common in speech than in writing. Many readers mistakenly take the label to mean that the dictionaries' editors frown upon these words. In fact, colloquial words can be accurate and expressive and are used freely in good general writing. Because misinterpretation of *colloquial* is common, the label is avoided in this book. If a usage is more common in speech than in writing, that fact is stated. If the word or expression is standard English but rarely appears in general or formal writing, it's labeled informal.

See **Spoken and written English.**

 ## Colon

 Use a colon here. Or reconsider the use of this colon.

The colon is a mark of anticipation. It indicates that what follows the mark will supplement what came before it.

1. Introductory uses. Use a colon before a series of illustrative or explanatory words, phrases, or clauses when the series is not preceded by an introductory word or phrase or when it's formally introduced by a set phrase like *as follows* or *the following:*

> There are two modes of thinking, two poles by which one can orientate one's life: politics and religion.—H. Saddhatissa, *The Buddha's Way*

> Classifying the poetry written from 1500 to 1900 in accordance with this distinction, we discover a sequence which runs as follows: predicative, then balanced; predicative, then balanced.—Josephine Miles, *PMLA*

Do not use a colon after less formal introductory words *(like, such as, for example, namely)* that make what follows a part of the clause:

> The shop carried a lot of ethnic recordings, like[:] West African, Moorish, Egyptian, and Arabian.

Do not use a colon between a verb and its object or complement:

> The reason I went broke freshman week was that I had to buy[:] books, furniture, and tickets to a lot of things I knew I'd never go to.

> My three immediate goals are[:] to survive midyear exams, to get to Colorado, and to ski until my legs wear out.

When appropriate, use a colon to introduce quotations in factual writing, especially if they run to more than one sentence. The colon is more common in formal than in general or informal writing, and its appropriateness depends in part on the way you introduce the quotation. If it's built into the sentence, a comma is usual. If it's more formally introduced, a colon fits the context. Both situations are illustrated in this example:

> For example, the report cannot say, "It was a wonderful car," but must say something like this: "It has been driven 50,000 miles and has never required any repairs."—S. I. Hayakawa, *Language in Thought and Action*

2. Between clauses. Particularly in a formal paper, you may decide to use a colon between the clauses of a compound sentence when the second clause illustrates, restates, or amplifies the first:

> The supposition that words are used principally to convey thoughts is one of the most elementary of possible errors: they are used mainly to proclaim emotional effects on the hearers or attitudes that will lead to practical results.—H. R. Huse, *The Illiteracy of the Literate*

(Note that here a semicolon could be used instead of a colon, with a slightly different effect. A semicolon cannot introduce a series or a quotation.)

3. Capitals following. In most cases, use a lowercase letter to begin an independent clause after a colon. (See the example in **2** above.) Use a capital letter when what follows is a question, a lengthy, complex statement, perhaps comprising more than one sentence, or a statement that you want to give special prominence: ''This is how to dispose of the pending bill: Kill it'' (James J. Kilpatrick, syndicated columnist).

4. Conventional uses.
a. After the salutation of formal letters: Dear Sir:
b. Between hours and minutes in figures: 11:30 A.M.
c. Between Bible chapter and verse: Genesis 9:3–5.
d. In ratios and proportions when the numbers are written as figures: concrete mixed 5:3:1. Two colons are used between the pairs in a full proportion: 1:2::3:6.

Comma

Insert or remove a comma at the place marked.

''Should there be a comma here?'' is the question most often asked about punctuation. The general advice of this book is to use commas wherever established conventions demand them and to use them elsewhere only if they'll help the reader or serve some other specific purpose. When there's a choice, your decision should be based on appropriateness: the complex structures and deliberate pace of much formal writing call for more commas than the simpler, brisker sentences of general English.

The following list of uses of the comma outlines the treatment in this article. The numbers and letters refer to sections and subsections.

1. To separate independent clauses in a sentence
a. Clauses connected by *and*
b. Clauses connected by *but*
c. Clauses connected by *for*
d. Clauses not connected by a coordinating conjunction

2. With preceding and following elements
a. After a dependent clause or long phrase preceding the main clause
b. Before a dependent clause or long phrase following the main clause and not essential to its full meaning

3. To set off nonrestrictive modifiers

4. To enclose interrupting and parenthetical elements
a. Around interrupting elements
b. Around conjunctive adverbs within clauses

5. In lists and series
a. Between units in lists and series
b. Between coordinate adjectives

6. For clarity

7. For emphasis and contrast

8. Between main sentence elements
a. Subject and verb
b. Verb and object
c. Compound predicate

9. In conventional practice
a. In dates
b. In addresses
c. After salutations in all but formal letters
d. After names in direct address
e. In figures
f. With degrees and titles
g. With weak exclamations
h. To show omission

10. With other marks of punctuation
 a. With parentheses
 b. And dash
 c. With quotation marks **(Quotation marks 4b, 4c)**

C₁ **1. To separate independent clauses in a sentence.**
a. And. Use a comma before the coordinating conjunction *and* when the clauses are rather long and when you want to emphasize their distinctness, as when they have different subjects:

> Descriptive linguists tended to be condescending, if not downright censorious, toward notions of correctness in language, and a certain amount of the "permissiveness" they inspired has seeped into the English classroom, arousing the ire of purists.— Dwight Bolinger, *Aspects of Language*

When the independent clauses are short and closely related in meaning, the comma is often omitted: "Who will live and who will die?" *(Time)*. But there's no rule that forbids using a comma to separate the clauses in a compound sentence, no matter what their length or relationship. Many experienced writers automatically place a comma before the coordinating conjunction and so guard against the momentary confusion that a sentence like this one invites: "A crowd of spectators lined the walkway to see him[ ] and the President, in standard fashion, passed along the crowd" *(New York Times)*.
b. But. Use a comma between two independent clauses joined by *but*, regard-

less of their length, to emphasize the contrast: "His achievements in office have been difficult to assess, but they have been formidable" (John David Hamilton, *Atlantic*).

c. For. Use a comma between independent clauses connected by the conjunction *for* to avoid confusion with the preposition *for:* They were obviously mistaken, for intercollegiate sports are always competitive. Without the guidance provided by the comma, a reader might stride through "They were obviously mistaken for intercollegiate sports," then stumble and have to begin all over again.

d. Use a comma alone in place of a coordinating conjunction or a semicolon when you have good reason to do so. Thoughtless use of such punctuation is likely to produce a comma splice (see **Comma splice**), but under certain conditions a comma can appropriately stand between independent clauses not joined by a conjunction:

> The intellect gets busy, means and methods are studied, purposes are assessed.—Gerald Warner Brace, *The Stuff of Fiction*

> Weasels not only take over prey nests, they also remodel them.—Mikael Sardell, *Natural History*

The clauses here are short, parallel in form, and closely bound together in meaning. Semicolons, the traditional punctuation between independent clauses not joined by coordinating conjunctions, would slow the pace and make the style more formal.

Sentences punctuated like these are common in print. Not all are successful. If the clauses are neither short nor similar in structure, and if one or more of them contains internal punctuation, the reader may have a hard time grasping the meaning. In "The strongest and luckiest private constituencies win, social needs get pushed aside, as in the 50s, to explode a decade later" (Bill Moyers, *Newsweek*), a reader who assumes that the writer is building a series (The strongest and luckiest private constituencies win, social needs get pushed aside, and the gulf between haves and have-nots widens) is brought up short and forced to reread the sentence.

Between two independent clauses, then, you can put a coordinating conjunction (with or without a comma or a semicolon before it), a semicolon alone, or a comma alone. The choice is a matter of style. But you need to take convention into account. Before using a comma alone, consider your audience. Some very conservative readers are invariably uneasy about such punctuation. If you can assume that your audience won't automatically condemn the practice, then be sure you're using the comma for a purpose. Most important, be sure that your use of a comma alone won't make your reader's task more difficult.

See **Fused sentence, Semicolon 1.**

C2   **2. With preceding and following elements.**

a. Use a comma after an introductory dependent clause or a long introductory phrase:

> While the CIA sometimes is able to refute publicly allegations and criticism, usually it must remain silent.—Robert M. Gates, *Foreign Affairs*

> With the waning of the Middle Ages and the initiation of the voyages of discovery, the European mind shifted its focus from the hereafter to the world beyond the horizon.—Anne W. Tennant, *Américas*

When the preceding phrase is short or when the dependent clause has the same subject as the independent clause, the comma is often omitted:

> From France this second wave of flu spread west to England and south to Spain.—Jack Fincher, *Smithsonian*

> As I drive I see small lots staked off and a road newly graveled in one of the creek bottoms.—Wendell Berry, "The Journey's End"

Some professional writers put commas after all introductory clauses and after all introductory phrases that contain verbals. In that way they establish a consistent pattern and avoid risking the momentary confusion that may result from the absence of punctuation.

b. Use a comma before a dependent clause or long phrase that follows the main clause if the subordinate element isn't absolutely essential to the meaning of the main clause:

> And as I said earlier, the rear ones should probably be snow tires, even if you get the truck in May.—Noel Perrin, *First Person Rural*

> Over the past few years, her behavior has been increasingly erratic, culminating last May in her arrest and conviction for shoplifting.—Patricia Morrisroe, *New York*

C3 **3. To set off nonrestrictive modifiers.** Use a comma to set off word groups that don't restrict the meaning of the noun or verb or clause they modify. The italicized word groups in the following sentences are nonrestrictive:

> *With these numbers in hand,* he studied certain factors in each week's game, *which he referred to as a "test."*—Mike D'Orso, *Sports Illustrated*

> After we had discussed the Donell trial, I asked about the Houston litigation, *which is how the family-trust fight is usually referred to.*—John Davidson, *Vanity Fair*

See **Restrictive and nonrestrictive modifiers.**

C4 **4. To enclose interrupting and parenthetical elements.**
a. Use commas around a word, phrase, or clause that interrupts the main structure of the sentence:

> Of course, changes in military posture and strategy should be made if assessments of the threat change.—Henry Kissinger and Cyrus Vance, *Foreign Affairs*

> Industry as a whole, however, is still not sensitive enough to either the plight or the value of great numbers of older workers.—*Modern Maturity*

The American Cancer Society, formed in 1945 from the American Society for the Control of Cancer, which was founded in 1913, pioneered public education to reduce irrational fear of the disease and encourage consultation with a physician when a suspicious symptom appeared.—Arthur I. Holleb, *The American Cancer Society Cancer Book*

Enclosing calls for two commas. Forgetting the second one can cause confusion: "If factory workers and farmers became more efficient, Soviet citizens were told this week[ ] they would get more domestic goods, food, housing, hospitals and schools" *(Newport Daily News)*.

Usage is divided over setting off short parenthetical expressions like *of course*. Enclosing them in commas is more characteristic of formal than of general writing. There's often a difference in emphasis as well as tone depending on whether or not commas are used:

As one of the second generation of boppers, he had of course learned the new harmonic system the founders had invented.—James Lincoln Collier, *The Making of Jazz*

The question, of course, is not whether the family will "survive."—*Time*

b. Use commas around a conjunctive adverb that stands after the first phrase of its clause: It was this ridiculous proposal, however, that won majority approval. At the beginning of a sentence, conjunctive adverbs may or may not be set off, depending on whether the writer wants the separation a comma would provide: Therefore[,] I have decided to withdraw my application. *But* and other coordinating conjunctions are a part of the clauses in which they appear and should not be set off: But[ ] a solution must be found. See **however.**

C5 5. In lists and series.

a. Use commas to separate the units in lists and series: "He has read everything he could lay his hands on, manuscripts and printed, that was written during the period: plays, sermons, ballads, broadsides, letters, diaries, and, above all, court records" (Edmund S. Morgan, *New York Review of Books*). See **Semicolon 2.**

Usage is divided over the use of a comma before the conjunction in a series: "letters, diaries, and records" or "letters, diaries and records." A comma is often a safeguard against boners. Here a comma would prevent a misreading that might bring on a giggle: "He had small shoulders, a thick chest holding a strong heart[ ] and heavy thighs" (Richard Mandell, *Sports Illustrated*). See **Series.**

b. Use a comma between adjectives modifying the same noun. In the sentence "Though it was a hot, sticky, miserable day, Mrs. Marston looked cool in her fresh gingham dress," there are commas between *hot* and *sticky* and between *sticky* and *miserable* because each stands in the same relation to the noun *day*. "Hot *and* sticky *and* miserable" would make sense. There's no comma between *fresh* and *gingham* because *fresh* modifies *gingham dress*, not just *dress*. "Fresh *and* gingham" would not make sense.

Some writers use no comma when two adjectives modify the noun: a hot sticky day; the tall dark woman. There's no loss of clarity, but if you never use a comma between such adjectives, you deprive yourself of a rhetorical resource. By separating, a comma provides emphasis. Compare these two versions:

> His long, greasy hair hung down to the shoulders of his worn, faded jacket.
>
> His long greasy hair hung down to the shoulders of his worn faded jacket.

In the first, *greasy* and *faded* stand out as separate modifiers of their nouns.

C6 **6. For clarity.** Use a comma to help readers interpret a sentence correctly as they go along, so that they don't have to go back over it to get its meaning.

A comma between clauses joined by *for* makes it clear that the word is being used as a conjunction rather than as a preposition. Similarly, a comma can prevent a reader from even momentarily mistaking the subject of one verb for the object of another:

> When the boll weevil struck, the credit system collapsed and ruined both landowners and tenants. (*Not* When the boll weevil struck the credit system . . .)
>
> Soon after the inspector left, the room was crowded with curious onlookers. (*Not* Soon after the inspector left the room . . .)
>
> While I was surveying, the ice, which was sixteen inches thick, undulated under a slight wind like water (Henry David Thoreau, *Walden*). (*Not* While I was surveying the ice . . .)

Here a comma marks the end of a phrase and keeps *general* from being misread as an adjective: "In general, concerns about income are more political than economic" (*New Yorker*). (*Not* In general concerns . . .)

A comma can also make immediately clear whether a modifier goes with what precedes or with what follows: A great crowd of shoppers milled around inside, and outside hundreds more were storming the doors. (*Not* . . . milled around inside and outside . . .)

In all the preceding examples there is justification other than clarity for using a comma. In the following sentence commas would simply make reading easier: "Another positive step would be to require as many people as are able[,] to work for a living[,] and to find or create jobs for them" (Carll Tucker, *Saturday Review*). And a comma helps when a word is used twice in a row: What he does, does not concern me.

C7 **7. For emphasis and contrast.** When *and* connects two words or phrases, there's no need to set them apart with a comma. But because a comma tends to keep distinct the elements it separates and to emphasize slightly the element that follows it, you may occasionally want to use commas for these purposes alone: ''Savannah was a port, and a 'good town' as he remembered it'' (Stanley Dance, *The World of Earl Hines*).

Here the last comma slows the sentence movement and gives emphasis to *always:* ''A youthful voice, raised over questions of art, even the dumbest of art, impresses me, always'' (Mark Jacobson, *Esquire*).

C8 **8. Between main sentence elements.**
a. Subject and verb. Though it sometimes occurs in old-fashioned formal prose, don't use a comma between a subject and its verb: ''All that democracy means[,] is as equal a participation in rights as is practicable'' (James Fenimore Cooper, *The American Democrat*).
b. Verb and object. Don't use a comma between a verb and its object. (Words and phrases that must be set off by pairs of commas may, of course, come between subject and verb and between verb and object. See **4** above.)
c. Compound predicate. Use a comma between the verbs of a compound predicate only when the sentence is so long and involved that it's difficult to read or when you feel a need for special emphasis or contrast. This is a sensible rule and one that many writers, teachers, and editors insist on, though in published prose the verbs in a compound predicate are frequently separated by a comma when no need for aid to the reader or for special emphasis or contrast is apparent: ''Those who study gender may revise our concepts of humanity and nature, and enlarge our sense of the human predicament'' (Jill K. Conway, Susan C. Bourque, Joan W. Scott, *Daedalus*).

C9 **9. In conventional practice.**
a. In dates, to separate the day of the month from the year: May 26, 1990. When the day of the month isn't given, a comma may or may not be used: In September 1846 *or* In September, 1846. If a comma precedes the year, punctuation should also follow it: In September, 1846, the government fell.
b. In addresses, to separate small units from larger: Washington, D.C.; Chicago, Illinois; Hamilton, Madison County, New York; Berne, Switzerland.
c. After salutations in all but formal letters: Dear John,
d. To set off names in direct address: Spin it, Henry.
e. In figures, to separate thousands, millions, etc.: 4,672,342. In some styles no comma is used in figures with four digits: 2750.
f. To separate degrees and titles from the names they follow: Gerald F. Rogers, D.D.S.; William Lamb, Viscount Melbourne. The comma before *Jr.* after a name is now sometimes omitted: Charles Evans Hughes[,] Jr.
g. After a weak exclamation like *well, why, oh:* Oh, what's the use?
h. Sometimes to show the omission of a word or words required to fill out a construction: He took the right-hand turn; I, the left.

C10 **10. With other marks of punctuation.**
a. When parentheses come at the end of a phrase or clause that's followed by a comma, put the comma after the *closing* parenthesis: After returning from Italy (in 1988), she lived in Oconomowoc.

b. Use a comma or a dash, not both.

c. For the use of commas with quotation marks, see **Quotation marks 4b, 4c.**

☞ Comma splice

Revise the sentence marked by changing the comma to a semicolon or a period, or by inserting an appropriate conjunction, or by rephrasing to make a more satisfactory sentence.

A comma splice (comma blunder, comma fault) occurs when, without good reason, a comma alone is used to separate the independent clauses of a compound or a compound-complex sentence: He stared at his visitor, it was a dark, snowy night. Such punctuation may be justified by the matching structure of the clauses or by the close relationship of their content or the rhetorical impact (see **Comma 1d**):

> I was awed by this system, I believed in it, I respected its force.—Alfred Kazin, *A Walker in the City*

> Not only are women put off, they are also put down, numerically and otherwise. —Francine Frank and Frank Ashen, *Language and the Sexes*

There are various ways to correct a comma splice:

1. Replace the comma with a period or semicolon.

> He stared at his visitor, it was too dark to see who it was.

> *Revised:* He stared at his visitor. It was too dark to see who it was.

This is the simplest remedy but not always the best one. Inserting a period in the following sentence would simply produce two weak sentences in place of one:

> I think Americans should read this book, they would get a more accurate picture of problems in the Middle East.

> *Revised:* I think Americans should read this book; they would get a more accurate picture of problems in the Middle East. (For a better revision, see **3** below.)

2. Join statements that belong together with a conjunction that makes their relationship clear. If you choose a coordinating conjunction, you should probably keep the comma (see **Comma 1a**). If you choose a conjunctive adverb, replace the comma with a semicolon (see **Semicolon 1b**):

> An increase in student fees would enable us to balance the budget, this is clearly not the time for it.

> *Revised:* An increase in student fees would enable us to balance the budget, but this (*or* budget; however, this) is clearly not the time for it.

3. Rewrite the sentence, perhaps subordinating one of the clauses, perhaps making a single independent clause. Work to produce a good sentence, not just to correct the comma splice:

> I think Americans should read this book, they would get a more accurate picture of problems in the Middle East.

> *Revised:* I think Americans should read this book for a more accurate picture of problems in the Middle East.

> One part receives the stimulus from outside and transmits the impulse to the cell, this is known as the dendrite.

> *Revised:* One part, known as the dendrite, receives the stimulus from outside and transmits the impulse to the cell.

If you can make a sure distinction between an independent clause and a dependent clause, you should find it easy to spot any comma splices in your sentences. Look first to see how many independent subject-verb combinations you have in each group of words punctuated as a single sentence. If there are two independent clauses, see if you have a connective between them. If there's no connective but only a comma, you've probably produced a comma splice. For exceptions, see **Comma 1d.** Compare **Fused sentence.**

Commands and requests

Direct commands are also called imperatives: Hurry up; Shut the door; Fill out the coupon and mail it today. Punctuate emphatic commands with an exclamation mark: Stop! Let's go! Punctuate less emphatic ones with a period: Stop at the next gas station.

Commands and requests are often expressed in the form of questions. Use question marks after those that you intend as questions: Would you be willing to take part in the program? Use periods after those you mean to be orders: Will you please report no later than 9:15.

committee

Committee is a collective noun, usually construed as singular. When the logic of the sentence makes it clear that you're not thinking of the committee as a single unit (The committee, men and women alike, were bustling around, collecting their papers and other belongings), it's better to use "the members of the committee."

Comparative form

Thinner and *more happily* are the comparative forms of *thin* and *happily*. See **Comparison of adjectives and adverbs.**

compare, contrast

Compare with *to* points out likenesses: He compared my writing to Allen's (said it was like his). *Compare* followed by *with* finds likenesses and differences: He compared my writing with Allen's (pointed out like and unlike traits). *Contrast* always points out differences.

When the things compared are of different classes and when the likeness is figurative, use *to:* He compared my stories to a sack of beans. In the common construction with the past participle, use either *to* or *with:* Compared with (*or* to) Allen's, mine is feeble. *In comparison* is followed by *with:* In comparison with Allen's, mine is feeble. *Contrast* ordinarily takes *with:* He contrasted my writing with Allen's. But *contrast* sometimes takes *to,* and *in contrast* usually does: In contrast to Allen's, my writing is magnificent.

Comparison and contrast

To compare and contrast is to establish the similarities and the differences between two or more objects, people, places, institutions, ideas, and so on. Comparing is a natural way of explaining. You can inform a reader about a subject that's unfamiliar to her by telling her how it's like and how it's unlike something she knows well. And you use contrast automatically in argument when you set out to prove that one thing is better than another.

To write a comparison, first select the points that are significant for your purpose. (If you're comparing makes of cars for potential purchasers of your own age, is cost a significant factor? Is safety? Fuel consumption? Speed? Color?) Then find out how your subjects (the makes you're comparing) are alike and how they differ in each of these respects. In organizing your discussion, you might treat one of your subjects *(A)* fully before taking up the corresponding points in another *(B)*. Or you might compare *A* and *B* point by point. Or you might set out all the likenesses between *A* and *B* and then all the differences, or the reverse. In any case, it's not enough to offer a collection of details about each of the subjects. You must work out the comparison, relating details about one to corresponding details about another, so that the reader understands the ways the subjects differ and the ways they're alike.

See **Logical thinking.**

Comparison of adjectives and adverbs

Comp

Correct the fault in comparing the adjective or adverb marked.

To express degrees of what is named, adjectives and adverbs are compared— that is, their forms are changed by adding *-er* or *-est* to the root, or base, form *(long, longer, longest)* or by preceding it with *more* or *most (beautiful, more beautiful, most beautiful)* or with *less* or *least.*

1. Choosing the form. We say "a longer walk," not "a more long walk." We say "a more beautiful picture," not "a beautifuller picture."

a. To the root form (the positive degree), some adjectives and adverbs add *-er* to make the comparative degree, *-est* to make the superlative degree.

	Positive	*Comparative*	*Superlative*
Adjective	early	earlier	earliest
	hoarse	hoarser	hoarsest
	unhappy	unhappier	unhappiest
Adverb	fast	faster	fastest
	soon	sooner	soonest

b. Other adjectives make the comparative and superlative degrees by preceding the root form with *more, most.*

	Positive	*Comparative*	*Superlative*
Adjective	exquisite	more exquisite	most exquisite
	afraid	more afraid	most afraid
	pleasing	more pleasing	most pleasing
Adverb	comfortably	more comfortably	most comfortably
	hotly	more hotly	most hotly

Three-syllable adjectives and adverbs are ordinarily compared with *more* and *most,* one-syllable adjectives and adverbs with *-er* and *-est.* Two-syllable adjectives and adverbs are usually compared with *more* and *most,* but many can take either form: *able—abler, more able, ablest, most able; empty—emptier, more empty, emptiest, most empty.* When you're in doubt, *more* and *most* are the safer choices. In earlier times, it was all right to use both methods of comparison at once, as in Shakespeare's "most unkindest cut of all," but now double comparatives and double negatives (except for such locutions as "not unhappy") are classed as nonstandard.

Some points of usage raised by irregular forms of comparison are discussed in **former, first–latter, last** and in **last, latest.**

2. Using the comparative. The comparative expresses a greater or lesser degree (It is *warmer* now) or makes specific comparison between two people or things (He was *kinder* [or *more kind*] than his brother). The things compared must be truly comparable:

> *Comparable:* His salary was lower than a shoe clerk's (salary). *Or . . .* than that (*or* than the salary) of a shoe clerk.

> *Not comparable:* His salary was lower than a shoe clerk.

(This rule holds true when the root form of the adjective is used: His salary was low, like a beginner's. *Not . . .* like a beginner.)

Logic calls for *other* with *any* in comparisons between a single unit and the group it belongs to: She's a better dancer than *any* of the *other* girls. But the comparative is frequently used when no actual comparison is involved: *higher education, older people, the lower depths*. In advertisements the job of providing a comparison is often left to the reader or listener: *cooler, fresher, stronger, faster, more economical*—than what?

3. Using the superlative. In formal writing and in most general writing, the superlative is used to indicate the maximum or minimum degree of a quality among three or more people or things: She was the *calmest* one there; That's the *loudest* shirt in the showcase. Informally, the superlative is common with two, and this usage isn't rare in general writing: Roy and Joe do push-ups to see who's *strongest;* the two nations compete to see which can be *most critical* of the other's policies. Use of the superlative as a form of emphasis is also informal: She has the *loveliest* flowers; We saw the *best* show!

Don't use *other* to complete a superlative: Television won the largest audience for Shakespeare's plays that they had ever attracted in any (*not* any other) medium.

4. Comparing absolutes. Some grammarians raise objections to the comparison of *black, dead, excellent, fatal, final, impossible, perfect, unique* on the grounds that, logically, there can be no degrees of deadness or blackness or impossibility. But competent writers frequently compare these words: a *more equal* society, a *more complete* victory, a *more impossible* situation. And the Constitution speaks of "a more perfect union." Many absolutes are used figuratively with meanings that naturally admit comparison: This is the *deadest* town I was ever in. When applied to people, *black* and *white* are obviously not being used in a literal, absolute sense. See **Divided usage.**

complected

Justifiably or not, there is considerable bias against *complected* (a dark-complected man), and it seldom appears in print. Neither does *complexioned*. Instead, writers use *light-* or *fair-* or *dark-skinned*.

Complement

In grammar, *complement* refers to the noun or adjective that completes the meaning of a linking verb and modifies the subject: He became *the real head of the business;* She was *busy*. See **Linking verbs, Predicate adjectives.**

complement, compliment

As a noun, *complement* means "that which completes or is called for" (a full complement). As a verb, it means "to make complete" or—of two things—

"to fill out each other's lacks" (the scarf and blouse complemented each other perfectly). *Compliment* is the noun (He received many compliments for his work) and the verb (He complimented her on her victory) having to do with praise and congratulations.

Complex sentence

A complex sentence has one independent, or main, clause and one or more dependent clauses, ordinarily introduced by relative pronouns or subordinating conjunctions: She married the man *who* picked her up *when* she fell. See **Clauses.**

Compound-complex sentence

When one or more of the independent clauses of a compound sentence are modified by dependent clauses, the sentence is called compound-complex. Here the dependent clause modifies the second independent clause: "The dances are mutating without him, and as they do, we are losing them forever" (Stephen Schiff, *Vanity Fair*). See **Clauses.**

Compound predicate

Two or more verbs with the same subject, together with their objects and modifiers, form a compound predicate: "Field's ornate speech in *Poppy* caught the proper spirit of carnival fakery and did much to influence the comedian's dialogue in subsequent appearances" (Stanley Green, *The Great Clowns of Broadway*). Compound predicates help make writing economical. See **Comma 8c.**

Compound sentence

A compound sentence contains two or more independent clauses.

1. With coordinating conjunction. Usually the clauses of a compound sentence are connected by one of the coordinating conjunctions: "We all know that Shakespeare's Romeo and Juliet commit suicide, and I daresay most of us feel pretty sorry for them" (H. W. Matalene, *College English*).

2. Without coordinating conjunction. A compound sentence may have a semicolon instead of a coordinating conjunction between the clauses: "Young people should neither smoke nor drink; nearly everyone gave lip service to that rule" (Ross Gregory, *America 1941*). For the use of a comma instead of a coordinating conjunction, see **Comma 1d.**

3. With conjunctive adverb. The clauses of a compound sentence may be connected by a conjunctive adverb (*however, moreover, then, indeed, consequently, therefore,* and so on) that is preceded by a semicolon: "In imitation, she tries to coax Boris to kiss her; then, impatient with his reluctance, she kisses him'' (Edward Wasiolek, *Tolstoy's Major Fiction*). A comma before *then* would produce a comma splice.

See **Clauses, Conjunctive adverbs.**

Compound subject

Two or more elements standing as subjects of one verb make a compound subject: "Flake knives and scrapers, large core choppers, and one-handed grinding stones . . . characterize the tool kit" (Dorothy K. Washburn, "The American Southwest"). The verb following a compound subject is usually plural: Inflation and recession occurring simultaneously create stagflation. See **Agreement 1c.**

Compound words

Compound words are combinations of two or more words, usually written as one word or hyphenated: *doorknob, notwithstanding, quarter-hour, father-in-law, drugstore*. Some compounds continue to be written as separate words: *White House, high school, post office*. For the spelling of particular compound words, consult your dictionary. See **Group words, Hyphen, Plurals of nouns 5.**

comprise

Traditionally, *comprise* means "consist of" or "include": The whole comprises (*not* is comprised of) its parts. In current usage the nearly opposite senses of "constitute," "compose," and "make up" are very common: "The four states that at one time comprised French Equatorial Africa . . ." (Harold G. Marcus, *American Historical Review*). But many writers, editors, and teachers insist that *comprise* be used only in its traditional sense, and in the relatively formal contexts where *comprise* is appropriate, using it only with the meaning "include" would be wise. In most contexts the more general English verb *make up* can do double duty:

> The four states that at one time made up French Equatorial Africa . . .
>
> French Equatorial Africa was made up of what are now four separate states.

concept

Concept is often used for an idea that takes itself too seriously, as in "a new concept for cat food commercials." *Idea* would be a better choice.

Concrete words

Concrete words name things that can be seen and touched: *box, building*. See **Abstract language.**

Conditional clauses

A conditional clause states a condition (If she knows what she's talking about) that is necessary if what is expressed in the independent clause (there'll be more jobs next term) is to be true. Or it specifies an action (If the ransom is paid) that is necessary for what is expressed in the independent clause (the hostages will be freed) to take place. *If, unless,* and *whether* are the subordinating conjunctions that most commonly begin conditional clauses. Somewhat more formal introductory words and phrases are *in case, provided, provided that, in the event that.*

1. For real or open conditions—statements of actual or reasonable conditions under which the main statement will hold true—use the indicative verb forms:

> *If the red light is on,* you know a train is in that block of tracks.
>
> He will be there *unless something happens to his car.*
>
> *Whether they come or not,* Kate will go just the same.

2. For hypothetical conditions—theoretical but still possible—use *should* . . . *would* or the past tense: *If he should offer another $100,* I would take it. Or *If he offered another $100,* I would take it.

3. For contrary-to-fact conditions—those that can't be met or are untrue—use the past tense of the verb if you're writing in a general style: If he *was* here, we would have seen him by now. In formal English, the plural form of the past tense, usually called the subjunctive, is firmly established in the first-person singular (If I *were* you . . .) and isn't uncommon in the third-person singular (If he *were* here . . .).

See **if, whether; Subjunctive mood.**

Conjunctions

Conjunctions join words, phrases, clauses, or sentences. In this *Index* conjunctions are further defined and discussed according to their conventional classification:

> *Coordinating conjunctions* (*and, but, for,* etc.)
> *Correlative conjunctions* (*either . . . or, not only . . . but,* etc.)
> *Conjunctive adverbs* (*however, therefore, consequently,* etc.)
> *Subordinating conjunctions* (*as, because, since, so that, when,* etc.)

conj Conjunctions and style

Make the conjunction marked more accurate or more appropriate to the style of the passage.

1. Accurate choice. In everyday speech we get along with a relatively small number of conjunctions—*and, as, but, so, when,* and a few others—because we can indicate shades of meaning and exact relationships by pauses, tones, and gestures. In writing, we don't have these means of relating ideas, and we need to use connectives more thoughtfully.

Choose your conjunctions with care. Don't toss in *but* when there's no contrast between your statements (see **but 2**). Responding to a waitress who disliked being called ''Hon'' by customers, ''Dear Abby'' wrote: ''It is your right, of course, to nip it in the bud since such familiarity irritates you. However, I'll print your letter to let my readers know that not everyone appreciates pet names.'' *However* is illogical and should be omitted.

Decide whether your meaning can be conveyed better by a coordinating conjunction or by a construction that uses the corresponding subordinating conjunction—*but* versus *though,* for example. And note distinctions between subordinating conjunctions. *As* can mean ''because,'' but it's a weak *because* (see **as**). *While* can mean ''although'' or ''whereas,'' but the core of its meaning is related to time. Sometimes, if your thinking has been logical and you've reproduced it on paper without skipping essential steps, the relationships are apparent, and a *therefore* or a *consequently* will be unnecessary and unwelcome. See **Transition** and the articles on the particular conjunctions.

2. Strategic use. Conjunctions should be appropriate to other traits of style. Often simple *but* is a better choice than *however:*

> The trail is easy walking as far as the canyon; from there on, however, it's no route for Sunday strollers.
>
> *Better:* . . . the canyon, but from there on . . .

See **Conjunctive adverbs 1.**

Repeating a conjunction at the beginning of each item in a series makes each one distinct, avoids possible confusion, and gives the sentence strong rhythm and clear-cut parallelism:

> I took an old shutter and fixed a sort of porch roof on it, and nailed it to a locust tree nearby, and set the nest with the eggs carefully in it.—Wendell Berry, *The Long-Legged House*

On the other hand, omitting *and* before the last element in a short series may build a strong climax:

> The most important of these, the most characteristic, the most misleading, is called *Some Glances at Current Linguistics.*—William H. Gass, *New Republic*

Or it may suggest that the series is only a sample, not a complete list:

> Many were the Northerners who, during and after the Civil War, went south to train, to educate, to rehabilitate Negro refugees and freedmen.—William H. Pease, *Journal of Southern History*

See **Conjunctive adverbs, Coordinating conjunctions, Correlative conjunctions, Subordinating conjunctions.** See also **Coordination, Subordination.**

Conjunctive adverbs

Conjunctive adverbs are used as connectives after a semicolon between independent clauses or after a period to introduce a new sentence. These are some of the most common:

accordingly	furthermore	moreover
also	hence	nevertheless
anyhow	however	otherwise
anyway (*informal*)	incidentally	still
besides	indeed	then
consequently	likewise	therefore

All these words are primarily adverbs. They become conjunctive adverbs when they join together, or provide connection:

Adverb: Though the danger was great, the policy was *nevertheless* adopted.
Conjunctive adverb: The action proposed by the government meant risking military action; *nevertheless,* public opinion supported it.

1. Style. The heavier conjunctive adverbs—those with three or four syllables—are best suited to formal writing, in sentences of some length and complexity. In general writing, the shorter adverbs are more appropriate and are more likely to serve as transitional devices between sentences than to connect clauses within a sentence. Writing that is straightforward and easy to read seldom needs conjunctive adverbs in any position.

Note these appropriate and inappropriate uses:

The believer in truth, on the other hand, is bound to maintain that the things of highest value are not affected by the passage of time; *otherwise* the very concept of truth becomes invisible.—Richard M. Weaver, *Ideas Have Consequences.* (Appropriate to the formal sentence structure and content.)

In the morning I still felt sick; *nevertheless,* when the bugle sounded, I got up. (Inappropriately heavy in this simple context. Could substitute *but.* Better to rewrite as a complex sentence: Though I still felt sick the next morning, I got up when the bugle sounded.)

2. Position. Placing a conjunctive adverb inside its clause instead of at the beginning gives initial stress to the word or words that precede it: The action proposed by the government meant risking military action; public opinion, however, supported it.

3. Punctuation. Whether a conjunctive adverb introduces or comes inside the second independent clause of a compound sentence, the two independent clauses are separated by a semicolon. In either position, it is sometimes but not always set off by a comma or commas. See **Comma 4b.**

Connotation

The associations a word or phrase has are its connotations, as distinguished from its denotation—what it refers to. Connotation makes the difference between *house* and *home,* between a *dutiful* child and an *obedient* one.

A writer needs to be conscious of what words connote as well as what they denote. Although *flush* (in the sense "turn red") and *blush* are so close in meaning that they can often be substituted for each other, the overlap of the two words isn't complete. We say, "He flushed with anger," but we don't say "He blushed with anger."

The context a word regularly occurs in, the variety of usage it belongs to, the prevailing social attitude toward what it refers to and toward the people who use it (politicians, advertisers, children) all contribute to the public connotations a word has. Beyond that are private connotations resulting from personal experiences. For one person *school* has connotations of confinement; for another, intellectual excitement; for still another, sociability.

Heavily connotative words are sometimes called slanted or loaded, and writers are sometimes urged to replace them with words that are more nearly neutral. The advice is not always sound. We use words not only to give information about things but also to express our feelings about them and to influence the attitudes of others. It's natural to describe an action we admire as *courageous* and one we deplore as *foolish* or *disgraceful*. Neutral terms are preferable only when we are in fact neutral or when the rhetorical situation calls for us to write as if we are.

See **Denotation.**

consensus

Consensus is a troublesome word. It's easy to misspell, and it tempts users to add *of opinion*. Since *consensus* means "agreement," *of opinion* simply repeats what the word already conveys. So let *consensus* (spelled with three *s*'s) do the job on its own.

Construction

A construction is a group of words that stand in some grammatical relationship to each other, like that of modifier and word modified (black cat), preposition and object (to the roof), or subject and predicate (They walked slowly). Any grammatical pattern may be spoken as of a construction.

contact

As a verb, *contact* means "get in touch with" (I was told to contact the superintendent). Like *get in touch with, contact* covers all means of communication (face-to-face, telephone, letter, cable, computer, etc.), and it's more economical—one word instead of four. Stylistically, the word still bothers some readers, who associate it with business jargon, but it is established as standard English. See **Jargon.**

Context

The word *context* is used in different ways.

1. Verbal context. In writing, a sentence may provide the context for a word, a paragraph may provide the context for a sentence, and so on. The context is the setting—the combination of content and style—that gives meaning to what's being said and determines its appropriateness. Context is extremely important in conveying the sense in which a word is being used. For example, dictionaries record forty or more senses in which people use the word *check,* yet when *check* appears in specific contexts, as in the following sentences, we have no trouble understanding it:

> They were able to *check* the fire at the highway.
> The treasurer's books *check* with the vouchers.
> He drew a *check* for the entire amount.
> I like the tablecloth with the red-and-white *check.*
> He moved his bishop and shouted, *"Check!"*
> She had difficulty holding her temper in *check.*
> *Check* your suitcase through to Seattle.

A great many words are used in more than one sense. To convey the particular meaning she intends, a writer must—and usually can—rely on the context. And besides establishing the denotative sense of the word (as illustrated with *check*), context gives clues to its connotation. We recognize this when we say, "By itself her remark couldn't possibly give offense, but in that context it was downright insulting."

2. The context of quotations. An honest writer makes sure that the quotations she uses are true to the context in which they originally occurred and that they accurately represent the ideas of the people who wrote or spoke them. Complaints by government officials that they've been quoted "out of context" are often justified.

3. Rhetorical context. Every piece of writing occurs in a rhetorical situation, or context, which includes the writer, the subject, the writer's purpose, and the audience. The choice of material, the organization, and the style of a good paper all reflect the writer's sense of the rhetorical context. See **Rhetorical situation.**

continual(ly), continuous(ly)

In the sense "uninterrupted," with reference to time, formal stylists prefer *continuous(ly)* (For weeks we observed the almost continuous eruption of the volcano), but *continual(ly)* is also used. In the sense "occurring rapidly and often," the situation is reversed—formal writers prefer *continual(ly)* (The governor broke his promises not just repeatedly but continually), but *continuous(ly)* too is standard.

Contractions

In writing, contractions are forms that show pronunciation, usually by the substitution of an apostrophe for one or more letters of the standard spelling: *can't, you're, I'm, don't, they've.* They occur regularly in informal usage but far less often in formal writing. In general styles, a writer should use them or avoid them just as he makes other rhetorical choices, considering the rhythm of the particular sentence, whether the occasion calls for a relaxed or a restrained style, and how much distance he wants between himself and his readers. (In this book contractions are used, in part, to show that writing about a serious subject doesn't call for a style that keeps the audience at arm's length, if not out of reach.) Contractions are necessary in representing actual speech, as in dialog (but see **Apostrophe 4**).

contrast, compare

Contrast points out differences; *compare to* points out likenesses; *compare with* does both. See **compare, contrast.**

controversial

Controversial (a controversial person, a controversial book) labels the subject a source of disagreement, of argument. But there can be disagreement about almost any subject, and no one needs to be told that certain subjects (abortion, capital punishment) and individuals are controversial. So use the label sparingly, and don't use it as a warning. Controversy is often what makes a subject interesting enough to write about.

convince, persuade

For a long time some uses of *convince* and *persuade* have overlapped: She persuaded (*or* convinced) me of the necessity for action; She convinced (*or* persuaded) me that I should act. *Convince* is now common in still a third context, where *persuade* is traditional:

> It must have contributed to the general merriment when later it was written . . . that the invasion failed because Adlai Stevenson convinced the President to cancel the air strikes so vital to the success of the invasion.—Ward Just, *New York Times Book Review*

The use of *convince . . . to* instead of *persuade . . . to* (persuaded the President to cancel) is deplored by many conservative stylists.

Coordinate

Two or more grammatically equivalent words, phrases, or clauses are said to be coordinate: *bread* and *butter; in the sink* or *on the stove; dancing, singing, laughing; When she lectured* and *when she prayed*, everyone listened; *He wrenched his back*, and *she broke her leg.*

Coordinating conjunctions

The coordinating conjunctions—*and, but, for, nor, or, so,* and *yet*—are used to connect two or more elements of equal grammatical rank:

> *Words:* books *and* papers; books, pamphlets, *or* magazines

> *Phrases:* in one ear *and* out the other

> *Dependent clauses:* She . . . wrote to young Lewis Rutherford cheerfully enough that his sister looked lovely *and* that the new baby was delightful.—R. W. B. Lewis, *Edith Wharton*

> *Independent clauses:* There is no evidence that Elizabeth had much taste for painting; *but* she loved pictures of herself.—Horace Walpole, *Anecdotes of Painting in England*

> *Sentences:* Perhaps I should wish that I had liked him better. *But* I do not wish it.—Renata Adler, *New Yorker*

See **Conjunctions and style, Coordination, Series.**

coord # Coordination

Correct the faulty coordination.

Faulty coordination is not a lapse in grammar or usage. It's a failure to make logical relationships clear. Coordination is faulty when, in a particular context, the material calls for a relationship or emphasis different from the one implied by the writer's use or arrangement of independent clauses.

1. Faulty coordination may result from joining two statements that don't belong together: The condition of the house is deplorable, and the dining nook seats six comfortably. Revision should put the two statements in separate—and separated—sentences.

2. Sometimes faulty coordination can be corrected by turning one of the independent clauses into a dependent clause. "He went to France for the summer, and his novel was published" suggests a causal relationship between his going to France and the publication of his novel. In some contexts this might make sense. But if the only relationship is a temporal one—two events happening at the same time but not otherwise related—the sentence needs to be revised: "During his summer in France, his novel was published," or "At the time his novel was published, he was spending the summer in France,'' or in some other way.

3. Coordination may be confusing or misleading, as in the example above. Sometimes it's worse than ineffective:

> The bold reds and greens of hats, scarves, and jackets and the bright fall foliage made it a colorful scene, and the driver lay propped against the wrecked car.

The final clause—"the driver lay propped against the wrecked car"—needs to be taken out of the coordinate relationship and made into a separate sentence. Even if the injured driver contributed to the color, coordination ignores his plight and strikes the reader as illogical and heartless.

See **Subordination.**

Correlative conjunctions

Some coordinating conjunctions are used in pairs: *both . . . and, either . . . or, neither . . . nor, not only . . . but also, whether . . . or.* Of these correlatives, *neither . . . nor* and *not only . . . but also* suggest more conscious planning than is common in informal or general English: "The attack not only had left him blind, and in need of plastic surgery which would require years to complete, but also had deprived him of his sense of smell" (Joe McGinniss, *Going to Extremes*).

Like coordinating conjunctions, correlatives normally join elements of the same grammatical rank:

> *Nouns:* He said that both *the novel* and *the play* were badly written.
>
> *Adjectives:* She must have been either *drunk* or *crazy.*
>
> *Prepositional phrases:* They can be had not only *in the usual sizes* but *in the outsizes.*
>
> *Verb phrases:* The wind scoop not only *caught the cool breezes* but also *picked up the captain's conversation.*
>
> *Clauses:* Whether *Mitch thumbed a ride through the mountains* or *Jenny made the long bus trip,* they were determined to be together during the vacation.

Like similar rules, the rule that constructions built on correlative conjunctions must be strictly parallel should be broken when it gets in the way of natural, rhythmic expression.

See **Shifted constructions.**

could(n't) care less

Formerly (and too frequently) a lack of concern was expressed by "I couldn't care less." Recently the negative has been dropped, and "I could care less" is used to mean the same thing: "kids who never heard of Little Richard and could care less" (Ellen Willis, *New Yorker*). Neither form is suited to college writing, except perhaps to point up triteness in dialog.

Count nouns

Count nouns name things that can be counted as separate units. See **Mass nouns, Nouns 3c.**

couple

The primary meaning of the collective noun *couple* is "a pair, two persons or things associated in some way," as in "a married couple." In general and informal usage *couple,* usually followed by *of,* is equivalent to the numeral *two* or to *a few:* "A couple of things happened" (James J. Kilpatrick, syndicated columnist). The *of* is frequently omitted in speech and informal writing and sometimes in general writing, but many readers object to the omission. *Couple* is not common in formal prose. If used, it should be followed by *of.*

Course names

In general discussions, only the names of college subjects that are proper nouns or proper adjectives are capitalized. In writing a list of courses that includes one or more of these terms, all the course names may be capitalized for consistency, but usually the distinction is kept: I am taking biology, chemistry, European history, English composition, and French. Names of departments are capitalized (the Department of Psychology), and so are the names of subjects when accompanied by a course number (History 347).

credibility

In journalese, *credibility* ("believability") was joined to the vogue word *gap* to refer to public loss of faith in President Johnson's statements about the Vietnam War. In the Nixon administration the gap became a gulf, and *gap* went out of vogue. But *credibility* moved into officialese and flourished. Both writers and readers should remember that *honesty* and *credibility* are by no means synonymous. In college papers it's better to say that a person's word isn't trusted, or that he lies, than to say he lacks credibility.

criterion, criteria

Criteria is heard so often, particularly in college classrooms, that it's possible to forget the singular form *criterion.* As a result we run into references to "this criteria" or read that certain criteria "is important." Base your judgment on *a criterion* or on *several criteria* (or *criterions*).

Cumulative sentence

A cumulative sentence makes its main statement at or near the beginning, usually in a short independent clause, and then goes on to add details in modifiers that are parallel or roughly so and that can be added to or omitted. Here is a very simple version of the cumulative sentence, with three verbal phrases modifying the opening clause:

> All of the town's big shots were there in their tuxedoes, wolfing down the buffet foods, drinking beer and whiskey and smoking black cigars.—Ralph Ellison, *Invisible Man*

The next two examples illustrate the cumulative sentence in more elaborate form:

> He'd be out there in full view, on the circular driveway of the Bachelor Officers Quarters, togged out in his sweatsuit, his great freckled face flaming red and shining with sweat, going around and around, running a mile, two miles, there was no end to it, in front of everybody.—Tom Wolfe, *The Right Stuff*

> There are those of us for whom the best part of a baseball game is not the action, but the prelude—the rattle of the bat against the spiked shoes to remove mud clots, the pulling of caps, the peerings of pitcher and catcher, the waggles of the upraised bat as it explores the air through which the ball soon is humming, the hitching of the umpire's chest protector, the unwinding of the pitcher's body.—Heywood Hale Broun, *Travel & Leisure*

For Wolfe and Broun, the cumulative sentence offers an economical way of presenting a mass of details, especially suited to descriptive and narrative writing. It also occurs, sometimes with great effect, in expository prose on ceremonial occasions. Here the modifiers enrich the initial declaration:

> Let the word go forth from this time and place, to friend and foe alike, that the torch has been passed to a new generation of Americans, born in this century, tempered by war, disciplined in a hard and bitter peace, proud of our ancient heritage, and unwilling to witness or permit the slow undoing of those human rights to which this nation has always been committed, and to which we are committed today at home and around the world.—John F. Kennedy, Inaugural Address

Because it observes the natural order of speech—main statement first, then qualifications and particulars—a cumulative sentence can and often does give the impression of ease and naturalness. But unless the modifiers add strength or richness, or support the initial assertion, the sentence may wander off into insignificant or irrelevant detail. What counts in a cumulative sentence, then, is the skill with which it's constructed and the effect that it produces.

Compare **Periodic sentence.**

curriculum

Curriculum (the courses offered or the courses required in a field of study) has the Latin plural *curricula* and the English plural *curriculums*. The adjective is *curricular*. The compound adjective with *extra-* is almost always written as one word: *extracurricular*.

dm Dangling modifiers

Revise the sentence so that the expression marked is clearly related to the word it is intended to modify.

A phrase is said to dangle, or to be misrelated, if its position makes it seem to modify a word that it can't sensibly modify or if, in a context that demands an explicit relationship, it has no clear relation to any word in the sentence.

In "Looking farther to the left, we saw the spire of a church," *looking* obviously modifies *we*. If the phrase "looking farther to the left" is turned into a clause, *we* is the subject of the verb: [*We* were] looking farther to the left. That is, the reconstructed subject is identical with the subject of the main clause. When the phrase does *not* refer to the subject—that is, when the phrase has a different subject from the subject of the main clause—then the modifier dangles.

In the sentence "To get the most out of a sport, the equipment must be in perfect condition," reconstruction of the subject of the introductory phrase would produce something like "[For *someone*] to get the most out of a sport, *the equipment* must be in perfect condition." But since *someone* is different from *equipment*, it can't safely be omitted. If the sentence "At eleven, my family moved to Denver" is reconstructed, it reads "[When *I* was] eleven, *my family* moved to Denver." *I* doesn't equal *my family*, so *I* should not be left out.

In the following examples, try to reconstruct the subject of the introductory phrase:

> Rising from the shallows, water streams off his chest, and he picks his way among his teammates with hardly a word.—Trip Gabriel, *New York Times Magazine*

> Associated with basketball for a half century, his coaching included Brown, Rogers High, St. George's school and De La Salle Academy.—George Donnelly, *Newport Daily News*

In both examples, the introductory phrase dangles. In the second, the phrase refers to a coach who is represented only by the possessive *his*. This type of dangling modifier occasionally appears in print.

Modifiers that dangle may also follow the independent clause: Signs reading "Visit Our Snake Farm" are seen, driving toward the city.

You should avoid dangling modifiers in your writing chiefly because educated readers don't expect to find them. As a rule there's no real question of the intended meaning of the sentence, and in context the dangling phrases are not apt to be conspicuously awkward or as nonsensical as they appear in isolation. But they're distracting in any writing that's meant to be read carefully. And when they force the reader to search for or guess at the related noun, they make a piece of writing needlessly difficult.

Such dangling constructions shouldn't be confused with absolute phrases, in which the phrase has its own subject. Here, for comparison, are an absolute phrase, a correct modifier, and a dangling modifier:

> *Absolute phrase:* The car paid for with my last dollar, I was at last out of debt.
>
> *Correct modifier:* Paid for with my last dollar, the car became my first piece of personal property.
>
> *Dangling modifier:* Paid for with my last dollar, I drove the car away.

Though prepositional phrases sometimes dangle—"As an institution, he cordially detested the Spanish Church" (Scott Donaldson, *By Force of Will: The Life and Art of Ernest Hemingway*)—the phrases that cause most trouble are those that begin with participles (particularly *being*) or infinitives or that contain gerunds. So in revising your papers, examine every verbal phrase. If you continue to have trouble relating such phrases to the words they should modify, you might try substituting clauses.

See **Absolute phrases, Gerunds, Infinitives, Participles.**

Dash

The dash—typed as two hyphens without space before or after—can be used singly to link a following word or word group to the main structure of the sentence or in pairs to enclose a word or word group that interrupts the main structure. Use enclosing dashes when you want greater separation from the core of the sentence than enclosing commas would provide but less separation—or less formality—than you'd get with parentheses.

At its best, the dash is a lively, emphatic mark. If used sparingly, it suggests a definite tone, often a note of surprise or an emphasis equivalent to a mild exclamation. If used regularly in place of commas, colons, and semicolons, it loses all its distinctiveness and becomes a sloppy substitute for conventional punctuation.

1. Before a kicker. The single dash is often used to throw emphasis on what follows, which may be dramatic, ironic, humorous: "The old nations still live in the hearts of men, and love of the European nation is not yet born—if it ever will be" (Raymond Aron, *Daedalus*). Robert Gates describes a book review as "neat, unambiguous, clinical, noncontroversial, even commendable—and highly misleading" *(Foreign Affairs).*

2. Before an explanation, illustration, or listing. The dash is used singly or in pairs with word groups that summarize what's just been said or provide details or examples:

> Long before 1961 many people—linguists and grammarians—realized that certain rules of school grammar were out of harmony with educated practice.—Edward Finegan, *Attitudes toward English Usage*

> Storms come announced by what old-timers call "mare's tails"—long wisps that lash out from a snow-cloud's body.—Gretel Ehrlich, *The Solace of Open Spaces*

3. Between independent clauses. A dash is sometimes used to link independent clauses when the second expands, develops, completes, or makes a surprising addition to the first. In this function a dash is less formal than a colon:

> Bessie was no longer the Queen of the Blues—she was the Empress.—Chris Albertson, *Bessie*

> In one respect, Welles was unique among the Cabinet members—he did not think himself a better man than the President.—Margaret Leech, *Reveille in Washington*

4. Enclosing interrupting elements. Dashes are used to set off words and word groups, including complete sentences, that break with the main structure of the sentence:

> Many farmers still had to wrestle with older machines—more than one-third were at least ten years old—built purely for functional purposes, with little attention to comfort or fashion.—Ross Gregory, *America 1941: A Nation at the Crossroads*

data

Formal usage follows the Latin, treating *datum* as singular and *data* as plural. In general usage *datum* is rare, and *data* is treated as a collective noun. So used, it takes a singular verb to emphasize the whole—"Data so far available makes it seem doubtful" (John Mecklin, *Fortune*)—and a plural verb to emphasize the parts—"There were still a good many data in the 33-page report" (William H. Honan, *New York Times Magazine*).

Dates

The typical American form of writing dates is "August 19, 1983." The form "19 August 1983" prevails in British usage and American military usage and has gained popularity in the United States. If the full date is given within a sentence, the year is usually set off by commas. If the day of the week is also given, it's separated from the month by a comma: The legislature met on

Wednesday, December 13, 1905. When only month and year are given, no commas are necessary (In August 1983 he died).

The year is not written out in words except in formal social announcements, invitations, wills, and some other ceremonial situations. At the beginning of a sentence usage is now divided. (See **Numbers 2.**) Most writers manage to avoid beginning sentences with the year. In lists and charts, months having more than four or five letters are often abbreviated: Jan. 3, 1989.

In writing dates in figures only, American practice is month-day-year: 9/17/76. European practice is day-month-year, sometimes with the month in Roman numerals: 17-IX-76.

Deadwood

Words or phrases that add nothing to the meaning or effectiveness of a statement are deadwood. See **Wordiness.**

Declension

As applied to the English language, *declension* refers to the listing of the forms of nouns and pronouns to show number, gender, and case. See **Case, Gender, Inflection, Nouns, Number, Pronouns.**

Deduction

Deduction is the process of drawing a conclusion from propositions known to be true, or accepted as true, or assumed to be true. You're reasoning deductively when you notice a ring around the moon and say, "We're in for some bad weather." Your unspoken premise, based on your own experience or on what you've read or heard, is that the appearance of a ring around the moon means that bad weather is bound to follow. From two related propositions— (1) a ring around the moon forecasts bad weather, and (2) there's a ring around the moon—an inevitable conclusion is drawn: the weather will be bad.

For the conclusion of a deductive train of reasoning to be both valid and true, correct inferences must be made from true premises. See **Fallacies, Logical thinking, Syllogisms.** Compare **Induction.**

Deep structure

Transformational grammarians distinguish between the surface form of a sentence and the more abstract relationships in its deep structure. In the five sentences "Bill bought Jane a stereo," "Bill bought a stereo for Jane," "Jane was bought a stereo by Bill," "A stereo was bought for Jane by Bill," and "It was a stereo that Bill bought for Jane," the surface subjects are *Bill, Bill, Jane, stereo,* and *it.* But at a deeper level all the sentences have the same subject, or agent—Bill—since Bill did the buying regardless of the form the expression of the fact is given.

Such a concept of sentences may enlarge your view of the sentences you write. You can experiment with ways of expressing the same deep grammatical relationships through different surface structures, noting the varying rhetorical effects. The sentences about Bill and Jane and the stereo offer an example. Each of these could also be embedded in a larger structure in various ways:

> When Bill bought Jane a stereo, he surprised her.
> Bill's buying Jane a stereo surprised her.
> Jane was surprised by Bill's buying her a stereo.
> That Bill bought Jane a stereo surprised her.
> For Bill to have bought Jane a stereo surprised her.

These are only a few of the possibilities. Usually such considerations as focus, tone, transition between sentences, and the rhythm of the sentence in its context will help you choose between one surface structure and another.

See **Clauses 2, Grammar 3c.**

Definition

1. Types of definition. Definitions are of two main kinds.

a. A lexical, or dictionary, definition tells how a word is used in different contexts. Lexical definitions that appear in everyday prose often use the verb *means* or *expresses* or, when connotations are being emphasized, *suggests: expectorate* means "spit"; *hooked,* applied to drug use, suggests hopeless addiction.

b. A real definition (sometimes called a formal definition) identifies the essential characteristics of the thing the word refers to. It joins subject and predicate with a form of the verb *be* on the model of the equation

term-to-be-defined	=	*genus*	+	*differentia(e)*
A ballad	is	a song		that tells a story.

Thus, in "Logic is a specialized language dealing with the relationship of truth and falsity within a language" (Dwight Bolinger), *language* is the genus, and the two differentiae (distinguishing characteristics) are *specialized* and *dealing with the relationship of truth and falsity within a language.*

Logicians have formulated rules for real definitions. One is that the definition must include all things designated by the term but exclude anything the term doesn't properly apply to. "A bachelor is a person who is unmarried" is unsatisfactory because the genus is too broad. In "A shoe is a leather covering for the foot," one of the differentiae—*leather*—is too restrictive. Shoes can be made of various materials.

Other traditional rules are these: A definition should not be circular (Hostility is the state of being hostile). Except when loss or lack is a distinguishing characteristic (as in *baldhead* and *bastard*), a term should not be defined negatively (Liberty is the absence of restraint). A term should not be defined metaphorically (Television is the opiate of the people), nor should a term be defined by a synonym (A pail is a bucket).

These rules have all been laid down in the interest of precision, and in writing assignments that call for precision—as in answering examination questions on the special terms of a subject matter—you should observe them. But not all definitions require the rigor of formal logic, and often you'll want to say more about a term than can be compressed into the *genus + differentiae* formula.

2. Definition in exposition and argument. As a writer, you'll have occasion to use both lexical and real definitions. When you do, you should make clear which kind you're using.

a. In the stipulative definition, a variety of lexical definition, the writer gives a word a special, limited sense that is necessary for his specific purpose:

> I do not use the word "myth" to imply something entirely false. Rather, I use it to connote a complex of profoundly held attitudes and values which condition the way men view the world and understand their experience.—Richard Weiss, *The American Myth of Success*

A stipulative definition shouldn't be so remote from ordinary usage that it won't be taken seriously. Most readers will go along with the writer who says, "In this paper I will use the word *teenager* to include twenty-year-olds," but they'll probably stop reading if they find, "In this paper *teenager* means everybody who knows what's really happening."

b. An extended definition gives information about the essential nature of a thing, like the one-sentence formal definition, but it's not restricted to the processes of classification and division that yield the genus and differentiae. It may use *description,* telling what a thing looks like; *chronology,* giving its origin and development; *example,* giving instances of it; *comparison,* saying what it's like; *contrast,* saying what it's not; *causal analysis,* indicating what circumstances produced it and what consequences it has; and *testimony,* telling what authorities have said about it. Etymologies (histories of words) and synonyms may also be used to develop a definition. What the central elements are depends on what's being defined and also on where the writer's interest lies. A psychologist and a biologist define *man* in different ways.

An extended definition may be simply explanatory, with the aim of giving information about the subject in a readable, interesting essay. Or it may pave the way for further analysis. Having established a definition of comedy, a writer can go on to show that a new play or movie is, or is not, a comedy. Defining is also one way of conducting an argument. When opponents of legalized abortion argue that abortion is murder and its proponents argue that it's not, the issue is one of definition. Defining is often geared not to the purpose of explaining but to proving that a belief is sound or a policy wise.

3. Phrasing a definition. Definitions may be introduced casually:

What economists call total factor productivity—the amount of output produced by given amounts of labor and private capital—grew at a healthy 1.8% annual rate.—Alan S. Blinder, *Business Week*

Boom boxes, or portable stereo radio tape players, may be more useful for what they do than for how well they do it.—*Consumer Reports*

When a definition is presented in a separate sentence, the subject and the complement should normally be the same part of speech—noun matched by noun, adjective by adjective, and so on. In "Defining is to locate a thing in its class and then separate it from other members of the class," the meaning is clear, but the sentence would be easier to read if the two parts matched: "To define is to locate . . ." or "Defining is locating . . . and then separating . . ."

Definitions that begin with *where* or *when* (Erosion is when rain washes away the topsoil) are objected to in formal contexts. But they occasionally occur in literary works of established reputation—in this example, metaphorically: "Morning is when I am awake and there is a dawn in me" (Henry David Thoreau, *Walden*). See **when, where.**

Degrees

Ordinarily, academic degrees are not given with a person's name except in college publications, reference works, and articles and letters where the degrees offer proof of competence in a particular field, as in a physician's comment on a medical matter. When used, the names of the degrees are abbreviated, and the abbreviations are separated from the person's name by a comma. In alumni publications they are often followed by the year in which the degrees were granted:

Harvey N. Probst, A.B. (*or* B.A.)   Harvey N. Probst, A.B. '78
Jane Thomson, Ph.D.   Jane Thomson, Ph.D. '81
Royce Walton, M.B.A., was master of ceremonies.

As a rule, except in reference lists, only the highest degree in an academic professional field is mentioned. If the institution granting the degree is named, the following form is usual: George H. Cook, A.B. (Grinnell), A.M. (Indiana), Ph.D. (Chicago).

Demonstrative adjectives and pronouns

This, that, these, and *those* are traditionally called demonstrative adjectives or demonstrative pronouns, according to their use in a sentence:

Adjectives: This car is new. *Those* people never think of others.
Pronouns: These cost more than *those. That*'s a good idea.

See **Determiners; kind, sort; Pronouns 6; that; this.**

Denotation

The denotation of a word is what the word refers to, as described in a dictionary definition: fuel = a substance that is burned to produce heat or power. When heating oil is in short supply or gasoline doubles in price, *fuel* takes on overtones, or shades of meaning, that go far beyond this literal definition. See **Connotation.**

depart, exit, leave

Airline jargon has invaded general English, with people as well as planes "departing" places—and jobs: "Swearer plans to depart his current position on December 31 and spend a six-month sabbatical traveling and studying" *(Brown Alumni Monthly)*. Traditionally we depart *from.* We also arrive *at* or *in:* Sue departed from (*or* left) Ithaca Thursday and arrived at (*or* reached) Towanda in time for her appointment.

   Exit is another poor substitute for *leave:* He left (*not* exited) the house around noon.

Dependent clauses

A dependent, or subordinate, clause has a subject and predicate but doesn't normally stand alone as a sentence: If he comes today. One exception to the general rule is the exclamation: If we had only called! See **Clauses.**

Description

Description usually deals with the visible and tangible, telling how a thing looks or feels or tastes or smells. Abstractions can be described, too, but when you set out to produce a word picture of grief or pride or chaos, you're likely to find that you can best do the job in terms of physical sensations. Description feeds on concrete detail.

   Although most common in narration, description is used in all types of writing. Discussions of all subjects, except perhaps the most theoretical, include patches of description, for only description can help the reader visualize the subject or otherwise share the writer's sensory experience.

1. Kinds of description. In describing an object or a scene, you may try to present what any impartial observer would see, to come as close as you can to putting into words the image a camera would record. Or you may try to present a scene as it appears to an observer whose perception is highly colored by emotion—for example, a fire in which you were temporarily trapped or a fire as you imagine it appeared to someone who was trapped in it. Descriptions range from the precise, informative reports of technical writing to impressionistic sketches.

2. The function of details. Most descriptive passages fall somewhere between factual reporting and emotional (or imaginative) recreating. Writers try to provide a picture of reality so clear that the actual scene or object would be immediately recognizable. In addition, they try to make the reader aware of how they (or their imagined observer) feel about it and understand why they feel as they do.

Such description, if successful, will make the subject particular and individual. You won't describe Sachuest Beach in Middletown, Rhode Island, in details that apply equally well to other beaches along the Atlantic coast. Instead, you will search out the details that give this beach its special character and convey them in words that communicate what you feel as well as what you perceive. It's always best to make the details evoke the feelings. Outright statements of emotions (The big surf scared me) or judgments (The beach is best in late September) are unconvincing on their own. If you supply the details that triggered the emotions or that led to the judgments, such assertions become unnecessary. The appropriate generalization will form in the reader's mind. Good description shows; it doesn't need to tell.

3. The selection and organization of details. When you begin to write about a subject you have looked at long and hard (even in memory), you have far more details than you can use. Selection is vital. A crowd of unrelated details will only bewilder the reader. You won't name all the shore birds any more than you'll count the waves. Which birds? What details about the sea? Leo Rockas gives a clue: "The night club in Mozambique needs only be plainly presented; the corner supermarket had better be invested with novelty." As in every writing situation, then, the audience must be taken into account. What's commonplace to one group will be new and strange to another.

How you organize your details should be determined by the subject and your purpose. Does the reader need to understand the spatial relations in order to picture the scene? The directions must be made clear through the use of indicators such as *here, there, on top, in the middle, below, to the left, on the right, beyond, in the distance, on the horizon.*

4. The language of description. Again, selection counts. Descriptive prose should be neither flat nor excited to the point of incoherence. A rush of adjectives may call attention away from the scene to the writing. The language you use should suit the subject and the feelings you want the subject to arouse. You can convey details most directly and compellingly in language that's concrete and specific. Concrete diction gives things color, shape, and texture. Specific terms given them particularity and individuality.

See **Abstract language, Adjectives and style, Details, Point of view.**

det Details

Develop the passage or the topic more fully by giving pertinent details.

The symbol *det* is shorthand for "Give an example" or "What's your evidence?" or "Make this specific" or "Don't just *say* the house is in bad condition; make me *see* that it is." In revising a paper so marked, you need to supply particulars that will make your ideas or impressions clearer, your argument more convincing, or your essay more readable.

The details of a physical object are its parts (the *webbed feet* of a duck) or its attributes or qualities (*scorching* wind, *smooth* leather). The details of an abstraction like pride are the words and attitudes and actions that justify our saying that someone is proud. The details of a novel are specifics of plot, character, style, and so on. In short, the details of any subject are its particulars. In a good paper they fit together, making a pattern, leading to a generalization, or encouraging the reader to draw an inference. Besides giving substance to a paper, details make writing lively, so that it captures and holds the reader's interest. See **Description, Induction.**

Determiners

Some grammars apply the label *determiners* to a group of words, other than descriptive adjectives, that precede nouns. The group usually includes what traditional grammars call articles, demonstrative adjectives, and possessive pronouns (or adjectives), as well as such words as *some, few, several, many, each, both, half, first,* and *last.* In the phrase *"the first two* installments," the three italicized words are determiners.

Diacritical marks

Diacritical, or accent, marks are used in many foreign languages as guides to pronunciation. The more common marks that have carried over to English are the following:

acute accent	é	cedilla	ç
grave accent	è	circumflex	ê
dieresis or umlaut	ö	tilde	ñ
breve	ĕ	macron	ō

An accent mark is sometimes used in poems in English to indicate, for example, that an -*ed* ending is to be pronounced *(blessèd).* For a long time *cooperate* was printed with a dieresis *(coöperate)* to show that the sounds of the two *o*'s are separated. Later a hyphen was substituted *(co-operate),* and now the word is written solid, without any clue to its pronunciation.

Foreign words that become fully established in English are likely to lose their diacritical marks. *Naive,* from French, has lost its dieresis in virtually all publications. But the noun *exposé,* also from French, retains its acute accent, which distinguishes it from the verb *expose;* and while another French noun, *résumé,* retains both marks in formal styles, it also appears with only the second mark (to distinguish it from the verb *resume*) and even with no marks at all. The Spanish *mañana* retains the tilde; the Spanish *cabana* has lost it. Your best guide is an up-to-date dictionary.

See **Foreign words in English, Origin of words 2b.**

Dialects

A dialect is the speech (sounds, forms, meanings) characteristic of a fairly definite region or group. It is speech that doesn't attract attention to itself among the inhabitants of a region (regional dialect) or among members of a group (group or class dialect) but that an outsider would notice immediately. All of us speak a dialect of one sort of another, and many of us have command of several.

The term *dialect* is also applied to written expression: there are written dialects as well as speech dialects. Standard written English, based on educated middle-class usage, is the appropriate dialect to use in college work.

Though most of the writing you do in college will follow the rules and conventions of standard written English, you shouldn't set out to rid your writing of all the words and word forms and phrases of the regional or group dialect you grew up with. The guiding principle should be appropriateness. What are you writing about? Who's your audience? If you're reminiscing about your childhood or describing your homesickness, don't resist an impulse to use dialectal expressions. If your instructor and your classmates are familiar with the dialect you grew up using, you may also use it successfully in other papers. The more formal and impersonal your topic and the broader your audience, the less appropriate dialectal usages will be. In any circumstances, avoid those that are likely to mystify your readers or strike them as simply ungrammatical. See **grammatical, ungrammatical.**

 ## Diction

Replace the word marked with one that is more exact, more appropriate, or more effective.

Diction means choice of words. Good diction is exact, appropriate, and effective. Faulty diction either doesn't convey the writer's meaning fully or accurately or in some other way fails to meet the reader's expectations.

1. Choose the exact word. The exact word is the one that conveys better than any other the meaning you intend. Some mistakes in word choice result from confusing two words that resemble each other in some way: *delusion* for *illusion, predominate* for *predominant.* Others result from confusing two words that, though similar in basic meaning, are not interchangeable in all contexts. We can speak of a *durable* friendship or a *lasting* friendship, but though we may describe shoes as *durable,* we don't say they're *lasting.* Idiom allows "the oldest existing manuscript" but not "the oldest living manuscript."

In some instances, finding the exact word means looking for a more specific one (*complained* is more specific and may be a better choice than *remarked*). Often it means settling for a simpler expression. If you reach for a fancy phrase, you may come up with one that has nothing to do with your meaning: During midyear exam week, a *disquieting aura pervades* me even when I am relaxing. See **Connotation, Dictionaries, Idiom, Meaning, Wrong word.**

2. Choose the appropriate word. The words you choose should fit both your subject and your relationship with your audience. If your subject is technical, complex, and serious and if you're addressing readers who know something about it and want to learn more, you'll probably use a rather formal vocabulary. If your subject is light or humorous and if you know your readers well or want to establish a sense of intimacy with them, you'll express yourself more informally.

Though a style can certainly be too informal, probably the most common fault in college papers is inappropriate formality—"big" words selected more to impress the reader than to express meaning. Big words needn't be long; *deem* for *think* is as big as *domicile* for *house*. They're big in the sense of "pretentious"—too fancy for the writer or the audience or the subject. Such words as *ignominious, cantankerous, lachrymose, inscrutable, mortified,* and *chronicled* can be "big" in one context and not in another.

You can catch the big words in what you write by reading your papers aloud. If you've used words that you'd be unlikely to speak in or out of the classroom, reconsider them. See if you can't substitute words that are just as precise but more natural to you.

Though formal, general, and informal English overlap and are often successfully mixed in print, you can seriously weaken what you write if you mix them carelessly. When informal name-calling interrupts a thoughtful paper on welfare, when high-flown poetic clichés break the mood of an honest piece of descriptive writing, when *know-how* is applied to a great artist's technique or *finalize* to a composer's efforts, readers will be distracted and disturbed. If you mix usage deliberately, have a good reason for doing so—to amuse or startle your reader, perhaps, or to emphasize the point you're making. Keep your audience in mind, and avoid overkill. If you find yourself being criticized for mixing usage, read and reread your papers before turning them in, and maybe ask a friend to read them, too, with an eye open for sore thumbs and an ear cocked for sour notes.

See **Dialects, "Fine" writing, Formal English, Informal English.**

3. Choose the effective word. If your words convey your meaning accurately and if they're appropriate to the rhetorical situation, your diction will be competent, and it may be effective as well. But you'll probably move beyond competence only if you pay some attention to style. Effectiveness in writing factual prose nearly always means choosing words that convey your meaning directly and economically. But that isn't to say that you should always pick the shortest, plainest words you can find and use them in the simplest way. In a particular writing job, you may find it effective to repeat a word or put it to a new use, or to choose a word for its sound as well as its sense.

Using words well often means using them imaginatively. The challenge is to avoid the trite and tiresome without making your prose so fancy that your reader pays less attention to what you're saying than to how you're saying it. See **Abstract language, Adjectives and style, Adverbs and style, Conjunctions and style, Euphemisms, Figurative language, Imagery, Nominalization, Repetition, Style, Triteness, Vogue words, Wordiness.** See also articles on individual words: **claim, contact, drunk, finalize, hopefully, however, massive, relate,** and so on.

Dictionaries

Next to a well-stocked mind and a good ear, your dictionary is your chief resource in writing papers. Refer to it to check spelling and word division. Consult it when you're trying to choose the word that conveys what you want to say most precisely. Browse in it to increase your own word hoard.

A good dictionary tells what a word denotes in various contexts (see the several meanings of *office, cast, culture, critical* in your dictionary). It gives linguistic information about the word (its part or parts of speech, its inflections), something of its history, and sometimes its synonyms and antonyms and the idioms in which it appears. It may also suggest some of the connotations the word has. Watch for the labels that indicate restrictions on the use of a word or of some of its senses—subject labels like *chemistry,* temporal labels like *archaic,* geographical labels like *British,* and usage labels like *nonstandard.* And be sure you know what the labels mean. Some dictionaries use *colloquial* to mark words that are characteristically used in conversation and in informal writing. Others use *informal* for the same words.

Because dictionaries differ in the labels they apply and in the amount of labeling they do, determining the status of a word isn't always easy. You may be told that *plenty* as in "plenty hot" is informal or colloquial and therefore inappropriate for a formal essay, but you won't be warned that *adumbrate* is too formal and literary for general writing. A dictionary can give you a great deal of information, but it can't substitute for a good ear and good judgment. These you must develop for yourself.

The following dictionaries, listed alphabetically, are recommended for college work. Always use the latest editions.

> *The American Heritage Dictionary of the English Language* (Houghton)
> *The Random House College Dictionary* (Random)
> *Webster's New Collegiate Dictionary* (Merriam)
> *Webster's New World Dictionary of the American Language* (Collins and World)

Each of these dictionaries has its own policies, procedures, abbreviations, restrictive labels, and order of definitions. To use your dictionary well, become familiar with the explanatory notes in the opening pages.

Your college library will have unabridged dictionaries—the most recent include *Webster's Third New International Dictionary of the English Language* (Merriam) and *The Random House Dictionary of the English Language* (Random)—as well as dictionaries in a variety of special subjects such as law, business, psychology, and economics. The *Oxford English Dictionary,* now in its second edition, is the great storehouse of information about English words—their origins, their forms, their meanings, and the ways in which they have been used by writers from their first appearance.

See **Connotation, Definition 1a, Denotation, Diction.**

different from, different than

Formal usage prefers *different from:* The rich are different from you and me. General usage is divided between *different from* and *different than:* "The young TV generation has a completely different sensory life than the adult generation which grew up on hot radio and hot print" *(Newsweek). Different than* is especially common when the object is a clause: "The story would be different for an investigator who accepts the verdict of the court than for one who doesn't" (Meyer Shapiro, *New York Review of Books*). The formal alternative would be the longer, wordy expression: . . . verdict of the court from what it would be for one who doesn't.

Only *different than* can be used in such elliptical constructions as "a different make than [the car that] I drive."

dilemma

Dilemma has a range of meanings. The narrowest is "a choice between equally unpleasant alternatives." A broader meaning is "any difficult choice." And finally there's "any difficult problem." Since *dilemma* is a rather formal word, giving it so broad a meaning as this last is likely to be criticized.

Direct address

In direct address, the audience being spoken to is named:

> *My friends,* I hope you will listen to me with open minds.
> What do you think about his coming home, *Doctor?*

Words in direct address are usually set off by commas. See **Indirect discourse.**

Direct objects

In "Dogs chase cats," *cats* is the direct object of the transitive verb *chase.* See **Objects 1, Transitive and intransitive verbs.**

discreet, discrete

Here's a case in which a mistake in spelling can result in a change in meaning. *Discreet* means "prudent, circumspect": They were so discreet in public that no one suspected a thing. *Discrete* means "separate, distinct": Further analysis revealed that the issue could be divided into discrete parts.

disinterested, uninterested

From its first recorded uses in the seventeenth century, *disinterested* has had two senses: "indifferent, uninterested" and "impartial, not influenced by personal interest." But the first meaning gradually disappeared from educated usage, and its revival in this century has met strong opposition. Restricting *disinterested* to the meaning "impartial" sets up a distinction between *disinterested* and *uninterested* and thereby prevents ambiguity. Ignoring the distinction creates ambiguity and can cause serious misunderstanding. The disinterested observer of a competition may be intensely interested even though he favors neither side.

Though *disinterested* in the sense "uninterested" is established in general styles, writers who use it in that way should know that they risk upsetting some readers: "I began to hate someone once who habitually said 'disinterested' when he should have said 'uninterested' " (Alexander Cockburn, *New Statesman*).

Divided usage

Usage is said to be divided when two or more forms are in reputable use in the same dialect or variety of English. *Divided usage* doesn't apply to localisms like *poke* for *sack* or *bag* or to differences like *ain't* and *isn't,* which belong to separate varieties of the language. It applies to different practices in spelling, pronunciation, and grammatical form by people of similar educational background. In addition to hundreds of instances of divided usage in pronunciation, most dictionaries record forms like these:

In spelling: buses or busses, millionaire or millionnaire, catalog or catalogue

In past tenses: lighted or lit, sang or sung, stank or stunk

In past participles: shown or showed, proved or proven

The point about divided usage is that each of the alternatives is acceptable. A person who's learned to say "It's I" doesn't need to change to "It's me," and one who says "It's me" needn't change to "It's I." When there's a choice between variants of equal standing, choose the one that you use naturally, that's appropriate to your style, or the one that's customary among the people you want to reach. Before criticizing anyone's usage, make sure that it's not a variant as reputable as the one you prefer—which is usually the one you're used to.

The entries in this *Index* include divided usages and give fair warning when one or the other of two acceptable variants is likely to disturb some readers or listeners and arouse emotional attitudes. For examples, see **can, may; different from, different than; disinterested, uninterested; dove, dived; due to; enthuse; farther, further; like, as; Principal parts of verbs; reason is because; Sexist language; slow, slowly.**

div Division of words

Break the word at the end of the line between syllables.

To keep the right-hand margin of a manuscript fairly even, you have to divide some words at the end of a line with a hyphen. When you're not sure how to divide a word, consult a dictionary. Here are the basic rules:

1. Both the divided parts should be pronounceable. The break should come between conventionally recognized syllables: *mar gin, hy phen, chil dren, hi lar i ous, ad min is tra tive.* Words of one syllable *(matched, said, thought)* shouldn't be divided.

2. Double consonants are usually separable *(ef fi cient, com mit tee, daz zling, bat ted),* but they're kept together if there's no syllable break *(im pelled)* or if both belong to a root that a suffix has been added to *(stiff ly,* not *stif fly; yell ing,* not *yel ling).*

3. A single letter is never allowed to stand alone. Don't divide words like *enough.*

4. Words spelled with a hyphen *(half-brother, well-disposed)* should be divided only at the hyphen, to avoid the awkwardness of two hyphens in the same word.

dock

A few people will have conniptions if you write of tying up to a dock. A dock, they'll tell you, is the waterway between piers. But *dock* now also means the pier or wharf you tie up to.

doctoral, doctor's, doctorate

Doctoral is an adjective, *doctorate* a noun. A person who has earned a doctorate has earned a doctor's degree (a Ph.D.) in a doctoral program.

Documentation

The purpose of documentation is to make plain what sources—books, articles, personal interviews, and the like—a writer has drawn on in the course of composing a paper or a longer work. Methods of documentation vary. One system uses notes keyed to the text, with an accompanying bibliography, arranged alphabetically. A note referring to a book gives the author, title, facts of publication, and the page or pages on which the relevant fact or discussion appears.

The general principle is that you must be scrupulous about providing readers with whatever information they need to locate the source of statistics, data, statements, and inferences that are neither the product of your own firsthand investigation nor common knowledge. (Common knowledge includes undisputed facts—the dates of Theodore Roosevelt's birth, marriage, and death, for example—that anyone can find without difficulty.) The quality of your sources and the uses to which you have put them enter into a reader's evaluation of your work.

Formal acknowledgment of sources is particularly important in those research papers that refer to or build on the investigations of others. In writing such papers, take care to identify the author and source not only of every direct quotation but of all major statements of fact, interpretations, opinions, and conclusions that you have derived from the work of others.

See **Bibliographical form, Note form, Plagiarism, Research papers.**

don't

Don't is the contraction of *do not*. It is universally used in conversation and is often used in writing when *do not* would be too emphatic or when the shorter form gives a more comfortable rhythm. Until about 1900 *don't* was the usual third-person singular *(he don't, it don't, that don't)* in informal speech, but that usage is now nonstandard.

Double negative

In nonstandard English two or more negatives are very often used to express a single negation: There a*in't no*body home; Could*n't no*body find the body; I do*n't* have *no*thing to lose. But standard English insists on a single negative in such constructions. Instead of "They could*n't* find it *no*where," use "They could*n't* find it anywhere" (or possibly the formal "They could find it *no*where").

Some say a concealed double negative occurs with *hardly* or *scarcely.* When *hardly* means "almost not" or "probably not" and *scarcely* means the same a little more emphatically, "There's hardly nothing in the campus paper" should read "There's hardly anything," and "For a while we couldn't scarcely breathe" should read "could scarcely breathe."

At one time two negatives were used in all varieties of English. Today the usage is nonstandard, not because "two negatives make an affirmative" but simply because the double negative is no longer acceptable to educated people—even to those who say and write, "I was not unfamiliar with the plot."

Double prepositions

The *of* in a double preposition like *off of* is unnecessary. See **Prepositions and style 2.**

doublespeak

Doublespeak is the use of language not to express but to obscure, disguise, or deny the truth. Dwight Bolinger suggested that the label be applied to "jargon that is a sophisticated form of lying." Doublespeak is common in the pronouncements of governments and government agencies, corporations, and special-interest groups of all kinds. In some cases doublespeak in the form of euphemisms is used to protect the feelings of the old, the poor, the mentally retarded, the crippled, or the criminal, but the inaction encouraged by bland doublespeak does more harm than hurt feelings. See **Euphemisms, gobbledygook.**

doubt

After the verb *doubt* used negatively, a clause is introduced with *that:* I don't doubt that he meant well. After the verb *doubt* used positively, a clause is also introduced by *whether* or, less often, *if:*

> A couple of days ago, Walter Heller . . . said that he doubted whether that level could be reached.—Richard H. Rovere, *New Yorker*

> I doubt if this was ever a really important reason for his leaving London.—George Woodcock, *Esquire*

> For *doubt but,* see **but that, but what.**

dove, dived

Both *dove* and *dived* are acceptable as the past tense of *dive*.

drunk

It seems to take courage to use the word *drunk*. We either go formal *(intoxicated)*, or grab at respectability through euphemism *(under the influence, indulged to excess),* or try to be funny with any one of the dozens of slang expressions like *looped, bombed, smashed*. But *drunk* is the word.

due to

No one complains when *due* (followed by *to*) is used as an adjective firmly modifying a noun: "The failure was due to a conceptual oversight" (William Jaffé, *Journal of Political Economy*). But there has been strong objection to the use of *due to* in the sense "because of" to introduce prepositional phrases functioning as adverbs: Due to the coal miners' strike, a lot of stores were sold out of long underwear. Although this usage has been standard for decades, prejudice against it persists. As a result, some writers hesitate to use *due to* in any context.

each

1. The pronoun. Though the pronoun *each* is singular (To each his own), we use it to individualize members of a group (each of the joggers). As a result, it attracts plural verbs and pronouns:

> Each of the stages in child development produce typical conflicts.—Selma Frailberg, *New York Review of Books*

> Each of these people undoubtedly modified Latin in accordance with their own speech habits.—Albert C. Baugh, *A History of the English Language*

In cases like these, the writers have treated *each* as a collective because the plural idea has been uppermost in their minds. The practice is common in informal English and increasing in general English. But in formal usage *each* is ordinarily singular, and conservative stylists insist that it must be: "Each of them was asserting its own individuality" (John Hingham, *American Historical Review*).

Sometimes when *each* refers to both men and women, a writer will use *their* to avoid *his* or *his or her:* Each of the weekend guests brought their own climbing gear. See **Agreement 2, Collective nouns, every, Sexist language.**

2. The adjective. As an adjective, *each* does not affect the number of the verb or related pronoun. When *each* follows the plural subject that it modifies, the verb and related pronoun are also plural: "Two entrants will each win $500 and publication of their stories" *(Mademoiselle).*

each other, one another

Some textbooks have insisted that *each other* refers to two only and *one another* to more than two, but writers regularly ignore the distinction. See **Pronouns 3.**

Echo phrases

An echo phrase calls to mind a passage in literature, a song, or a popular saying. See **Allusion.**

Editorial *we*

Traditionally the anonymous writers of editorials use *we* and *our* (We believe that . . . ; It is our recommendation that . . .) rather than *I* and *my*. This is because editorials supposedly speak not just for the individuals who write them but for the publications in which they appear. See **I, we.**

educationese

Educationese is the label applied to the jargon of professional educators by those who find many of their speeches painful to listen to and much of their writing almost impossible to read. See **Jargon.**

effect, affect

The common noun is *effect,* meaning "result." As verbs, *effect* means "bring about" (The shortage has effected a change in driving habits), and *affect* means "influence" or "put on" (She affected a Southern accent). See **affect, effect.**

e.g.

E.g. stands for the Latin words meaning "for example." It is appropriate only in technical and scholarly writing. Generally "for example" is the right choice. See **Abbreviations 1, i.e.**

either

Though in speech a plural verb is common after *either* (I don't think either of them are going), in formal writing a singular verb is expected: Either of them was almost certain to reach the Pole. Usage is divided.

Either-or arguments

A legitimate procedure in arguing is to pose alternative courses of action (Either A or B) and then argue for one of them. This procedure is subject to abuse—resulting in a false dichotomy or false dilemma—when the claim that there are two and only two alternatives is, in fact, untrue. When the militant says, "You're either with me or against me," he is canceling out neutrality. When the economist offers a choice between inflation and recession, he overlooks the possibility that the country may be plagued by both. See **Fallacies, Logical thinking, Syllogisms.**

either . . . or, neither . . . nor

When one element of a compound subject joined by *either . . . or* or *neither . . . nor* is singular and the other is plural, make the verb agree with the nearer subject. See **Agreement 1c.**

elder, eldest

These forms of *old* survive in references to the order of birth of members of a family—"the elder brother," "our eldest daughter"—and in some honorific senses like "elder statesman."

Ellipsis

The three periods—each preceded and followed by a space—that are used to indicate the omission of one or more words within a quotation are called an ellipsis: "Four score and seven years ago our fathers brought forth . . . a new nation . . . dedicated to the proposition that all men are created equal." When the last words in a quoted sentence are omitted and the quotation is to continue, the end punctuation precedes the ellipsis: "We have come to dedicate a portion of that field, as a final resting place for those who gave their lives. . . . It is altogether fitting and proper that we should do this."

Current practice does not require an ellipsis at the beginning or end of a quotation when what remains forms a complete sentence. In such cases, a capital letter may be made lowercase or the reverse, as is appropriate: As Lincoln observed, "Our fathers brought forth on this continent a new nation."

Phrases run into the text should not be preceded or followed by ellipses: It is worth asking whether we continue to be "dedicated to the proposition" (*not* ". . . dedicated to the proposition . . .").

In dialog an ellipsis indicates hesitation in speech. It may also be used as an end stop for a statement that's left unfinished or allowed to die away: "Now, if you've got a moment, let me tell you a thing or two about Benny Carter . . ." (Daniel Okrent, *Esquire*).

Elliptical constructions

An acceptable elliptical construction omits a word or two that the reader can supply, usually from a neighboring construction: I work much harder than you [work]. The choice between longer and shorter forms is a matter of style. Formal writing uses relatively few elliptical constructions; general and informal styles use them freely. Compare **Clauses 2a.**

else's

In phrases with pronouns like *anyone, nobody,* and *someone, else*—not the preceding pronoun—takes the sign of the possessive: The package was left at somebody else's house.

empathy, sympathy

Empathy and *sympathy* overlap in referring to regret at the misfortunes of others. Both imply a sharing of the victims' unhappiness, with *empathy* suggesting a particularly close identification with those in distress.

emph Emphasis

Strengthen the emphasis of this passage.

Rightly used, emphasis indicates the relative importance of the points you're making, so that your readers recognize the most important as most important, the less important as less important, the incidental as incidental. If you don't provide emphasis, you fail to guide your readers. If you place it where it doesn't belong, you mislead or confuse them.

1. Proportion. Ordinarily, allot space on the basis of importance. Give the point you want to emphasize the space and development its significance calls for. If you write a paper at the last minute, you may give the preliminaries more space, and therefore more emphasis, than they deserve and then, realizing that you're running out of time, leave your major point undeveloped and unemphatic. Budget your time so that you won't mislead your reader in these ways.

2. Position. As a general rule, the most emphatic position in a sentence, a paragraph, or a full paper is the end (hence the danger of leaving the final point undeveloped). The second most emphatic position is the beginning. In writing long papers and answering examination questions, you'll often want to use both these natural positions of emphasis—stating your thesis in the opening paragraph and, after presenting the arguments that support it, restating it in your conclusion. In any case, don't let your major point get lost somewhere in between, and don't announce it at the beginning and then fail to get back to it. See **Beginning, Ending.**

3. Separation. Punctuation can emphasize a part of a sentence by setting it off. Occasionally you may want to use a comma for light emphasis where normally no punctuation would appear (see **Comma 7**). In other cases you can use a colon or a dash in place of a comma to give more emphasis (see **Dash 1**). Or you can begin a separate sentence or a new paragraph to achieve the same purpose.

4. Repetition. As long as you don't overdo it, you can gain emphasis by repeating significant words and by repeating ideas in different words. Repeating a structural pattern, such as a *who* clause, is an excellent device for emphasizing: "It continues to be men who predominate in the running of government, men who both manage and present news (and men's games that find the prominent position in national and local news programs), men who run the world of business and finance" (Carolyn Hardesty, *North American Review*). See **Parallelism, Repetition, Series.**

5. Economy. In the condensing that's a regular part of revision, pay special attention to the way you express ideas that deserve major emphasis. Strip sentences of unnecessary words that blur their clarity and blunt their impact. Emphatic statement needn't be brusque, but it must be direct and uncluttered. See **Wordiness.**

6. Mechanical devices. Used very sparingly, underlining can add emphasis: "Always Thoreau tells us, *You can change your life*" (Joyce Carol Oates, *(Woman) Writer*). But unearned italics, capitals, and exclamation marks for emphasis are likely to bore, annoy, or amuse the reader. Telling him that he should be interested ("It is interesting to note") or impressed ("Here is the really important point that everyone should recognize") is likely to irritate him. "Big" words have the same effect, and the intensifiers used in speech—*terribly, extremely, incredibly*—are almost always ineffective in writing. On paper "a terribly shocking incident" turns out to be less, not more, emphatic than "a shocking incident." So earn your reader's attention. Don't try to grab it with mechanical hoots and verbal hollers.

end Ending

Revise the ending of your paper to round out the discussion.

When you reach the end of your discussion, wrap it up. Don't just stop, so that a reader wonders if the last page is missing. And don't ramble on until your audience is missing.

If your paper is long, you may want to review the ground you've covered, preferably in fresh phrasing. If the material is complex, you may need to pull together the points you've made and show how they add up and what they add up to. Short papers, as well as long ones, must add up to something.

If the reader of a paper you've written finishes the last sentence and thinks "So what?" either you've produced a paper that has no point, or—more likely—you've failed to make clear what the point is. A conclusion can't save a pointless paper by simply announcing a point, but by clarifying the essential argument, by bringing out what has only been implied, the final paragraph or two can strengthen a paper greatly.

If your paper has been a voyage of discovery in which you've tried to define your own attitudes, you may end up with something like, "What I feel now is that my parents gave too much to me without thinking enough about me." Whether such a conclusion works depends on what's gone before. If that point has been gradually emerging throughout the paper, fine. If it hasn't—if, for example, you've only told about the size of your allowance, your charge accounts, the gifts on birthdays and at Christmas—then your ending will leave the reader perplexed and dissatisfied.

Final sentences should avoid tag ends and anticlimax as well as irrelevance. They should build to a firm conclusion, not trail off into silence. They should wrap up the discussion in such a way that the reader not only recognizes its completeness but feels satisfied that the last words were the right ones.

End stop

An end stop is the mark of punctuation—usually a period, exclamation mark, or question mark—used at the end of a sentence. When two end stops would come at the close of a sentence, use only the more emphatic or more necessary for meaning. Here a question comes at the end of a sentence that would normally close with a period; only the question mark is used: "When we say, for example, that Miss A plays well, only an irredeemable outsider would reply 'Plays what?' " (C. Alphonso Smith, *Studies in English Syntax*).

English language

The earliest records of English date from the seventh century A.D., two centuries after invading Germanic tribesmen from northwestern Europe—Angles, Saxons, Jutes, and Frisians—had made their homes in the British Isles, bringing with them the dialects that are the direct ancestors of the English language. Through those dialects English is connected to a prehistoric past—to an unrecorded language called Germanic, parent of the Low and High German languages, the Scandinavian languages, and English. Through Germanic, English is connected to a still more ancient and unrecorded language called Indo-European, the parent of (among others) most of the language groups on the European continent.

The history of English is often divided into three main periods: Old English (OE), c. 450–1100; Middle English (ME), c. 1100–1450; Modern English or New English (MnE or NE), c. 1450–, with this last period sometimes subdivided into Early Modern English (EMnE), c. 1450–1700, and Modern English, c. 1700–.

See **Dialects.**

enormity, enormousness

Because *enormity* looks like a more compact way of expressing the idea of "enormousness," it's often used in that sense, as most dictionaries indicate. But this use is deplored by those who restrict *enormity* to the traditional meaning "enormously evil" or "great wickedness," as in "the enormity of the crime."

enthuse

Enthuse is a back formation (see **Origin of words 3d**) from *enthusiasm*. Though widely used in general and informal writing, the word is still avoided in formal usage, and many readers object to it. The only other locutions we have for the idea are the longer *be enthusiastic over* or *be enthusiastic about*.

equally as

Though *equally as* is an established idiom (Color is equally as important as design), one of the words can often be deleted. *Either* Color is as important as design *or* Color and design are equally important.

-ese

The suffix *-ese* is used to make new nouns (*journalese, educationese, bureaucratese, officialese*) that have the disparaging sense of "lingo" or "jargon": His mastery of sociologese left us impressed but uninformed.

Establishment

In the 1960s *Establishment* (sometimes not capitalized) became a vogue word for the powers that be. Though no longer in vogue, it survives both as shorthand for the complex of power—economic, political, military, scientific—that runs things and as a scare term for sinister inner circles that supposedly control our national destiny.

et al.

In documenting sources, you may be expected to reduce a list of four or more authors of a single work to the first author named and *et al.* "Nina Baym et al." serves as an economical substitute for listing the seven authors of a textbook. Current practice favors *and others*, the translation of Latin *et alii*, for which *et al.* is the abbreviation.

etc.

Though sometimes a convenient way to end an incomplete list, *etc.*, the abbreviation of the Latin phrase *et cetera* ("and the rest"), belongs primarily to business and reference uses: This case is suitable for large photographs, maps, charts, etc. In most writing, *and so forth* or *and so on* is preferable when the reference is to things, and *and others* is preferable with lists of people. The fact that a list is incomplete can also be indicated by naming the category and then using *such as* or a similar introductory term: This case is suitable for graphics such as large photographs, maps, and charts. Don't use *etc.* to hide the fact that you've run out of material.

Ethnic labels

American English has its full share of slang terms for members of racial and ethnic groups, but many of the older labels for peoples for foreign origin have practically disappeared. Casual use of racist terms is now rare in writing, and it is far less common in speech than it was a few decades ago.

Etymology

Etymology is the study of word origins. See **Origin of words 1.**

Euphemisms

A euphemism is a term used in place of one that names more explicitly something unpleasant or something regarded as not quite nice: *perspire* for *sweat, passed on* for *died, senior citizens* for *old people, lavatory* or *powder room* or *comfort facility* for *toilet*. Political, military, and promotional vocabularies offer countless examples. Occasionally euphemisms are warranted, to avoid causing pain or embarrassment, but in most cases honesty is better—and makes for better writing—than evasion.

every

1. *Every, everybody,* and *everyone* were originally singular and continue to take a singular verb: Every player on the team deserves our praise; Everybody loathes the mayor; Everyone takes the freeway. But for related pronouns that follow, usage is divided. The singular is perhaps more common in formal writing, but the plural appears in all varieties: "Everyone who ever learned to write . . . began by using writing . . . as a way of expressing themselves" (Harvey A. Daniels, *Famous Last Words*). The plural *themselves* is reasonable, since the reference is to a number of people. Instead of substituting *himself* for *themselves,* formal written usage might replace *everyone* with an explicit plural: All those who ever learned . . .

A plural pronoun is also used for clarity when the *every* phrase is the object of a verb with a singular subject: "The traditional leader then comes forward and thanks everyone for their attendance and invites them to lunch" (John A. Woodward, *Ethnology*). Treating the *every* words as collectives can sometimes prevent confusion and also avoid the awkward *he-or-she* locution. But some conservatives continue to insist that, in writing, related pronouns must be singular. See **he or she.**

2. *Everybody* is always written as one word. *Everyone* is usually written as one word, but when the *one* is stressed, it's written separately: Everyone knew what the end would be; God bless us, every one.

3. *Everyplace,* meaning "everywhere," is inappropriate in formal writing. *Everywheres* is nonstandard.

Examples

Examples are instances that illustrate general statements. They clarify explanations, strengthen assertions, and provide support for arguments. See **Details, Induction.**

except, accept

Except as a verb means "leave out, exclude": In making the new assignment, the teacher excepted those who had made an honest effort on the last one. It's decidedly formal. *Excused* would often be more appropriate for the same meaning in general writing.

Accept means "receive" or "respond to affirmatively" and is slightly formal: I accept with pleasure; He accepted the position (as contrasted with "He took the job").

Exclamation mark

An exclamation mark (or point) is used after an emphatic interjection; after a phrase, clause, or sentence that's genuinely exclamatory; and after forceful commands. Clear-cut exclamations are no problem:

Oh! Ouch! No, no, no!
Damn those mosquitoes!
It's the chance of a lifetime!

But many interjections are mild and deserve no more than a comma or period: "Well, well, so you're in college now." Often sentences cast in exclamatory patterns are simply statements (What a memorable experience that was), and the mark of punctuation is optional.

In deciding whether to use an exclamation mark, you should first ask yourself whether you intend to exclaim—to express strong feeling or give special emphasis. Walt Kelly said, "Using the exclamation point is like wearing padded shoulders." But when used sparingly, to signal genuine emotion, the mark can serve the writer as the raised voice or dramatic gesture serves the speaker:

The Sun Also Rises is a major work, brilliantly constructed and colored—though last year I was taken aback to hear some students complain that Jake Barnes indulges himself in too much self-pity. How imperious the young can be when judging the victims of disasters they don't even trouble to learn about!—Irving Howe, *Harper's*

Exclamations

What distinguishes an exclamation from other kinds of utterance is its purpose: emphatic expression. In form, an exclamation may be a declarative sentence (She's late again!), a question (Can she be late again!), a command or request (Be ready when I call! Please be on time!), a verbless sentence (How terrible for you!), or an interjection (Ugh!). See **Exclamation mark.**

expect

In general and formal writing, *expect* is ordinarily limited to the senses "anticipate" (He expects you to be a great success) and "require as reasonable"

(Winsock, Inc., expects its employees to arrive on time). In American usage the sense "to suppose, presume, believe" in reference to past or present (I expect there were times when Lincoln was heartily fed up) is unlikely to be found in formal contexts.

Exposition

Most factual writing is explanatory—intended primarily to inform and enlighten the reader. *Exposition* (or *expository writing*) is the traditional term for writing of this kind. When extended to include argument, *exposition* refers to all factual prose, in contrast to fiction. See **Argument, Forms of discourse, Rhetoric.**

fact

The fact is often deadwood and should be deleted: The study demonstrates [the fact] that workers can become affluent. Sometimes phrases with *fact* can be replaced by single words: in spite of the fact = *although;* due to the fact that = *because. True fact* is redundant. Omit *true.*

factor

Windy phrases with *factor* should be deleted: Determination and imagination [were the factors that] brought the program its popularity. *Factor* itself, meaning "something that helps produce a result," can often be replaced by a more precise or expressive word: A major factor (stimulus? influence? resource?) in creating the system was the artisan class. Used in the plural, it may give the reader no specific information and arouse suspicion that the writer doesn't have any.

In the political journalism of the late 1980s, "the sleaze factor" and "the wimp factor" gave *factor* new and excessive life, spawning such analogous combinations as "courage," "anger," and "comfort" factors.

Fallacies

As the term is used in logic, a fallacy is an error in reasoning. If a college announces that it awards scholarships only to students who are needy, then we are reasoning correctly when we assume that a particular student who receives a scholarship at that institution is needy. But it would be fallacious to say, on the basis of the same announcement, that every needy student in the college is receiving scholarship aid. Similarly, a person who acts on the premise that an X-rated movie is not fit to see can't confidently assume that every movie with a different rating *is* fit to see. *Non sequitur* ("it does not follow") is a comprehensive category covering all those errors in reasoning in which the stated conclusion doesn't follow from the premises, or starting points.

Popularly, *fallacy* is extended to include all misleading statements and errors in interpretation, intentional or unintentional. In this sense, speakers or writers who deliberately withhold facts, slant evidence, use a term inconsistently, draw an unjustified inference, or argue beside the point commit a fallacy. So do speakers or writers who can't reach a sound conclusion because they don't know enough about a situation or because they make a mistake in interpreting what they do know.

The common fallacies go by names that are almost self-explanatory. *Hasty generalizing* means basing a conclusion on inadequate evidence: The fact that two of every three students in my physics class are interested in a career in engineering indicates that engineering is the first choice of science majors these days. *Faulty generalizing* is generalizing that's based on weak or unrepresentative instances. It may take the form of *card stacking* (suppressing data that do not support the conclusion).

Fallacies in *part-whole relationships* result from the twin errors of assuming that what is true of the part is always true of the whole and vice versa. A common form of the fallacy, called *stereotyping,* typically generalizes about a whole class of people (Swedes, Rotarians, plumbers, poets) on the basis of very limited personal experience or, particularly when ethnic or religious groups are concerned, acceptance of widely held biases.

Either-or fallacies often originate in a faulty analysis of the issue under debate. To assume that there are only two possible courses of action is risky; to ignore the existence of other alternatives is to make productive discussion impossible.

Ignoring the question is an umbrella term for many different ways of shifting the grounds of the argument to a topic that is not under debate. One form of this fallacy is *begging the question*—assuming something is true that has not been established. "When is the administration going to stop leading the country into illegal wars?" begs the question of whether the administration has led the country into wars and, if it has, whether the wars were illegal. A related tactic is *arguing in a circle:* "In our society it is necessary to keep up with the latest styles because it is essential to be fashionably dressed."

Another way to ignore the question is to engage in *ad hominem* ("to the man") argument. This popular label originally meant appeals, often emotional, tailored to the beliefs and circumstances of the audience, at the expense of arguments on the issue. The term is now widely used in the quite different sense of argument *against* the man—an attack on the character, actions, or motives of the opponent rather than a debate on the issue. Such attacks often amount to *name-calling,* the irresponsible use of epithets and labels chosen for their connotations for particular audiences. (For some audiences, *liberal* is inflammatory; for others, *conservative* is.) A *red herring* introduces an issue that sidetracks attention from the argument. Like *ad hominem,* the term *red herring* is in general circulation: "College administrators say this argument is a red herring. To them, the issue is not freedom of speech but harassment and intimidation'' (Tamar Jacoby, *Newsweek*). Still another way of ignoring the issue is to set up a *straw man,* a distortion or caricature of the opposing position, and then launch a devastating attack on the caricature.

Fallacies that ignore or distort the real issue are often accompanied by a smokescreen of *irrelevant emotional appeals.* Appeals to emotions and ideals—to pride, to justice, to morality, even to anger—can be a legitimate part of an argument. Stirring up dissension by reinforcing the jealousies, hatreds, fears, and prejudices is a reprehensible method of swaying an audience.

An *argument from authority* recommends a position or an action solely because it is supported by somebody presumed to be better informed or wiser than either the writer or the intended audience. This is another legitimate and powerful means of persuasion when the authority's competence on the particular issue is beyond question. But the tactic is subject to abuse when, for instance, a television star is offered as an authority on medication or an evangelist as an expert on fiscal policy. It is also subject to abuse when the authority is a general class: ''Scholars tell us . . . ,'' ''Everybody knows . . .'' The next step—the fallacy of *hypostatization* or reification—is the appeal to an abstraction as the authority: ''Science tells us'' instead of ''Heisenberg tells us in *Physics and Beyond* . . .''

Because fallacies masquerade as sound arguments, audiences are often taken in by them, as successful advertising campaigns and victorious political strategies frequently prove. In fact, many fallacies can be interpreted as good arguments gone wrong: hasty generalizing is a classic example. In scrutinizing your own arguments for flaws, you need to do more than hunt for logical fallacies; you need to deal with the substance of what you have written and your motives for writing it. Sooner or later, ethical considerations enter into the evaluation of any argument.

See **ad hominem, Begging the question, Cause and effect 2, Either-or arguments, Non sequitur, Part-whole relationships, Stereotyping.** See also **Argument, Logical thinking, Syllogisms.**

famous, famed

Word worriers prefer *famous* to *famed,* but as an adjective before a noun (the famous, or famed, actor) often neither term is necessary: the reader doesn't need to be told that what is publicly acclaimed is famous. So avoid both unless you're telling how someone or something became renowned or explaining what someone or something is celebrated for.

farther, further

Some careful writers make a distinction between *farther,* referring to physical distance (Farther north there was heavy snow), and *further,* referring to more abstract relations of degree or extent (Nothing could be further removed from experience). The useful distinction is not consistently maintained, even in formal English.

feel

Though one of the accepted meanings of *feel* is "think" or "believe" (I feel that Barnum was right), *feel* shouldn't replace those verbs. Readers need to be reminded now and then that a writer thinks and has convictions.

female

In current usage the noun *female* seems most appropriate in somewhat formal or technical contexts, as in "biologically determined females of the species." It is usually a poor substitute for *woman*, though it serves a writer well in calling attention to sexual stereotypes, as here: "I'm blaming myself for their lack of a good time, as if I, the female, am supposed to keep them entertained and happy" (Kathleen McConnell, "Memoirs of an Oilfield Smoothneck"). The adjective *female* also focuses on classification by sex, whether human or nonhuman. See **Sexist language.**

fewer, less

The rule is that *fewer* refers to number among things that are counted (fewer particles) and *less* to amount or quantity among things that are measured (less energy). Formal usage ordinarily observes the distinction except when units of time (hours), distance (miles), money (dollars), or other items are being discussed: They won by less than a hundred votes. In general writing *less* is applied to countables fairly often: "I suggest they sell two less tickets to the public" (Dwight Macdonald, *Esquire*). Usage is divided.

field

The phrase *the field of* can almost always be omitted: He has long been interested in [the field of] psychiatry.

Figurative language

We use figurative language when we transfer a word from a context in which it's literally true (a *smelly* cheese) to one in which it isn't (a *smelly* scandal). Everything we say and write is peppered with such transfers (*peppered,* for instance). We *play ball* when we cooperate, *chime in* when we join in a conversation, *tax* the patience of others when we talk too much. Many of these word transfers have been around so long that they've lost all their figurative, or image-making, power. (Do you picture an animal when you hear that someone has *weaseled* out of a situation?) Though *foot* continues to serve as the name for a part of the body, its reference has been extended to include the bottom or lowest part of a tree, a bed, a path, and a mountain, among many other things. In these uses, *foot* is a petrified, or dead, figure. (*Dead* is used here figuratively. So is *petrified.*)

A live figure is created when a word is extended to a new referent. We speak routinely of peeling an apple or a potato. Paul Auster, writing of the poet Laura Riding, speaks of her "trying somehow to peel back the skin of the world" *(New York Review of Books)*. The yoking of things not ordinarily thought of as alike or the phrasing of a perception in a fresh way can serve the double function of seizing the attention and of informing or persuading. Two radically different comparisons—one to an ancient empire, the other to a modern technological phenomenon—are packed into this brief description of Bangkok: "Bangkok is Byzantine in its complexity, intricate and elaborate as a computer chip" (Erin McGraw, *North American Review*).

Traditionally, distinctions among figures of speech are made on the basis of the way the meaning of the word or phrase is transferred. In a metaphor the transfer is often direct: loud music *becomes* a secular religion. In a simile it's made through *like* or *as: like the scarecrow,* listeners have their brains turned to sawdust. In other common figures the part stands for the whole (*wheel* for bicycle) or the whole for the part (*tails* for a full-dress suit) or the author for the works (*Shakespeare* for Shakespeare's plays). Hyperbole uses extravagant language for emphasis: I almost *died* of shame. Understatement seeks the same effect by the opposite means: Enthusiasm for conscription was *not overwhelming*.

Personification gives life to abstractions and inanimate objects. In this elaborate figure General Motors, Ford, and Chrysler, losing sales to foreign automakers after years of total dominance, are pictured as pompous aristocrats being hard pressed by snapping dogs:

> The Auto Lords of Michigan continue to stride about the interior, making gruff and manly sounds, but their legs are beset with Saabs and Volvos, their ankles nibbled at by Datsuns and Volkswagens.—Michael Arlen, *New Yorker*

For other figures of speech, see **Analogy, Hyperbole, Imagery, Irony, Metaphor, Metonymy, Oxymoron.** For figures of sound, see **Alliteration, Assonance, Onomatopoeia, Puns.** See also **Figures of speech.**

Figures

Figures are the symbols for numbers. See **Numbers.**

 ## Figures of speech

This figure of speech is trite, inconsistent, or inappropriate. Revise the passage.

A good figure of speech can add color, humor, interest, or information and may convey meaning more economically than its literal equivalent. But literal expression is always preferable to a figure that doesn't work.

1. Replace trite figures. Use figures of speech that represent your own perceptions. Many figures that once were fresh and vivid are now clichés: *cool as a cucumber, a ribbon of concrete, sick as a dog, fresh as a daisy, Old Man Winter*. Writers who think about what they're setting down on paper either avoid them or at least try to give them a new look. "Cucumber-cool" might get by where "cool as a cucumber" would bore or irritate the reader. But there are dangers in trying to disguise clichés. Though "a lot of water has flowed under the bridge" takes on some new life in "all the water, and war, that had flowed under the bridge" (Karl Miller, *New York Review of Books*), readers may feel that water and war don't mix.

Whenever possible, offer the reader an original figure, like James Thurber's road "which seemed to be paved with old typewriters." If you can neither freshen an old figure successfully nor invent a new one that works, stick to a literal statement of your meaning.

2. Untangle mixed figures. Sometimes, instead of coming up with no image at all, you may come up with too many:

> The noise, like an enthusiastic roar from a distant sports stadium, yet as insistent as the surge of distant surf, grew till it was galloping up the quadrangle in massive waves.

Here sports fans, the ocean, and horses create a catastrophe. To catch such incongruous mixtures before the final draft, read what you've written as objectively as you can.

More difficult to spot are the mixed figures that involve dead metaphors. Keep in mind that a figure that's dead in most contexts may revive in certain relationships, with ridiculous results. In the first of the following sentences, the student invents a figure that's apt. In the second, the word *faces,* which is regularly used to stand for "people," simply won't work with *sitting* or with suiting up:

> As we dressed, comments were tossed about the room as casually as the rolls of tape we were using to tape our ankles. The familiar faces, sitting in their usual corners, were all getting into their uniforms.

Don't just read what you've written before you turn a paper in. Think about what it *says.* When your figures of speech call up pictures of physical impossibilities or other absurdities because you've mixed images, they're likely to distract your readers from the point you're trying to make. If in speaking figuratively you seem to be speaking foolishly, your figurative language needs to be overhauled or abandoned.

3. Replace inappropriate figures. A figure of speech may be inappropriate to the audience, to the subject, or to you as the writer. Whether used to explain or to amuse, similes, metaphors, and analogies drawn from electronics or trout fishing or from the folklore of your home town won't work with readers who know nothing about these things. Describing bluegrass music with figures of speech appropriate to a discussion of Beethoven's symphonies, or vice versa, makes sense only if you're trying, perhaps desperately, to be funny. And using figures that don't match your own attitudes or temperament—poetic metaphors, for example, when your natural style is down-to-earth, or violent similes when you're typically peace-loving and thoughtful—gives them prominence that will seem off-key to your readers unless your content justifies the uncharacteristic emotion.

A figure of speech can be judged good or not good only in a context, a rhetorical situation. When you write your final draft, judge each of your figures by its appropriateness to the audience, the subject, and your prevailing tone. If you decide that a figure doesn't fit, replace it with a suitable figure or with the literal equivalent. But don't discard a figure simply because it startles you when you read over what you've written. In the context of your paper, "the moon crashed through the clouds" may be just right. See **Figurative language.**

finalize

Finalize has been in widespread use for more than a generation. Its near-synonyms—*finish, complete,* and *conclude*—lack the connotation "to make official" that gives *finalize* its usefulness in some contexts: "Before they finalize new guidelines they will consult listeners in East Europe to make sure the proposed changes are having the right effect" (Mary Hornaday, *Christian Science Monitor*). But no writer can afford to be ignorant of the prejudice against *finalize*. It was included in Maury Maverick's original list of gobbledygook in 1942, and some still consider it—and many newer *-ize* words—gobbledygook.

"Fine" writing

The adjective *fine* has long been applied to writing that's too pretentious for what's being said. "Fine" writing uses "big" words and strained, artificial figures of speech. If you write more to impress your readers than to express your ideas, you're likely to produce "fine" writing. Another aged term for an overripe style is *purple prose*. See **Diction, Figures of speech.**

fix

In formal usage *fix* in its broadest sense means "fasten in place," and this meaning is used metaphorically in such expressions as "fix the blame," "fix your eyes," "fix a time." In general usage it means "repair" or "put into shape": The VCR had to be fixed. As a noun meaning "predicament," *fix* has passed from informal to general: "In some respects economic theory is in the same fix as biology was years ago" (Henry M. Boettinger, *Harvard Business Review*).

flaunt, flout

Flaunt, to "wave, display boastfully," is frequently used with the sense "treat with contempt, scorn," the meaning traditionally assigned to *flout.* Readers aware of the traditional distinction deplore the confusion, which reverses the intended meaning.

folk, folks

In formal writing *folks* is uncommon. *Folk* is used in the senses "the common people" (usually of a certain region) and "people" (of a specified type). In general writing *folks* for "people," often with the connotation "ordinary, everyday," and for "relatives, parents" is carried over from informal.

Folk etymology

When people are puzzled by an unfamiliar word or phrase, they sometimes try to make it more regular or more meaningful by rephrasing it from familiar elements: from *aeroplane* they made *airplane;* from Spanish *cucuracha,* English *cockroach;* from *saler,* "a salt-holder," first the redundant *salt-saler* and then *saltcellar,* which has no more to do with a cellar than the *sir-* in *sirloin* has to do with a knight (the *sir-* in the cut of beef is *sur,* "above"). See **Origin of words 1.**

for

When *for* joins clauses, it is classified as a coordinating conjunction even though it may mean the same as subordinating *because:* He was exhausted, *for* he had gone two nights without sleep.

In some contexts, *for* differs slightly in meaning from *because.* It conveys the sense of giving the reason for an opinion or the evidence for an assertion. Here *for* is more precise than *because* would be:

> Komarov clearly had some control over his ship, for he was able to orient it well enough to accomplish re-entry.—*Newsweek*

Especially in this meaning, *for* is a rather formal conjunction.

A comma is usually needed between clauses joined by *for* to keep it from being read as a preposition: The tutors must love the work, for the pay, which is only $300 a year plus room and board, can't be very attractive. The comma prevents the misreading: The tutors must love the work for the pay.

See **because.**

Foreign words in English

1. Anglicizing foreign words. English has always borrowed words and roots from other languages, and it's still borrowing (from French, *duvet;* from Spanish, *macho;* from Japanese, *sushi*). Words usually cross the threshold of English with their foreign spelling, perhaps with un-English plurals or other forms, and with no established English pronunciation. The process of anglicizing brings them more or less in line with English usage, though they may keep some of their foreign quality, like the *i* of *machine,* the silent *s* in *debris,* the *t* where we are tempted to put a *d* in *kindergarten.*

The speed and degree of anglicizing depends on how frequently the word is used, the circumstances in which it's used, and the people who use it. Formal writers and conservative editors keep the foreign spelling longer than writers and editors of general English. If the words come in through the spoken language, like those of the automobile vocabulary, they're anglicized sooner than if they come in by way of literature: *chamois, garage, detour, chauffeur, coupe* (now rarely spelled with its accent mark—*coupé*—or pronounced as two syllables). Words that come in through and remain in literary, scholarly, or socially elite circles change more slowly, in both spelling and pronunciation: *tête-à-tête, faux pas, nouveau riche, laissez-faire.*

2. Using borrowed words.
a. Italics. Words that have not been completely anglicized are usually printed in italics in magazines and books and should be underlined in the papers you write. Consult your dictionary. Words on the borderline will be found sometimes in italics, sometimes not. Formal writers use italics more than general writers.
b. Accents and other marks. In books and magazines, words recently taken in from other languages are usually written with the accent marks they have in the language of their origin. After a time the accents are dropped unless they're needed to indicate pronunciation. But publications addressed to general audiences are more likely to drop accent marks *(expose, detente)* than are publications for scholarly audiences *(exposé, détente).*
c. Plurals. English usually brings borrowed words into its own system of conjugation and declension *(campuses,* not *campi),* though some words change slowly, especially those used mainly in formal writing *(syllabi* or *syllabuses).* See **Plurals of nouns 4.**

See **Origin of words 2b.**

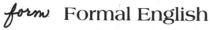

Formal English

The word or passage marked is too formal for the subject or for the style of the rest of the paper. Revise, making it more appropriate.

Formal written English is appropriate (though not mandatory) in discussions of ideas, in research papers and other scholarly works, in addresses to be delivered on ceremonial occasions, and in literary essays intended for well-educated readers. It's usually not appropriate in accounts of personal experience, in papers about campus issues, in comments on current books, movies, TV shows, or popular records, or in other writing intended for general readers.

The vocabulary of formal style includes many words not used in general written English. *Form* in the margin of your paper may refer to a word that's too formal for the context: For a while it looked as though the bad habits he had picked up were irremediable (*better:* could never be corrected). Or it may point to a sentence pattern that suggests the deliberate pace of formal English and therefore mixes poorly with sentences that suggest the spontaneity of speech:

> In addition to being younger than my classmates, I had retained, along with the babyish habit of sucking my thumb, a tendency to cry when I was not allowed to have my own way, thereby increasing their animosity toward me.

> **Possible revision:** Besides being younger than my classmates, I still sucked my thumb. This irritated them, and I made things worse by crying when I didn't get my own way.

See **General English, Informal English, Standard English.** For discussion and illustration of formal, general, and informal styles, see the Introduction.

former, first–latter, last

Traditionally, *former* and *latter* refer only to two units: "the former called the latter 'little prig' " (Ralph Waldo Emerson). Tradition holds for *former,* but the use of *latter* with more than two is common enough to be standard. Even so, some conservative readers would prefer "the last named" in references like this one: "The list of products . . . could include potassium, bromine, chlorine, caustic, and magnesium. The latter might become a very important lightweight metal" (Glenn T. Seaborg, *Bulletin of the Atomic Scientists*).

First and *last* refer to items in a series, usually more than two:

> The first president had set up a very informal organization.
> His last act was to advise his family on their future.

Latest refers to a series that's still continuing (the latest fashions). *Last* refers either to the final item of a completed series (their last attempt was successful) or to the most recent item of a continuing series (the last election). See **last, latest.**

Forms of discourse

Writing has traditionally been divided into four forms of discourse—narration, description, exposition, and argument. The classification is useful because it emphasizes purpose as the controlling element in a piece of writing, and examining the forms one by one enables the student of writing to concentrate on certain traits of content, organization, and style that are peculiar to each type. But the categories are not sharply distinct. Description contributes to the other three, particularly to narration; many papers that are primarily argumentative include stretches of exposition; and so on.

Formulas

Every language has some fixed phrases that have become customary in certain situations: Once upon a time, Ladies and gentlemen, Good morning, Best wishes, Yours truly, How do you do? Such phrases are too useful to be called clichés, and unlike most trite expressions they're not substitutes for simpler locutions. When called for, they should be used without apology. See **Idiom, Subjunctive mood 2a.**

fortuitous

Fortuitous means "by chance, accidental": My meeting with the talk-show host was entirely fortuitous. It does not mean "fortunate."

Fractions

Fractions are written in figures when attached to other figures (72¾), in a series in figures (½, 1, 2, 4), or in tables or reference matter. In most running text they're written in words: "Each board was thirty-six inches long, thirty-two inches wide, and a quarter-inch thick" (Robert Reich, *Atlantic*). Hyphens are normally used between the numerator and denominator if neither part itself contains a hyphen (seven-tenths), and hyphens should be used to avoid confusion; but they are less common than they used to be and are now omitted when the numerator functions as an adjective, as in "He sold one half and kept the other."

Decimals are taking the place of fractions in factual writing, because they are more flexible and permit greater precision in less space: .7; .42; 3.14159.

 # Fragment

The construction marked is not a satisfactory sentence. Revise by joining it to a neighboring sentence, by making it grammatically complete, or by rewriting the passage.

A sentence fragment is a part of a sentence—usually a phrase or dependent clause—that's carelessly or ineffectively punctuated as if it were a whole sentence. You can usually correct a fragment by joining it to the preceding or following sentence or by otherwise making it grammatically complete. But sometimes rewriting is the best solution.

Below, with suggested revisions, are three common types of fragments.

1. A prepositional phrase punctuated as a sentence:

The northern part of the city is mainly residential. On the eastern outskirts are the oil refining plants. And to the south beaches and parks.

Revision: The northern part of the city is mainly residential. On the eastern outskirts are the oil refining plants and to the south beaches and parks.

2. A participial phrase punctuated as a sentence:

For sixteen years I did pretty much what I wanted to. Being distrustful and avoiding anyone in authority.

Revision: For sixteen years I did pretty much what I wanted to, distrusting and avoiding anyone in authority.

3. A dependent clause punctuated as a sentence:

I still remember him as the best teacher I ever had. Because right then he sat down and helped me work all the problems.

Revision: I still remember him as the best teacher I ever had, because right then he sat down and helped me work all the problems.

In an unexpectedly heavy turnout, over 80 percent of the citizens voted. A fact that shows how strongly they felt about the issue.

Revision: In an unexpectedly heavy turnout, over 80 percent of the citizens voted— a fact that shows . . . Or: . . . voted. This fact shows . . .

The deliberate setting off of a phrase or dependent clause for rhetorical effect is common in print. Used sparingly and skillfully, it can do good service as an organizational road sign that briskly points the reader toward the next topic—"But first, the new troops" (Lucian K. Truscott IV, *Harper's*)—or provides informal notice of the progress of the discussion—"Which brings us back to the absurdity of the backlash accusations" (Letty Cottin Pogrebin, *Ms.*). Here the syndicated columnist Ellen Goodman makes good use of fragments in a personal report on vacationing (ellipses mark deletions to save space):

Only now am I finally, truly, totally unproductive. Able to just sit and watch. . . . It had begun to seem important to do things at once. To return calls while unloading the dishwasher. To ask for the check with coffee. To read a magazine in the check-out line. To use rather than waste time. . . . Friendship takes time. So does family. So does arriving at a sense of well-being. . . . On a porch in Maine, one American is carefully lowering the national productivity. And raising the absolute value of doing absolutely nothing.

A clutch of fragments can convey in a general manner mood, atmosphere, values: "From that point on, bliss, balance, good vibes. Wholesomeness with a touch of humor. Earnest innerquesting but not overearnest" (David Asa Rose, *Esquire*). And fragments of some length can sometimes be used effectively to pile up details in descriptive writing:

Prairie wool blue-green, spring wheat bright as new lawn, winter wheat gray-green at rest and slaty when the wind flaws it, roadside primroses as shy as prairie flowers are supposed to be, and as gentle to the eye as when in my boyhood we used to call them wild tulips, and by their coming date the beginning of summer.—Wallace Stegner, *Wolf Willow*

See **Clauses, Phrases.**

freshman, freshmen

The modifier is *freshman,* not only before nouns with an obviously singular reference (a freshman dorm) but before plural and abstract nouns (freshman courses, freshman orientation). The plural noun is *freshmen.*

-ful, full

When the adjective *full* (a full basket, a basket full of apples) is used as a suffix to nouns of measure *(basketful, spoonful)* or of feeling or quality *(peaceful, sorrowful),* it has only one *l.* The plural of nouns ending in *-ful* is usually made with *-s: spoonfuls, cupfuls.* With the adjective *full,* the noun is made plural: *full baskets, baskets full.*

fulsome

Fulsome has come full circle in meaning—from "abundant" centuries ago to "disgusting" and now to "abundant" again. But the return to "abundant" is by no means established. "Fulsome praise," in formal English, means "exaggerated, insincere, and therefore offensive praise"; and those who use it to mean praise that is full-bodied or full of enthusiasm may find themselves both embarrassed and embarrassing.

further, farther

Both *further* and *farther* are used in referring to distance. See **farther, further.**

Fused sentence

Fused, or *run-on, sentence* is the name sometimes given to two grammatically complete sentences written with no mark of punctuation between them: If you ask me why I did it, I can only say that at the time it seemed the right thing to do[] that is my only explanation. To correct the error, begin a new sentence with *that* or insert a semicolon after *do.* Compare **Comma splice.**

Future tense

English verbs don't inflect, or change their form, to express future time. Some of the means we use to refer to the future are illustrated in these sentences: I am leaving next week; He sails tomorrow; She is to speak on Saturday; He is about to resign; When I am elected, I will make an investigation; They will try to be on time; She is going to refuse; Shall I take this to the cleaners? See **Tenses of verbs.**

gender

In grammar, *gender* refers to the choice of pronouns—*he, she, it, who, which*—and to the meaning of the words that govern the choice. As a substitute for *sex* ("the female sex"), the term *gender* now regularly occurs in such phrases as "discrimination based on age or gender."

Some writers make a distinction between sex and gender:

> Sex is a biological category into which we are born as male or female infants, whereas gender is a cultural category specifying the characteristics of masculinity and femininity that shape our maturation into adult men and women.—Evelyn Fox Keller, *Daedalus*

And some guardians of the language object to any transfer of meaning from the grammatical term. Theodore Bernstein said, "Words have gender; people have sex." In fact, people have had gender for centuries.

See **Sexist language; woman, lady, girl.**

General English

General English is the core of standard English. Spoken general English is what we hear in most talks for general audiences, in news broadcasts, and in the ordinary conversation of educated people. Written, edited general English is what we read in newspapers, magazines, and most books. The main focus of this *Index* is on writing general English. See **Formal English, Informal English, Standard English.** For discussion and illustration of formal, general, and informal styles, see the Introduction.

Genitive case

The genitive, or possessive, case is indicated by the apostrophe, with or without *-s;* by the possessive form of the personal pronouns; and by the relative *whose*. See **Possessive case.**

Gerunds

1. Form and function. A gerund—also called a verbal noun—is the *-ing* form of a verb used as a noun. It can serve in any noun function: as subject or complement of a verb (*Seeing* is *believing*) or as object of a verb or preposition (He taught *dancing;* The odds are against your *winning*). Like a noun, a gerund can be modified by an adjective (Good *cooking* was rare) or used as a modifier (a *fishing* boat, a *living* wage). Yet, like a verb, a gerund can take a subject and an object and can be modified by an adverb: The city council despaired of the architect (subject) ever (adverb) *designing* affordable housing (object) for the homeless. See **2** below.

A gerund may be in the present or the perfect tense and in the active or passive voice: *seeing, having seen, being seen, having been seen.*

Though it has the same form as the present participle, the gerund is used differently:

> **Gerund:** *Running* a hotel appealed to him. (*Running* is the subject.)
> **Participle:** *Running* a hotel, he prospered. (The participle phrase modifies *he.*)

2. Subject of a gerund. The subject of a gerund is sometimes in the possessive case and sometimes in the accusative, or objective, case. (In nouns the nominative and accusative forms are the same—the "common" case.) Formal writing uses the possessive more than general writing does: "Such a view leads to the metaphor's becoming a brief poem in itself" (Alex Page, *Modern Philology*). General writing is likely to use the common case: "The Vice President's humorous remarks about Hofstra not picking up this ball are somewhat offset . . . by the record" (Clifford Lord, *College Board Review*).

When the subject is a personal pronoun or a proper noun, the possessive is more usual than the common case in both formal and general styles: They wanted to discuss *her quitting* her job; We overlooked *Joe's swearing.* When the subject is a personal pronoun and begins the sentence, the possessive is required: *Our* (not *Us*) *worrying* won't solve anything; *His* (not *Him*) *lying* deceived nobody.

3. Phrases with gerunds. Gerunds are often used in phrases that function somewhat like dependent clauses: *In coming to an agreement,* they had compromised on all points; *By refusing to sing,* she embarrassed her mother. The relation of the gerund phrase to the word it modifies should be clear. The reader shouldn't have to pause to make sure just what the writer intended:

> **Dangling:** *In coming to an agreement,* campaign promises were ignored.

> **Revision:** In coming to an agreement, both sides ignored their campaign promises.

> **Dangling:** *After sleeping sixteen hours,* my headache was finally gone.

> **Revision:** After sleeping sixteen hours, I was finally rid of my headache. *Or:* After I slept sixteen hours, my headache was finally gone.

See **Dangling modifiers, Idiom.** Compare **Infinitives, Participles.**

get up

In general English you get up when you stand up or get out of bed. See **arise, rise, get up.**

girl

To some, the use of *girl* in referring to an adult female is disparaging and insulting. Accepting this view is difficult not only for older men who still play golf or pinochle with "the boys" but also for women of the same generation who look forward to a weekly luncheon or bridge game with "the girls." But in writing, *woman* for any female over the age of sixteen is the safe choice. See **woman, lady, girl.**

go

Go in the sense "become" is used as a linking verb in a number of idioms. While some *(go broke, go native, go straight)* are informal to general, others *(go blind, go lame)* are fully established in all varieties of usage. *Go and,* as an intensive with no actual motion implied, is common in speech and turns up in some general writing: "He has gone and made a genuine commercial film" (Joseph Morgenstern, *Newsweek*). *Going for* in the sense "working to the advantage of" is general: "when women in England didn't have much going for them" (Emily Hahn, *New York Times Book Review*). Neither *go and* nor *going for* in these senses is appropriate in formal writing. See **Idiom, try and.**

gobbledygook

In the 1940s Maury Maverick, a congressman from Texas, coined the term *gobbledygook* for wordy, pompous, overweight prose that confuses and irritates more than it informs. Although government bureaus have earned their reputations as producers of gobbledygook, business, the military, the social sciences, and the humanities have shown an equal weakness for such jargon. Frequently gobbledygook serves the purpose of disguising the truth. See **doublespeak, Jargon.**

good, well

Good is usually an adjective in standard English. *Well* is either an adjective or an adverb. "I feel good" and "I feel well" (adjectives) are both usual but have different meanings. *Good* implies a feeling of well-being, physical or emotional or both; *well* refers merely to a state, "not ill." See **Linking verbs.** *Good* misused as an adverb in place of *well,* as in "He sings good," "She played good," "The car's running good now," should be avoided in writing except when quoting a speaker, real or imaginary.

got, gotten

Either *got* or *gotten* is usually acceptable as the past participle of *get*. But *got*—not *gotten*—is often added to *has* or *have* to emphasize the notion of "possess" (I haven't got a cent; She's got a letter from home) or of "must" (You've got to lend me a dollar). Though seldom used in formal writing, the emphatic *got* is fairly common in general writing: "A lot of adults are bored by Bach because they haven't got the faintest idea of what music is about" (Marya Mannes, *TV Guide*).

gourmet

A gourmet is a connoisseur of food and drink. As a vogue word, the adjective *gourmet* is regularly applied to food and restaurants, to cooking, and even to cutlery, thereby losing any definable meaning. If you mean "foreign," "expensive," or "fancy," use those words. To express enthusiasm for a good meal, *delicious* is available.

graduated

The idiom *to be graduated from* an institution has generally gone out of use except in formal and somewhat old-fashioned writing and has been replaced by *graduated from*: He graduated from high school in 1904. Omitting the *from*—"She graduated college in 1980"—is a common usage that causes violent reactions in some quarters: "To say 'I graduated college' . . . is to be a language slob and a discredit to whatever learning factory mailed you a diploma" (William Safire, *New York Times Magazine*).

Grammar

Grammar has several different senses. Just as *history* can mean a field of study, events in the past, or the book that describes those events, so *grammar* can refer to a field of study, a set of abilities in our brains, or the book that describes those abilities.

1. Philosophers in Greece had begun speculating about language and words long before the Stoics in 300 B.C. singled out grammar as a field of study separate from rhetoric and poetics. Since then scholars have continued to study the structure of language, not only because language is the central defining characteristic of the human race but because it seems possible that the very foundation of our knowledge and thought—perhaps even perception itself—is shaped by the grammatical structures of our language. Grammar thus becomes an entry to the study of the mind.

2. *Grammar* may also refer to the ability every normal human being has to speak and understand sentences. We can all understand an indefinite number of new sentences we've never heard before. We can distinguish between grammatical and ungrammatical sentences (see **grammatical, ungrammatical 1**). We can recognize sentences that are ambiguous. We also understand that some sentences are related to others, as this sentence is related to the next two.

> That some sentences are related to others is also understood by us. It is also understood by us that some sentences are related to others.

The goal of a linguist—a scholar who studies grammatical structure—is to describe in a written grammar this internalized grammar that we all share.

3. The history of linguistic study in the last hundred years falls very roughly into three schools.

a. Traditional. Although this label is applied to a great variety of approaches, most traditional grammars start by describing parts of speech and the inflections associated with them: nouns are names of persons, places, and things, and so on. Once the parts of speech have been described, the grammar describes functions: subjects, predicates, objects, modifiers, and so on. The definitions are illustrated by examples. Readers of the grammar are expected to understand the labeling through the descriptions and examples and then to use their native knowledge of the language to apply the label in any new sentence that might contain the pattern. For example:

> A sentence adverb modifies a whole sentence rather than any individual word or construction. It usually stands at the beginning of the sentence, though it may occur elsewhere: *Fortunately,* he left; He is *allegedly* still here; No one cares, *obviously.*

Confronted with the sentence "Apparently, she left," you could identify *apparently* as a sentence adverb on the basis of the explanation and examples. Such descriptions require the ability of a native speaker to make them work.

b. Structural. In the early part of this century, a new approach to grammar emerged. Structural linguists tried to devise objective techniques for discovering the structure of a language without relying on the meanings of words (as traditional grammars do). They began by cataloging the sounds produced by native speakers, then identifying the smallest units that seemed to have meaning (morphemes), and then arranging these units into larger classes, not according to their meanings but according to their customary relationships with other units. Once the parts of speech were classified, sequences of different parts were identified (noun-verb, verb-noun, preposition-noun, adjective-noun, etc.) and then further described functionally (subject-predicate, verb-object, modifier-head, etc.).

c. Generative-transformational. Through the 1940s and most of the 1950s, structural grammars were thought to be the new wave in English-language education. In 1957 Noam Chomsky, a linguist at the Massachusetts Institute of Technology, published *Syntactic Structures* and revolutionized the study of language. Chomsky turned linguists toward a model of language that tries to account in a formal set of rules for the ability of native speakers to produce and understand an infinite range of new sentences. Grammarians of the generative-transformational school assume the existence of a grammar in the mind of the native speaker. They seek to account for what all languages have in common, as well as for the peculiarities that distinguish English, say, from German; and they try to deal with the full range of language, from sounds to meaning, in an integrated theory.

Chomsky's initial formulations of generative theory have been considerably modified and revised, and there are adherents of other theories of language description—tagmemic grammars, stratificational grammars, dependency grammars, and others. But for at least two decades the dominant models for research into the structure of English and other languages were generative-transformational.

4. So far, we've ignored the most common meaning of *grammar*. This is grammar in the sense of "good grammar"—making the "right" choice between *who* and *whom,* not using *like* for *as,* avoiding sentence fragments, and so on. It concentrates only on those areas where usage varies from one social class to another or from the way English teachers believe educated people should speak to the way their students actually do speak.

How we communicate depends on our social class, our geographical roots, the social situation we happen to be in, and our mode of communication— speaking or writing. What most schools teach as grammar are those features that are said to distinguish written, fairly formal, supposedly upper-middle-class usage from other varieties. Linguistic scholars believe it a serious mistake to assume that this form of grammar alone defines "correct" usage.

Thus, when we use the word *grammar,* we have to distinguish a variety of senses:

Grammar is a field of scholarly inquiry dating back to ancient Greece.

Grammar is the knowledge of our language—whatever that language may be—that we all have in our heads.

Grammar is a set of rules for a language that can be written down and that will generate the sentences of that language along with a description of each sentence. The object of this grammar is to "model" or explain grammar in sense 2 above.

Grammar in the sense of "good grammar" is concerned with certain usages that are supposed to represent the standard of upper-middle-class speakers and writers. A grammar of good usage consists of the prescriptions found in grammar books that allow someone who wants to be a member of the "educated" community to speak and write as those already in that community are said to speak and write. This last, narrow sense of grammar as linguistic etiquette is the sense most familiar to Americans in and out of school.

grammatical, ungrammatical

Sentences can be grammatical in either of two senses:

1. Sentences are grammatical when they meet the structural requirements of the grammar used by an individual speaker. "Can't nobody tell me what to do'' is ungrammatical for some speakers, but it's grammatical for others, if the grammar they've incorporated into their nervous systems allows them to construct that sentence in ordinary conversation (see **Grammar 2**). ''Nobody can tell me what to do'' might be ungrammatical for those speakers who habitually say ''Can't nobody tell me what to do'' but grammatical for those who don't.

In this sense, *grammatical* simply describes the structure of a sentence that's normal for use by a particular person in ordinary speech. The made-up sentence ''I know the man who and the woman left'' is ungrammatical for all speakers of English.

2. In common usage and school usage, sentences are said to be grammatical when they meet the requirements set by or accepted by those who are in a position to enforce standards of usage—teachers, editors, employers. In this looser sense, ''Can't nobody tell me what to do'' is said to be ungrammatical for everyone, and a person to whom the construction is normal and systematic with reference to an internalized grammar (see **Grammar 2**) is said to be speaking ungrammatical English.

Such usages might more accurately be termed socially acceptable—meaning ''acceptable to those who are concerned about the rules of 'good grammar' '' (see **Grammar 4**). In many cases, advice based on this sense of *grammatical* is accurate. Most educated people in this country don't say ''Can't nobody tell me what to do.'' In writing, most make their subjects and verbs agree. Most avoid *ain't* in all but relatively informal situations. On the other hand, rules for usage that's grammatical in the ''socially acceptable'' sense also involve a good deal of folklore, as many of the articles in this book make clear.

See **Usage.**

Group words

In English many groups of two or more words (that is, phrases) function like single words. Examples:

Nouns: hay fever, back door, holding company, home run, sacrifice hit, school year, car wash, dry cleaner, gas station

Verbs: dig in, hold off, look into, flare up, follow through, follow up, close up, show up, blow up, back down

Prepositions: according to, in spite of, in opposition to, previous to, due to

In this book we usually ignore the superficial difference between a part of speech written as a single word and one that's written as a group of words. *Noun* (sometimes called *noun phrase*) or *verb* or *preposition* refers to both single words and to group words functioning as noun or verb or preposition.

guess

Formal usage limits *guess* to its sense of ''conjecture, estimate, surmise'': ''The employers can only guess whom the victims will choose to sue'' (Henry L.

Woodward, *Yale Law Journal*). But in general and informal usage *guess* is common in its looser senses of "think, suppose, believe": "They were foolish, I guess, in trying to hold history still for one more hour" (Larry L. King, *Atlantic*).

had better

Had better is the usual idiom in giving advice or an indirect command: You had better take care of that cold; You'd better go.

half

Though *a half* is traditionally considered more elegant, there's little distinction between *a half* and *half a/an* in current formal and general usage. For example, both "a half century earlier" and "nearly half a century removed" occur in a single issue of the *American Historical Review*. *A half a/an* (a half an hour) is an informal redundancy.

The noun accompanying *half* or *half of* in a subject determines whether the verb is singular or plural: Half of the *book is* . . . ; Half of the *men are* . . .

hanged, hung

In formal English, people are hanged, pictures are hung. In general English, usage is divided, with informal's *hang, hung, hung* often used in all senses: "Of course, McCarthy hung himself at the hearing" (Isidore Silver, *New Republic*). When writing about executions in the past tense, *hanged* is the right choice.

hardly

When *hardly* means "probably not" or "almost not," don't add another *not*. See **Double negative.**

have

1. Independent meaning. As a verb of independent meaning, *have* has a range of senses *(have a good time/a fight/a baby/a cold/breakfast)*, with "own, possess," both literally and figuratively, the most common: They have a new car. Because *have* occurs so frequently as an "empty" auxiliary word, its meaning as an independent word meaning "possess" is often reinforced by *got* (see **got, gotten**).

2. Auxiliary. *Have/had* functions as a signal of tense:

Perfect tense: They have come.
Future perfect tense: They will have gone by then.
Past perfect tense: They had gone before we arrived.

See **Tenses of verbs 2.**

3. Had ought, hadn't ought. In your writing, don't combine *had* with *ought* in either a positive statement (She had ought to take better care of herself) or a negative one (He hadn't ought to lie like that). *Ought* (or *ought not* or *oughtn't*) can do the job on its own.

For *have got,* see **got, gotten.** See also **had better.**

Headword

A headword, or head, is a word modified by another word, especially a noun modified by one or more adjectives (his first long *sleep*), a verb modified by one or more adverbs (*walk* carefully), or an adjective or adverb modified by qualifiers (very *old,* more *intelligently*). The headword of a construction is the word around which the rest of the construction is built: very old *men* in rain-coats who had been waiting outside.

healthful, healthy

The distinction between *healthful* ''conducive to health'' (places and foods are healthful) and *healthy* ''having good health'' (persons, animals, and plants are healthy) is observed in some formal and general writing, but by and large *healthy* is now used for both meanings.

help but

Conservative stylists usually avoid using *can't* (or *cannot*) *help but.* See **can't help but, can't seem to.**

hence

As a conjunctive adverb connecting independent clauses, *hence* means ''for this reason, therefore.'' As a formal adverb meaning ''from this place, or time, or life,'' *hence* is rarely used today.

he or she

Traditionally, the masculine pronoun *he* is used with indefinite pronouns like *anyone* and *everybody* and with noun antecedents that may refer to either men or women: Every *student* must accept responsibility for *his* acts. But feminists find this usage a prime example of sexist language and prefer *he or she* (or *he/*

she or *s/he*) and *his or her*. Sometimes antecedents make a masculine pronoun inappropriate and the double pronoun mandatory: "In enabling a young man or woman to prepare for life in a shorter period of time, we direct his or her attention to other values" (Edward H. Litchfield, *Saturday Review*).

For writers and readers to whom avoiding *he* and *his* after a sexually indefinite antecedent isn't a matter of principle, *he or she* and its variants may seem unnecessarily awkward: "Any individual who is a candidate for promotion or tenure should her/himself make sure that records are complete" (committee recommendation). When *he* or *his* is inappropriate, *they* is a frequent choice in general writing: In helping a young man or woman to prepare for life, we must direct their attention to other values. Switching to "young men and women" would avoid the problem by making *their* the obvious choice. See **Agreement 2, Sexist language.**

himself, herself

Himself and *herself* are used in two ways: as reflexive pronouns, referring to the subject of the sentence (George has always taken himself too seriously; She looked at herself in the window), and as qualifiers, for emphasis (He told me so himself; The senator herself told me so).

historic, historical

Historic and *historical* ordinarily have quite different meanings. *Historic* usually means "important in history," "noteworthy," "famous": "a historic act: the toast to the French fleet by which the archbishop . . . urged French Catholics to abandon royalist opposition" (James E. Ward, *American Historical Review*). *Historical* is much more neutral, meaning "based on the facts of history," "having occurred in the past," "suitable for study by historians or using their methods": "This autobiography . . . provides a wide range of historical persons and events" (Heinz E. Ellersieck, *American Historical Review*). Most historical persons and events are not at all historic.

hopefully

From an adverb with the established meaning "in a hopeful way, full of hope" (The dog waited hopefully for a handout), *hopefully* became a vogue word meaning "it is hoped": "Hopefully, they will reveal the thickness of the planet's ice cap" (Jonathan Spivak, *Wall Street Journal*). Sometimes it means no more than "with luck": Hopefully, she'll be down in a minute. As long as it's kept away from the verb and set off by commas, there's little chance of real ambiguity. The *hopefully* vogue has faded, giving the violent opposition it aroused a chance to cool. The usage is standard though still unacceptable to some— including those who accept *fortunately* and other sentence modifiers as a matter of course: "Happily, his worries ceased at about five in the afternoon" (Norman Hammond, *Archaeology*).

Hours

In formal writing, hours are often spelled out in words: at four o'clock, about five-fifteen. In newspapers and much other general writing, figures are used, especially if several times are mentioned and always in designations of time with A.M. and P.M.: at 4 P.M., just after 9 A.M., around 4:30 P.M., from 10 to 12.

however

As a connective between independent clauses, *however* is more characteristic of formal than of general styles and more common in assigned writing than in published prose. Set off by commas, it typically serves to relate a sentence to a point made in the preceding sentence:

> Murder is usually reported, and 86 percent of all reported murders lead to arrests. Among those arrested, however, only 64 percent are prosecuted.—Ramsey Clark, *Saturday Review*

However can either introduce the clause it modifies (However, among those arrested . . .) or, as in the example, follow the words the writer wants to emphasize (Among those arrested, however, . . .). To begin a clause, the simpler *but* is often the better choice.

When *however* is used in the sense "no matter how," it should never be separated by a comma from the words it modifies: However[] strongly you feel . . . ; however[] tired they become . . .

See **Conjunctive adverbs.**

human

As a noun meaning "person," *human* has come into general use by writers who reject generic *man.* The longer substitute *human being* is preferred by some.

hung, hanged

In formal English, pictures are hung, people are hanged. See **hanged, hung.**

Hyperbole

We all use this very common figure of speech—obvious and extravagant overstatement—when we describe our troubles as *ghastly,* our embarrassments as *horrible,* our vacations as *fabulous.* Such efforts to dramatize and intensify fail through repetition. Like other figures, hyperbole works well only when it's fresh. See **Figurative language.**

Hypercorrectness

Hypercorrect forms are used by speakers and writers who work so hard at being correct that they end up being wrong. Perhaps the most common example of hypercorrectness is the use of *I* for *me* in a compound object: It is a wonderful moment for my wife and I; They invited Bill and I; between you and I. Other common hypercorrect forms include *whom* for *who* (He is critical of the other members, whom he feels spend more time making accusations than solving problems), *as* for *like* (I always tried to behave as a gentleman), the ending *-ly* where it doesn't belong (She looks badly), some verb forms *(lie* for *lay)*, and many pronunciations.

Hyphen

In *Manuscript and Proof* John Benbow wrote, "If you take the hyphen seriously, you will surely go mad." To ward off madness, adopt a recent dictionary or stylebook as your guide and follow it faithfully.

1. Word division. The hyphen is always used to mark the division of a word at the end of a line (see **Division of words**). Other uses are in part a matter of style.

2. Compound words. Some compound words are written as two words *(post office)*, some as one *(notebook),* and some as a combination of words joined by hyphens *(mother-in-law).* The trend is away from hyphenation, toward one-word spelling. Even when a prefix ends and a root word begins with the same letter, the current tendency is to write the word solid: *cooperate, reelect, preeminent, nonnative.*

Compound adjective forms are hyphenated when they precede the noun they modify but not when they come after it:

A little-known poet interrupted the award ceremony.
The poet who interrupted the award ceremony was little known.

She presented a well-argued thesis.
Her thesis was well argued.

Compounds consisting of an adverb followed by a verbal are not hyphenated when the adverb ends in *-ly:* a well-marked trail *but* a poorly marked trail.

3. Noun phrases. The hyphen is well established in phrases used as modifiers, particularly in formal styles: seventeenth-century philosophy.

4. Miscellaneous uses. A number as part of a modifier (as extinct as the 5-cent cigar, nine-inch boards) is hyphenated, and a hyphen is used between a prefix and a proper name: pro-Doonesbury, anti-Israeli. A suspension hyphen may be used to hold together a spread-out modifier: the third-, fourth-, and fifth-grade rooms; both fourteenth- and fifteenth-century records. *Vice* is no longer joined by a hyphen to *president* in the executive branch of the federal government, but in other titles—with *admiral, consul, regent,* for example— usage is divided.

5. To avoid ambiguity. Occasionally a pair of modifiers is ambiguous without a hyphen. "A light yellow scarf" may be either a scarf that's light yellow or a light scarf that's yellow. *Light-yellow* makes the first meaning clear; *light, yellow* the second. Similarly, "new car-owner" and "new-car owner" prevent misunderstanding.

I

The notion that *I* (always capitalized) shouldn't be the first word in a sentence is groundless. *I* should be used wherever it's needed. Circumlocutions to avoid the natural use of *I* are usually awkward. "My present thinking is that nuclear power projects are unsound" is a clumsy way of saying "I think now [or "I think" or "I have come to think" or "At present I think"] that nuclear power projects are unsound." See **it's me, myself, we.**

ibid.

Ibid., an abbreviation of the Latin *ibidem* ("in the same place"), is used in the notes of some scholarly books, articles, and research papers. In most current styles of documentation *ibid.* has been replaced by the author's name or by the author's name followed by a shortened version of the title of the work. Those who continue to find *ibid.* useful often restrict it to a second reference on the *same page* of the manuscript or publication.

id Idiom

The expression marked is not standard idiom. Revise it, referring to an article in this *Index* or to a dictionary if you are not sure of the correct form.

Idioms are established phrases that are not easy to explain grammatically or logically. Some examples are "come in handy," "strike a bargain," "look up an old friend," "many's the time," "make good," "in respect to." We learn these phrases as units, and if we're native speakers, few of them cause us serious trouble, though a faulty analogy sometimes leads us astray: as well as I can *but* as best [as] I can. No native speaker is likely to say "hit a bargain" or "look down an old friend" or "the time is many." Idioms are often completely frozen. You can use thousands of different words as subjects and verbs of sentences, but you can't substitute any other adjective in the phrase "in good stead" (Her advice stood me in good stead).

We have trouble with idioms we haven't learned, and the most common trouble is choosing the right preposition. Because we know "conform to," we may be tempted to speak of a policy that's "in conformity to public opinion"; but the idiom is "in conformity with." Because logic is no help, we must learn idioms, including the prepositions, one by one. Dictionaries sometimes show the preposition that's conventionally used with a particular word.

Some words are idiomatically followed by gerunds, others by infinitives. For example:

Gerunds	Infinitives
can't help *doing*	compelled *to do*
capable of *painting*	able *to paint*
the habit of *giving*	the tendency *to give*
an idea of *selling*	a wish *to sell*
enjoys *playing*	likes *to play*

Some common words can be followed by either a gerund or an infinitive: the way *of doing* something, the way *to do* something.

See **ability to; acquiesce; agree to, agree with; compare, contrast; Diction 1; different from, different than; it; Logic and language; Prepositions and style 1; Subjunctive mood 2a.**

i.e.

I.e. is the abbreviation for the Latin words meaning "that is." It's appropriate only in scholarly writing. See **Abbreviations 1.**

if, whether

Writers have a choice between *if* and *whether* before interrogative clauses (indirect questions) and clauses expressing doubt or uncertainty. *Whether* is more common in formal contexts: "It is appropriate to ask whether these decisions are to be considered a victory for those who champion individual right" (Wayne F. LaFave, *Supreme Court Review*). Both words are used in general writing, but *if* is more common: The survey asked people if TV had influenced their vote.

ill, sick

Ill is the less common, more formal word. See **sick, ill.**

illiterate, illiteracy

Illiterate and *literate* are used to refer both to the ability to read and write (There were few schools, and most of the peasants were completely illiterate) and to familiarity with what's been written (Any literate person should know the name Kafka). Usage called nonstandard in this book is often loosely referred to as illiterate in the second sense—that is, uneducated.

The label *illiterate* is applied most freely by those who demand that others use language precisely. Of the critic John Simon, Dennis Baron writes: "By *illiterate* he means not those who are unable to read or write but those whose level of culture or refinement is not sufficiently elevated" *(Grammar and Good Taste)*.

Literacy and *illiteracy* are also used in an extended sense. Some guardians of high culture have denied literacy to college graduates who have not achieved familiarity with specified masterpieces that these scholars have adopted as criteria.

illusion, allusion

An illusion misleads, an allusion refers. See **allusion, illusion.**

image

Image meaning "a public conception or impression" (He was criticized for not projecting the image of a president) has moved from the jargon of public relations and advertising into general use. More recently, perception has been said by some political manipulators to have more importance than fact. Image (or perception) makers are experts at doublespeak. See **doublespeak.**

Imagery

An image is a word or group of words that makes an appeal to one of the senses: sight *(shiny, ghostly, mist, light green, thick brown hair)*; hearing *(creaking, faraway shouts, the pounding of surf)*; taste *(salty, dry, a pickled pear)*; smell *(jasmine, fresh paint, a blown-out candle)*; touch *(smooth, glassy, razor sharp, a stubbly bread)*; or the muscular tension known as the kinesthetic sense *(squirm, jerky, jogging heavily along)*. Though an image may appeal to more than one sense *(a rough, angry sea)*, in a specific context one sense is usually dominant.

Studying the images in poetry and prose will reveal what has impressed the authors in their experience and what appeals to them—colors, lines, odors, sounds. Your own writing will be richer and stronger if it includes images drawn from your own experience and based on your own taste. A borrowed image is likely to be a dead one. An image from personal experience is a live image; and a live image is like a good photograph: it reveals something of the photographer as well as showing what he has photographed.

See **Figurative language.**

Imperative mood

The form of the verb used for direct commands and requests is in the imperative mood: Bring the tapes when you come; Run! See **Commands and requests.**

imply, infer

A writer or speaker *implies* something in her words or manner, suggesting a conclusion without stating it. A reader or listener *infers* something from what she reads or hears, drawing a conclusion from the available information. Having a word for each of these acts contributes to clear communication, and careful writers make the distinction.

But for centuries, *infer* has also been used to mean "imply," and today many dictionaries recognize this meaning (as well as the traditional meaning) as standard. So when clarity is essential, the safe course is not simply to distinguish between *imply* and *infer* but to provide a context that underlines your meaning: From the president's words, I infer that he . . .

in, into, in to

In usually shows location, literal or figurative: He was in the house; He was in a stupor. *Into* usually shows direction: He came into the house; He fell into a stupor. But in informal and general usage, *in* is common when direction is meant: "Twice a week we get in the car, and drive down the Parkway" (Richard Rose, *St. Louis Post-Dispatch*).

The *in* of *in to* is an adverb and the *to* a preposition (They went in to dinner) or sign of the infinitive (They went in to eat).

Incoherence

A sentence or a paragraph or a whole paper is incoherent when a careful reader is unable to perceive the relationship between its parts. The cause may be that there actually is no relationship between the parts, or it may be that the writer has failed to make the relationship clear. See **Coherence, Transition.**

Incomplete sentence

Punctuating a phrase or a dependent clause as if it were a complete sentence is often the result of carelessness. See **Fragment.**

incredible, incredulous

A story or situation is incredible ("unbelievable"); a person is incredulous ("unbelieving"). Those who constantly hear and read *incredible* become incredulous. One way to avoid confusing the two words is to refrain from using *incredible,* a voguish example of trite hyperbole (I'm taking this incredible course!) unless you mean it literally (His claim to have read *War and Peace* in one evening is incredible). Except in this literal sense, *incredible* has no place in serious writing.

Indention

To indent in manuscript or printed copy is to begin the first line of a paragraph some distance to the right of the left-hand margin—an inch in handwritten copy, five spaces in typewritten copy. Hanging indention is indention of all lines below the first line, as in biblography entries, each main section of an outline, and many newspaper headlines. If a line of poetry is too long to complete on one line, the part brought over to the second line should be indented. For indenting quotations, see **Quotation marks 1d.**

Independent clauses

An independent clause (like this one) can stand alone as a simple sentence. See **Clauses.**

Indicative mood

Verb forms that make assertions or ask questions are said to be indicative or in the indicative mood. The indicative is the mood of most verbs in English sentences: They *sat* on the porch even though it *was* late October; *Will* you *come* if you *are* invited? Compare **Imperative mood, Subjunctive mood.**

Indirect discourse (indirect quotation)

In indirect discourse a person's words are reported in paraphrase or summary instead of being quoted exactly:

> *Direct:* He said, "I won't take it if they give it to me."

> *Indirect:* He said he wouldn't take it if they gave it to him.

An indirect question restates a question at second hand:

> *Direct:* "Is everyone all right?" she asked.

> *Indirect:* She asked if everyone was all right.

See **Commands and requests, Questions, Quotation marks 2b, Tense 3b.**

Indirect objects

An indirect object names what or whom something is given, said, or shown to: She gave *him* a prize. See **Objects 2.**

Induction

The process of reasoning known as induction originates in curiosity and ends in conviction. You're reasoning inductively when, after asking your friends how they feel about a proposed change in the pass-fail policy and after listening to what's being said about the subject on campus, you decide that the student body is strongly opposed to the change. Note that you haven't polled the student body. That would be nose counting, not inductive reasoning. Instead, at some point in your gathering of information, you've made the "inductive leap," assuming that what is true of the people you've talked to and listened to is true of the whole group.

You can't be certain that your conclusion is correct. But you can have confidence in it—you can assume that it's highly probable—if the evidence you've examined has been relevant, adequate, and representative.

In serious argument, induction usually takes the form of example after example offered in support of a generalization. As used in everyday life, inductive reasoning may seem to be little more than a hunch or an informed guess. In either case, it's indispensable: only by using induction can we spot trends, make predictions, and discover causal relations.

See **Cause and effect, Deduction, Fallacies, Logical thinking.**

infer, imply

The writer or speaker implies; the reader or listener infers. See **imply, infer.**

Infinitives

Infinitive is a Latin grammatical term for a verb form expressing the general sense of the verb without restriction as to person, number, or tense. In Modern English, the root form of the verb is the infinitive, often with *to* before it.

1. The *to* infinitive and the bare infinitive. More often than not, an infinitive is used with the preposition *to: He's the man to see; He was glad to come; She likes to be visited. (To* is not used after the modal auxiliary verbs or after some full verbs: I can *see;* She must *carry* it; We let him *go;* They can't make her *talk;* I heard them *sing.* See **Modal auxiliaries.)**

2. Functions of infinitives. Infinitives serve as subjects, as objects, as complements, and as modifiers:

> **Subject:** *To sit and read* was his idea of a holiday.
> **Object:** She prefers *to wait* until Tuesday.
> **Complement:** He seems *to be* happy.
> **Modifier:** My friend is the man *to see.*

Infinitives, in turn, may have subjects, objects, complements, and modifiers:

Subject of infinitive: For *you* to do that again would be a serious mistake.
Object of infinitive: The police tried to disperse *the crowd.*
Complement of infinitive: They seem to be *happy.*
Modifier of infinitive: He was reluctant to stay *longer.*

Infinitives and style

1. Infinitives in a series. In a short, unemphatic series, there's no reason to repeat *to:* He decided to shower, shave, and dress. When the series is complex or when separate verbs deserve emphasis, *to* should be repeated: These were her goals: to escape the city, to avoid routine, and to find contentment.

2. Case of pronoun with infinitive. For the pronoun after the infinitive of a linking verb that has no expressed subject, general English has the accusative case: I admired my father so much I would have liked to be *him;* In costume and makeup, the actor not only resembled the late president but actually seemed to be *him.* Strictly speaking, formal English calls for the nominative; but a writer who finds "to be he" stilted and unnatural will rephrase: I admired my father so much that I wanted to be like him in every respect.

3. Dangling infinitives. Infinitives that function as absolute phrases (to tell the truth, to be sure) are sentence modifiers and as such present no problems. But an infinitive, like a participle or a gerund, will dangle if it seems to be related to a word that it can't sensibly modify or if, in a context that calls for an explicit relationship, it has no clear relation to any word in the sentence:

Dangling: To learn to swim with confidence, water must be a friend rather than a foe.
Revised: To learn to swim with confidence, you must make water a friend rather than a foe.

See **Absolute phrases, Dangling modifiers.**

4. Split infinitives. In a split infinitive, a word or phrase (usually an adverb) comes between *to* and the verb: to actively pursue. Some infinitives shouldn't be split. Some should be, because splitting makes the meaning clear: "They need to carefully weigh predicted costs against benefits" prevents misreading "to weigh carefully predicted costs." In still other contexts, it's a matter of choice, with more splits occurring in general English than in formal. Whenever avoiding a split infinitive would result in ambiguous or unnatural wording, split the infinitive. See **Split infinitive.**

Inflection

Inflection refers to the change of word forms to indicate grammatical relationships, like singular and plural number for nouns or past and present tense for verbs. See **Case, Comparison of adjectives and adverbs, Plurals of nouns, Pronouns, Verbs.**

Informal English

The word or passage marked is too informal for the subject or for the style of the rest of the paper. Revise, making it more appropriate.

Informal written English is appropriate (though not mandatory) in letters to close friends and to members of your family and may be the style you use in a diary or journal. Its casual, intimate tone makes it unsuitable for most other writing, though informal usages may be successfully introduced into papers written in general English if they're chosen with taste and judgment.

You'd be unlikely to use the informal *pretty* (pretty big, pretty soon, pretty old) in a chemistry report or a psychology examination, and you probably wouldn't describe Robert Frost as "a pretty good poet" in a paper for a literature course. But in writing for an audience of classmates, you might call a local star "a pretty good volleyball player." Whether or not *inf* appeared in the margin of your paper would depend on the context. If your style was relaxed and conversational, *pretty* would be appropriate. If your style placed some distance between you and your readers, *fairly* would be a better choice.

As applied to sections of papers or to whole papers, *informal* usually implies sloppiness—rambling sentences, vague references, trite slang, repetition, incoherence. If something you've written has been so marked, the best solution is to rethink what you want to say and rewrite the passage, aiming for clarity and precision.

See **Formal English, General English, Standard English.** See also **Agreement, Colloquial English, Repetition, Slang, Spoken and written English, Triteness.** For discussion and illustration of formal, general, and informal styles, see the Introduction.

Intensifiers

Intensifiers are words like *very, greatly, terribly, much,* which intensify the meaning of adjectives and adverbs: He is much older than she; She ran very fast. See **Qualifiers.**

Intensive pronouns

Reflexive pronouns—the personal pronouns plus *-self* or *-selves*—may be used as intensives: We ourselves are responsible. See **myself, Pronouns 2.**

interface

Interface is a term from computer technology meaning "a place where independent systems meet and interact harmoniously." It has moved into general use both as a noun (the high school–college interface) and an intransitive verb (legislators and lobbyists interface). Conservative stylists use *interface* only in technical contexts.

Interjections

Interjections are expressions of emotion like *oh, ow, ouch, ah.* See **Exclamations.**

Interrogative pronouns

Who, whom, whose, which, what are interrogative pronouns. See **Pronouns 5.**

Intransitive verbs

An intransitive verb takes no object: The money *vanished.* See **Transitive and intransitive verbs.**

Inversion

Inversion usually means placing the verb, or some part of the verb phrase, before its subject. This is the regular pattern in questions: Will she go? Did they enjoy it? Inversion is also used with expletive *there* and *it* (There was a man at the door) and in a few other situations: What a fool I am; Long may it wave; Here comes the thunder. In a declarative sentence, any part of the predicate may occasionally be inverted for emphasis: Cabbage I hate; Down he went; This I know; That she was brilliant we had no doubt. But inverting the natural order of elements in a sentence can quickly become a bad habit.

Irony

Irony implies something markedly different, sometimes even the opposite, of what's actually said. Light irony is mildly humorous, as in the greeting "Lovely day!" in pouring rain. Heavy irony is usually a form of sarcasm or satire: "The most important argument for collecting taxes from the elderly is that it would lower the tax burden on helpless corporations and conglomerates who are struggling to make ends meet" (Art Buchwald, syndicated columnist). If you set out to be ironic in your writing, make sure your readers will see what you're up to and not mistake your irony for your actual point of view.

irregardless

Irregardless is redundant: both the prefix *ir-* and the suffix *-less* are negative. The standard word is *regardless.*

Irregular verbs

Verbs that don't form their past tense and past participle by adding *-ed* are irregular. See **Principal parts of verbs.**

it

The neuter third-person singular pronoun *it* is used most commonly to refer to inanimates but sometimes refers to living things. Typically it replaces preceding neuter noun phrases: Have you seen *the neighbors' new car?* Yes, isn't *it* a mess? The antecedent may be a clause or a sentence: Some people say *that more money will solve the problem of our schools,* but I don't believe *it.* Sometimes *it* has no antecedent and needs none:

> *It's* been three hours since *it* began to rain, and *it's* still five miles to camp.
> *It* isn't pleasant to live in Washington these days.
> Damn *it,* we'll have to play *it* by ear.

Though typically neuter, the antecedent of *it* may be an animal or a baby whose sex is unknown or irrelevant. *It* is also used with reference to collective nouns denoting persons (The faculty must decide for *it*self) and in sentences where individuals are identified (I'm not sure who the tenor was, but *it* could have been Domingo).

The more important uses of *it* stylistically are those in which it fills the position of a subject or object that's fully expressed later in the sentence. In such sentences *it* is called the anticipatory subject or object:

> *It* is *doubtful that she should be given so much freedom.*
> He found *it* painful *living in the same house with a person whose racial attitudes he detested.*
> *It* was *Wordsworth* who called his gun a "thundering tube."

The advantages of such constructions are that they offer an alternative to lengthy separation of sentence parts that belong together (He found living in the same house with a person whose racial attitudes he detested painful) and a means of assigning emphasis: "It was Wordsworth who . . . ." emphasizes *Wordsworth;* "Wordsworth called his gun a 'thundering tube' " emphasizes *thundering tube.*

See **its, it's; it's me; there is, there are.**

ital Italics

In handwritten and typewritten copy, underline words or passages to correspond to the conventions of using italic type.

In writing, words and statements that would be printed in italics are underlined. Though newspapers have generally abandoned italic type, most magazines and books use it, and in academic writing—course papers, articles in learned journals, dissertations, reference books—italics have standardized uses:

1. To indicate titles of books, periodicals, newspapers, operas, symphonies, paintings, plays, motion pictures, television series, and other complete works. See **Titles 2.**

2. To mark words considered as words rather than for their meaning: There is often a shade of difference between *because* and *for* used as conjunctions.

3. To mark unanglicized words from foreign languages: Good clothes were a *sine qua non*. See **Foreign words in English 2a.**

4. To indicate words that would be stressed if spoken. This device is most appropriate in dialog and should be used sparingly even there. As Thomas Byrne Edsall said, ''Italics: the very word invites polemic'' *(Atlantic).*

5. To indicate key words, phrases, or sentences in an argument or explanation. Here, too, italics should be used sparingly. See **Emphasis 6.**

its, it's

Its is a possessive pronoun and, like the possessive pronouns *his, her, our, your,* and *their,* has no apostrophe: A car is judged by *its* performance. *It's* is the contraction for ''it is'' (It's a long road) and ''it has'' (It's been said before). Like other contractions, *it's* is better suited to informal and general than to formal styles.

it's me

The argument over *it's me* illustrates a conflict between theory and practice. The theory—that after a finite form of the verb *be* the nominative, or subjective, case should always be used—is consistently contradicted by the practice of speakers, educated as well as uneducated. (Except in dialog, the choice between *it's I* and *it's me* is one that writers seldom face.) We tend to use the nominative form of a pronoun when it's the subject and stands directly before the verb, but we're likely to use the accusative in most other positions, especially when the pronoun comes after the verb—in ''object territory,'' as it's been called. (Compare **who, whom.**) All the major grammars of English regard *it's me* as acceptable. See **be.**

-ize

The formation of verbs from non-Greek nouns or adjectives by adding the Greek ending *-ize* (often *-ise* in British usage) has been going on since the sixteenth century. Some readers object to the addition of verbs ending in *-ize,* either because the new verbs duplicate in meaning verbs that are in common use *(fantasized, fantasied; formularize, formulate)* or because the proliferation adds to the stock of advertising jargon *(customize, optimize, personalize).* See **finalize.**

Jargon

Sir Arthur Quiller-Couch popularized *jargon* as the name for verbal fuzziness of various kinds—wordiness, a high proportion of abstract words, "big" words, and words that add nothing to the meaning. *Jargon* and *gobbledygook* are sometimes used interchangeably. Russell Baker satirizes current jargon (and current attitudes) in the following passage:

> "I could not love thee, dear, so much, lov'd I not honor more," the poet could write. Today he could only say, "I could not have so fulfilling a relationship with thee, dear, had I not an even more highly intensified mental set as regards the absurd and widely discredited concept known as honor."—*New York Times Magazine*

Jargon also means shoptalk, or the specialized language of a group—doctors, printers, sociologists, photographers, chicken farmers, and so on. So defined, jargon is appropriate in certain circumstances, as when a physicist writes for fellow physicists, but not in others, as when the physicist writes for a general audience. Physicians sometimes become so attached to medical jargon that they lose the ability to communicate with patients. Deploring such addiction, William Zinsser wrote, "Jargon is seldom necessary. There is almost no technical subject that can't be made accessible to the so-called average man" *(New York Times Magazine)*.

In many groups and many situations there's a tendency to go beyond technical jargon and create jargon in the first sense. Examples of the use of language to impress more than to inform include sociologese, psychologese, educationese, journalese, and bureaucratese.

See **doublespeak, gobbledygook, Shoptalk.**

job, position

Job is general English for the formal *position:* He got a job at the oil refinery. The word *position* has more dignity, though what it refers to isn't necessarily better paid. Because *position* can sound pompous, many writers use *job* for all levels of employment.

journalese

Roy Copperud defined *journalese* as "all that is bad in journalistic writing." (Journalistic writing today includes not only the writing that appears in newspapers and newsmagazines but the writing that's read to us by television and radio news reporters and commentators.) Journalese is journalistic jargon, loaded with clichés, vogue words, buzzwords, hyperboles, gobbledygook, and doublespeak and wholly lacking in character and conviction. It proves that even professional, "grammatical" writing can be awful.

just

The qualifier *just* is redundant in expressions like *just exactly* and *just perfect.* Omit it.

kid

The noun *kid* for "child" and the verb *kid* for "tease" are established in general usage. A problem with *kid* as a noun is that it now may mean not only someone past puberty but someone past adolescence. So loosely used, *kid* is informal. In many contexts a more specific term is needed.

kind, sort

The words *kind* and *sort* cause three different problems for writers.

1. Agreement. *Kind* and *sort* are singular pronouns with regular plurals. A problem arises only when singular *kind* or *sort* is followed by *of* and a plural noun. Then there's a strong tendency to treat the plural object of *of,* rather than *kind* or *sort,* as the headword of the construction and to use plural demonstratives and verbs: "those kind of overhead expenses" (Lewis H. Lapham, *Harper's*). But though the construction is common in speech and there are numerous examples of its use by respected writers, strong objection to it continues. For one kind (or sort), then: *That kind* of book *is* . . . For more than one: *Those kinds* of books *are* . . .

2. *Kind (sort) of a(n).* *Kind of a(n)* and *sort of a(n)* are general idioms: "People just didn't trust that kind of an approach" (Charles Mohr, *Esquire*). Formal style would have "kind of approach."

3. *Kind (sort) of.* As adverbs equivalent to imprecise qualifiers like *rather* and *somewhat* in more formal usage, *kind of* and *sort of* are informal to general: "She was kind of plump" (Claude Brown, *Commentary*); "Still, there are moments when the treatment sort of works" (Joe Klein, *New York*).

know-how

Though *know-how* occurs in every variety of English, for many readers its connotations remain commercial and technical. To speak of the know-how of a great violinist, for example, would be inappropriate.

lab

The clipped form of *laboratory* is now common in all but the most formal usage.

lady

In writing, stylists in general and feminists in particular consider *woman* the right term for an adult female. See **woman, lady, girl.**

last, latest

Both *last* and *latest* are used as superlatives of *late* (his last book; his latest book). But to avoid ambiguity, formal English uses *last* for the final item in a series (His last book was completed only weeks before his death), *latest* for the most recent of a series that may or may not be continued (His latest book shows steady improvement).

latter

The use of *latter* in referring to the last of more than two items is standard, but conservative stylists prefer "the last named." See **former, first–latter, last.**

lay, lie

One of the most common errors in grammar is the use of *lay* for *lie,* as in "I wanted to just lay down and do nothing." To avoid it, you need to learn and remember the correct forms of *lie.* I or you *lie* down; he or she *lies* down. It *lies* on the ground. In the past tense, *lie* changes to *lay:* Yesterday I, you, he, she, it *lay* down. The past participle of *lie* is *lain:* I or you *have lain* there for hours; he, she, or it *had lain* there before.

The verb *lay* takes an object: You can *lay* your briefcase on the table. The past tense and past participle are *laid:* Last week they *laid* the new carpet; the hen *had laid* an egg.

Keeping the two verbs distinct is required in educated usage.

learn, teach

Although *learn* meaning "teach" has a long history in English, it is now non-standard: He learned me how to tie knots. Standard English makes the distinction: He *taught* me how to tie knots; I *learned* how to tie knots from him.

leave, let

Let, not *leave,* is standard English for "permit" or "allow." See **let, leave.**

legalese

Legalese refers to that considerable portion of the language of law courts, lawyers, laws, and legal documents that is unintelligible to ordinary citizens, often to their very great cost.

lend, loan

In referring to material things, *lend* and *lends* are preferred to *loan* and *loans* in formal writing: "those who wished to lend" (George V. Taylor, *American Historical Review*). But the past tense and past participle *loaned* is preferred to *lent* in all varieties: "About $4 billion have been loaned" (Adolf A. Berle, *The American Economic Republic*). In general contexts *loan* and *loans* are as common as *lend* and *lends* and are entirely acceptable.

In the sense "grant, impart, furnish" or "adapt or accommodate (itself)," *lend* and *lent* are always preferred: "America always lent itself to personification" (Norman Mailer, *Harper's*).

less, fewer

Use *fewer* for things that can be counted, *less* for things that can't. See **fewer, less.**

let, leave

A common nonstandard idiom is the use of *leave* for "permit" or "allow," meanings that standard English assigns to *let*. Both uses are shown in this sentence by a writer making a transition between nonstandard and standard: "In high school I was cured of the practice of leaving [nonstandard] notebooks go, but I fell into the habit of letting [standard] homework slide."

In standard English, the two verbs are interchangeable only with *alone* and the meaning "refrain from disturbing": Leave (*or* Let) me alone; All they asked of their government was to be let (*or* left) alone.

Lexical meaning

In linguistics a distinction is often made between grammatical or structural meaning and lexical meaning. In "Birds were killed," the information that *bird* and *kill* give us is the sort provided by a dictionary or lexicon—hence lexical meaning. The information given by the *-s* of *birds* (plural), *were* (past tense, passive voice), and the *-ed* of *killed* (past participle in this position) is the sort provided by our awareness of the grammar or structure of the language—hence grammatical or structural meaning. When we fully understand the sentence, we have grasped its total meaning.

liable

In formal writing and most general writing, *liable* followed by an infinitive is used to predict only undesirable or uncertain results: The effects are liable to be disastrous. *Liable*-plus-infinitive to predict desirable results most often appears in informal to casual general contexts: "Walleyes are year-round sport and . . . they're liable to hit any time of the day or night" (Roger Latham, *Field and Stream*). *Likely,* which signifies simple probability, predicts both desirable and undersirable results in all varieties of English.

lie

The transitive verb *lay* shouldn't be substituted for the intransitive *lie*. You *lie*, not *lay*, down when you're tired. You *lay*, not *laid*, down yesterday. See **lay, lie.**

life-style

One way to avoid overusing *life-style* is to distinguish between what is truly a distinctive way of life—of attitudes and behavior—and a deviation from the norm in some specific respect. If you write about a person who sleeps all day and goes to work at night, don't refer to his life-style; say that he's on the night shift.

like, as

1. As prepositions. In all varieties of English, *like* is used as a preposition introducing a comparison: The description fits her like a plaster cast; Habit grips a person like an octopus; He took to selling like a bee to clover. Largely because of fear of misusing *like, as* is increasingly common as a hypercorrect form: "The Basenji is the size of a fox terrier and cleans itself as a cat" (Natalie Winslow, *Providence Sunday Journal*).

2. As conjunctions. In all varieties of English, *as, as if*, and *as though* are used as conjunctions introducing clauses of comparison: They moved across the floor as skaters glide over a frozen pond; He walked as though he had been hurt. *Like* as a conjunction is common in speech and appears frequently in informal and general writing: "Like a typical kid his age might do, Holden does violate some rules of grammar" (James Lundquist, *J. D. Salinger*). But opposition to *like* as a conjunction introducing a full clause (as opposed to an elliptical one: he was attracted to her like a bee [is attracted] to clover) remains strong, and it should be avoided in most writing: They love animals, like most children; they love animals as (*not* like) most children do.

The same holds true of *like* for *as if:* The pilot flew on as if (*not* like) nothing had happened.

3. *The way*. *The way* provides an escape from the *like-as* thicket for writers who think *like* is crude and *as* is prissy: "Hemingway once told Callaghan, 'Dostoevski writes like Harry Greb fights.' Unfortunately, Callaghan writes the way Hemingway fights" *(Time)*.

likely

"They'll probably be there" can also be expressed as "They'll likely be there" or "They likely will be there," though some formal stylists insist that *likely* in this usage must be preceded by a qualifier like *very* or *most*. "They are likely to be there" is entirely acceptable but expresses a bit less likelihood.

Linguistics

Linguistics is a broad discipline incorporating several perspectives from which language may be studied systematically. Linguists study the structures of languages and the universal structure of language. They study the histories and the varieties of language. They study how language is acquired and how it is used.

Linguistics differs from other disciplines devoted to the study of language by having at its center a theory of language derived from the study of formal, regular, and recurrent patterns in the structures of human languages. Theories of language differ, and therefore schools of linguistics exist; but all linguists are empiricists, sharing a desire to be as objective as possible and rejecting conclusions not based on consistent theory and verified by significant data.

See **Grammar.**

Linking verbs

When a verb like *be* functions chiefly as a bridge between a subject and another noun or a modifier, it's called a linking, or copulative, verb. A linking verb is followed by single words, phrases, or clauses that function as adjectives or nouns and are traditionally known as predicate adjectives (This bottle was *full*) or as predicate nouns or predicate nominatives (The man was a *carpenter*).

Some grammarians prefer to call them complements, or subjective complements.

Many verbs besides *be* are used as linking verbs. A few of them are italicized in the following sentences:

She *became* a doctor.	The bassoon *sounds* nasal.
The butter *tastes* rancid.	He *appeared* to be healthy.
They *felt* sad.	The dog *acts* old.
His story *seemed* incredible.	The weather *turned* cold.
This *looks* first-rate.	She *grew* moody.

Many verbs are used both with full meaning of their own (The tree *fell* into the water) and as linking verbs (He *fell* silent). Speakers who are not aware that the same verb can function both ways and who have been taught that verbs are modified by adverbs often make the mistake of substituting an adverb for the adjective that should follow a linking verb: "The bassoon sounds nasally" for "The bassoon sounds nasal." Such hypercorrectness also crops up in writing.

For the most common source of difficulty in using the linking-verb pattern, see **Predicate adjectives.** See also **bad, badly; be; Hypercorrectness; it's me; look.**

literally

Literally means "actually, without deviating from the facts," but it's so often used to support metaphors that its literal meaning may be reversed. In statements like the following, *literally* means "figuratively" and *literal* means "figurative":

All of this is taking place in Florida at a time when the nation is literally awash in oil.—Fred J. Cook, *Nation*

In this struggle, women's bodies became a literal battleground.—Martin Duberman, *Nation*

Taken literally, such statements create astonishing mental pictures. Use *literally* only when you're being absolutely factual.

loan

In referring to possession, *lend* is more formal than *loan* in the present tense. For the past tense, *loaned* is preferred to *lent* in all varieties of usage. See **lend, loan.**

Loan words

Loan words are words borrowed from other languages. See **Foreign words in English, Origin of words 2b.**

Localisms

A localism is a word or other expression in regular use only in a certain region, like *hoagie, submarine* (or *sub*), *hero, po' boy* for the same sort of sandwich in a roll. Localisms are appropriate in informal writing and in some general writing, particularly when the audience is local. In more formal writing they should be used sparingly, to provide a desired regional flavor, and should be defined whenever necessary. See **Dialects.**

Locution

Locution is a handy term for referring to a word or to a phrase or clause considered as a unit. In the preceding sentence "a handy term" is one locution.

logic # Logical thinking

Reconsider the logical relationship that is expressed or implied.

At some time or other everyone has protested, "That doesn't make sense" or "That doesn't follow from what you just said." Everyone, that is, has some notion of the difference between logical and illogical thinking, and when something is said or written that doesn't make sense or fails to show a logical progression, everyone's impulse is to dismiss it.

In a college paper illogical thinking is revealed in irrelevant material, faulty organization, incoherent sentences, and words that blur or skew the meaning of what's being said. More narrowly, it shows up in the faulty relationship between ideas. Often the seeming breakdown in logic is simply the result of careless writing. In taking issue with the statement "The true university is a collection of books," a student wrote, "If I were to agree that a true university is no more than a collection of books, I would graduate well-read but not socially mature." This makes no sense, because simply agreeing or not agreeing with the statement about a true university could not determine the kind of education a particular student would receive at a particular school.

Presumably the student meant, "If a true university is no more than a collection of books, and if this is a true university, then I can expect to be well-read but not necessarily socially mature when I graduate." If he intended to base an *if . . . then* relationship on his agreeing with the original statement, he might say, "If I agreed that a true university is no more than a collection of books, then I would spend all my time in the library."

You can avoid such apparent lapses in logic by giving what you write a careful reading—seeing what you've *said* rather than what you *meant* to say—and revising your sentences before preparing your final draft.

Much more serious are the kinds of illogical thinking that undercut a whole paper. When you write to express an opinion, defend a point of view, argue for or against something, or persuade or convince your readers, keep these recommendations in mind:

1. Limit your generalizations to what you can support with evidence.

2. Make sure that what you offer as evidence is authoritative and bears on the issue.

3. Make sure that you attack the actual issue instead of skirmishing around the edges or wandering off into another conflict.

4. Make sure you omit no links in the chain of reasoning that leads to your conclusion.

In reading over what you've written, take a hard look at your generalizations. Are they sound enough to support your argument? Are they based on fact and justifiable inferences, or are they no more than unexamined assumptions or expressions of prejudice?

When you find yourself saying that *A* caused *B* or that *B* is the result of *A*, think over your reasons for saying so. Are they convincing? Are there reasons for *not* saying so that you've deliberately omitted? Are your comparisons justifiable and your analogies plausible?

After enjoying the violent language you've used in condemning those who hold an opposing point of view, and after admiring the eloquence with which you've praised those whose side you're supporting, ask yourself whether the faults of the former or the virtues of the latter have anything to do with the issue itself. Unless they have, don't mistake what you've written for logical argument.

See **Cause and effect, Classification and division, Deduction, Fallacies, Induction, Syllogisms.**

Logic and language

Sometimes an item of usage is objected to as being illogical—for example, "the reason is because." But when the objection to "the reason is because" is elaborated, it's usually that an adverbial clause *(because . . .)* is equated with a noun *(reason)*—a criticism that has to do with grammar rather than logic.

Idiom illustrates particularly well the lack of correspondence between logic and usage. The meanings of many idioms—"hard to come by," "hold your own," "out of order"—are not the sum of the meanings of their separate words. These show, more clearly than the general patterns and rules of English, that language is a human development, the result of millions of speech situations, not a preplanned system. Language isn't illogical; it's simply alogical.

Arguments from logic probably had an influence in establishing the double negative as nonstandard English. In Old and Middle English the more negatives there were, the stronger the negation. But arguments from logic have had few such successes, and the term *logical* applies to language only in its most general, popular sense of "more or less systematic."

See **Double negative, Idiom, reason is because.**

Long variants

Some writers are tempted to add an extra prefix or suffix to a word that already carries the meaning they intend. They write *irregardless,* though *regardless* already means "without regard to," or they write *doubtlessly* for *doubtless.* Some like to use suffixes that add nothing to the meaning, like the *-ation* in *analyzation,* which means no more than *analysis.* Some other long variants that it's wise to avoid are *certificated* for *certified, confliction* for *conflict, emotionality* when only *emotion* is meant, *hotness* for *heat, intermingle* for *mingle, orientate* for *orient, ruination* for *ruin,* and *utilize* when *use* is entirely adequate. See **Diction 2, gobbledygook, Jargon.**

look

When used as an intransitive verb meaning "use the eyes, gaze," *look* is modified by a adverb: look longingly, look searchingly. As a linking verb, equivalent to *appear, look* is followed by an adjective that modifies the subject: He looks well (*or* healthy *or* tired *or* bad). See **Linking verbs.**

looking to

Looking to has been used to mean "expecting to" for more than a century. Recently it has flourished as a rather folksy "trying to" or "planning to" or "wanting to." Journalists have encouraged this broad vogue usage: "Companies are looking to grab the attention of workers" *(Newsweek);* "The networks are also counterattacking by looking to expand their advertising" *(Time).* Say what you mean instead of making your reader guess which of the possible meanings you intend.

lot, lots

In the senses "much," "many," "a great deal," *a lot (of)* and *lots (of)* have an informal flavor. Both are established in general usage but not in formal: "There is lots of talk" *(Fortune). A lot* is two words, not one: a lot of money.

lc Lowercase

Use a lowercase (small) letter instead of a capital.

As an alternative or supplement to *lc,* the correction may be indicated by a slant line through the capitals:

```
It was a Ǥreat Ɇxperience.
```

For the conventional use of capitals, see **Capital letters.**

Main clauses

Main clauses (like this one and the next) are independent clauses. They can stand alone as sentences. See **Clauses.**

majority, plurality

Technically, a majority in an election is more than half the total number of votes cast, while a plurality is the largest number of votes cast for any one candidate but not more than half the total. Though the distinction is sometimes neglected, it's worth preserving for clarity.

In formal usage *majority* is applied only to groups of at least three things that can be counted. In informal and general usage *majority* is sometimes used also of the larger part of a single thing or mass: "A majority of the LP is taken up with bouncy dance tunes" (Robert Palmer, *New York Times*). *Most* is preferable.

ms Manuscript form

Your manuscript is not in the proper form. Revise or rewrite as directed.

Instructors establish their own specifications for manuscript form at the beginning of the course. Whatever the details, the goal is a clean, legible copy that can be read easily. What follows is one instructor's statement of requirements.

If you use a typewriter, keep the type clean and change the ribbon regularly. Submit your assignments on inexpensive white $8\frac{1}{2}'' \times 11''$ paper (not bond, not erasable). Type on only one side of the sheet, double-spaced; indent the first line of paragraphs five spaces; leave $1\frac{1}{2}''$ margins at both left and right; center the title on the first line of the first page; number the pages, beginning with 2; use a paper clip (not a staple) to fasten pages together in the upper left; turn in the manuscript flat (not folded); and write your name nowhere except on the back of the last sheet.

Proofread carefully. Make corrections neatly, using a caret to indicate insertions. Erase and retype transposed letters or correct them with a curved line.

```
Strikeovers [not Strikeovers] are often hard to read.
```

If you are composing on a word processor, use the SAVE command often, since electrical surges and interference can wipe out your best efforts in seconds. Keep a current backup copy of your file on a separate disk in case your working file is damaged.

Many word-processing programs have preset margins, tabs, and other formatting options. Reset the options as necessary to meet the requirements for particular assignments. Follow your program manual for instructions on single-spacing and double-spacing options.

Select simple, legible type fonts and sizes. Odd fonts, like Old English, are distracting for readers, as are type sizes that are either unnecessarily large or very small.

Whatever kind of printer you use, make sure the printout is sharp. Choose the highest quality your print menu offers, or change cartridges when the quality deteriorates.

Some writers rely on spell-check programs to catch misspellings. Because these programs do not detect the improper use of words spelled correctly, they cannot substitute for a careful proofreading of your copy.

See **Caret, Division of words, Quotation marks.**

massive

Used with abstract nouns, *massive* became a vogue word during the 1960s: massive retaliation, massive resistance, massive inequality, massive unemployment. This usage continues, despite the unhappiness of those who would apply *massive* only to things with mass.

Mass nouns

Mass nouns name masses that are not counted as separate units: food, coal, health, water. See **Nouns 3c.**

may, can

In requesting or granting permission or expressing feasibility, *may* is the formal choice. *Can* expresses ability and is commonly used in place of *may* in general English. See **can, may.**

may, might

In sentences where the past tense is established, *might,* not *may,* is called for: If the candidate had spoken with more conviction, she might have won a majority of the delegates. Journalists in particular have an unfortunate tendency to use *may* in such sentences: "Lane stopped to search his car for drugs or other contraband that may have been planted by the police" *(Newsweek).*

When the past tense is not established, both *may* and *might* express possibility, with *may* carrying more likelihood: We may go to the concert, and we might stay for the reception.

Meaning

The word, phrase, or sentence marked does not make sense in this context. Replace it with one that communicates the meaning you intend.

For a reader to question the meaning of what you've written indicates a drastic failure in communication. Ordinarily the problem is not simply the use of one word for another that's reasonably close to it in sound or meaning—*comprehension* for *comprehensibility,* for example. *Comprehension* can be labeled *ww* (wrong word) because the reader knows what you intended to say. But *mng,* often followed by a question mark, means that the reader can't, or won't, make a guess at what you're trying to say in a sentence or even a paragraph. Rethinking and rewriting are in order. Compare **Ambiguity, Coherence, Wrong word.**

meaningful

Meaningful became a vogue word in the 1960s and still hangs on, particularly among those who are addicted to pop psychologese. Before using it, remind yourself that many readers consider the term vague or pretentious or both.

media, medium(s)

Medium and *media,* the Latin singular and plural forms, were taken directly into English, and formal usage consistently maintains the distinction in number, while recognizing the alternative plural *mediums:* "the moral possibilities of the mediums themselves" (Robert J. Reilly, *American Literature*). But *media,* like many other Latin plurals, has tended to become singular in American usage and is frequently so used in general writing: "with help from an enthusiastic media" (Edwin McDowell, *Wall Street Journal*). In your own writing you'd be wise to use *media* only when referring to more than one medium and to follow it with a plural verb.

Metaphor

Metaphor, now widely applied to any nonliteral use of language, traditionally refers to the figure of speech which implies that two things normally considered quite different are in some way identical or very much alike. When we're talking literally, we say it's people or machines that *polish,* flags that *unfurl,* liquids that *stream,* and flowers that *bloom.* But a writer can, through metaphor, put these words to new uses and so make a description of even the simplest things both fresh and pleasing:

> The wind continued to polish the grasses. And a purple finch unfurled his song. Twice, and now three times, its last sure note streamed into the sun-bloom.— Sally Carrighar, *One Day on Beetle Rock*

Metaphors give this description of surf its power:

> Far out to sea, the combers were coming in: the long, heavy rollers, curling over white across their green hearts; tearing themselves to smoke on the sandbars and the slimy rocks, rasping up the beach with a sound like fire.—Peter S. Beagle, *The Last Unicorn*

Metaphor can do more than please. It can provide a new view of things and so shape attitudes and change minds. It may create a sharp image with a single verb (White House action *defused* the demands of Congress), or it may set up instructive analogies that hold the reader's attention:

> Before prose rhythm can be sensibly considered, one must redefine reading. It cannot be a jet flight coast-to-coast. It must be a slow walk in the country, taken, as all walks should be, partly for the walking itself.—Richard A. Lanham, *Style: An Anti-Textbook*

> The demon which possesses us is our mania for correctness.—Donald J. Lloyd, *American Scholar*

> From politicians to business leaders, judges to sports figures, our public discourse is carried forward on the backs of a battalion of anonymous scribes.—Ari Posner, *New Republic*

See **Figurative language, Figures of speech, Mixed metaphors.**

Metonymy

Metonymy is a figure of speech in which the thing named suggests the thing meant, as in ''guns [war] or butter [peace].'' See **Figurative language.**

might, could

These two words express a lesser degree of possibility than *may, can:* I might go; They could turn up. See **can, may.**

Misrelated modifiers

The placement of a misrelated modifier makes it seem to modify the wrong word in the sentence. See **Dangling modifiers.**

Mixed metaphors

Speakers frequently run two inconsistent metaphors together: The new measure has gained a firm foothold in the eye of the public; What they need on the ticket is a fresh face that hasn't been straddling the economic issue. Writers, who can reconsider their words, have less excuse for such obvious blunders and—since what they put into their final draft can be read again and again—

more reason for avoiding them. But many metaphors that aren't logically consistent are run together in print without disturbing any but the most fussy readers: "Consider Walter Kerr, a highly visual critic steeped in the silent movies, who turned his back on the talkies to find more nourishment in, God help us, the Broadway stage" (Wilfrid Sheed, *New York Review of Books*).

Mixed usage

Indiscriminate, thoughtless mixing of vocabularies—formal with informal, poetic with technical—weakens writing. See **Diction 2.**

Modal auxiliaries

Can, could; may, might; must; ought; shall, should; will, would are called modal auxiliaries. They differ from other verbs in having no *-s* in the third-person singular, no infinitive, no participle, and therefore no compound or phrasal forms. Instead, they themselves always occur as part of verb phrases, complete or elliptical. The generally similar *dare* and *need* are also sometimes treated as modal auxiliaries. See **Elliptical constructions.**

Modifiers

A modifier typically limits the meaning of the word, phrase, or clause it modifies and makes it more exact (a *green* apple). In the following illustrations the words in italics modify the words in small capitals: A *cold windy* DAY; He FAILED *miserably;* She was *truly* SUPERB; *Undoubtedly* IT WAS THE CAT WHO STOLE THE BUTTERMILK; *Coming around the corner,* WE met him head on. See **Absolute phrases, Adjectives, Adverbs, Dangling modifiers, Gerunds 1, Infinitives and style, Participles 2, Phrases, Restrictive and nonrestrictive modifiers.**

Money

1. Exact sums of money are usually written in figures: 72¢, $4.98, $168.75, $42,810. Though round sums are likely to be written in words (two hundred dollars, a million dollars), figures may be used for them, too, particularly when several sums are mentioned.

2. Except in lists and tables, amounts are usually spelled out when they're used as modifiers: a million-dollar project. Informally, figures are often used: a $10 seat.

3. For amounts in millions and billions, a dollar sign followed by the number followed by the word is most common: $50 billion. Instead of "three and a half million dollars" or "$3,500,000," "$3.5 million" is now standard.

4. A sum of money is usually thought of as a single unit: More than $9 million *was* invested in paintings.

Months

Abbreviate the names of months only when you're compiling data and your space is limited. In that situation "3/19/43" may be preferable to "Mar. 19, 1943." See **Dates.**

Mood

The mood of a verb, indicated by its form, tells whether the writer or speaker regards what he's saying as a statement of fact or a question concerning fact (indicative mood), as a wish or an expression of possibility or doubt (subjunctive mood), or as a command (imperative mood). See **Commands and requests, Imperative mood, Indicative mood, Subjunctive mood.**

more, most

Preceding the base forms of adjectives and adverbs with *more* and *most* is one way of expressing their comparative and superlative degrees. See **Comparison of adjectives and adverbs 1.**

most, almost

In speech *almost* is often reduced to *most:* A drop in prices would suit most anybody. So used, *most* occasionally appears in factual prose for general audiences: "But most everything is acceptable" (Gael Greene, *New York*). In more formal writing, if you can substitute *almost* for *most* in a sentence (almost always, almost everywhere), *almost* is the word to use.

most, majority

In referring to mass nouns like *time,* use *most:* most (*not* the majority) of the time. See **majority, plurality; Nouns 3c.**

Ms.

Ms. is a substitute for both *Miss* and *Mrs.* Its use is favored by those who believe that a woman shouldn't be labeled married or unmarried any more than a man is. If a first name is used after *Ms.* for a married woman, the name is hers, of course, not her husband's: Mrs. John Doe becomes Ms. Jane Doe. Not all married women prefer *Ms.* When you know a woman's preference, use that title.

In writing for college courses a choice between *Ms.* and *Miss* or *Mrs.* is most often necessary when the topic is a biographical or critical essay about a woman or her work—for example, an analysis of Frances Trollope's *Domestic*

Manners of the Americans or a review of the poetry of Sylvia Plath. It would be absurd to abandon "Mrs. Trollope," as Frances Trollope was known to her contemporaries, for "Ms. Trollope." But Sylvia Plath can be called Ms. Plath or Miss Plath. (As a poet, she remained Sylvia Plath during her marriage.) She can also be called Sylvia Plath or simply Plath. The latter usage is now common in published writing about women.

must

In general English, but not in formal, *must* is accepted as a noun meaning "necessity" (Their latest film is a must for movie fans) and an adjective modifier meaning "essential": "This book is a must assignment for reporters" (Robert O. Blanchard, *Columbia Journalism Review*).

myself

In compound subjects and objects, writers sometimes use *myself* instead of *I* or *me,* perhaps to give an impression of objectivity:

> Then the two of us, President Johnson and myself, walked out.—Malcolm Kilduff, *Columbia Journalism Review*

> The social chairman invited my wife and myself to dinner.

Many stylists find this use pompous and call for the regular nominative (*I* in the first example) and the accusative (*me* in the second). Opinion is divided. See **himself, herself; Pronouns 2; self.**

naked, nude

Naked and *nude* mean the same thing, but *nude* has classier connotations. It's "nude" in art. It's "naked" in the shower.

namely

Introductory *namely* is rarely needed in general writing: The topic was a particularly unpleasant one—[namely,] rising prices. See **that is.**

Narration

Stories (factual as well as fictional), autobiographies, biographies, and histories are all narratives. Like accounts of natural or mechanical processes and reports of laboratory experiments, they relate a sequence of events. In college papers you'll frequently be called on to narrate such sequences.

1. Chronological order. As a writer of narrative, you may have reasons for changing actual chronological order. To arouse interest, you may decide to begin in the middle, making the reader want to find out how a character got into a certain situation. Or you may give the ending first and then show the reader how each step led toward the final outcome. Or you may use a flashback (*Six years ago we had had a similar experience*) to explain causes or to draw a parallel.

Though the events in a narrative can be told in any order, the reader must finally be able to understand the order in which they actually took place. To make that order clear, use appropriate indicators of time (*then, later, after that, and so on*) and the right verb tenses (*had said* instead of *said* in a flashback, perhaps). And if the reader is to understand why an event took place or what effects it had, you need to use indicators of causal relationships (*in order to, because, as a result*).

2. Place. In narration you can compress the events of a decade into a single sentence or extend the happenings of an hour through ten pages. You may slow your narrative with patches of description so that the reader can visualize the scene or gain a vivid sense of what's taking place. Or you may vary the pace by using dialog to dramatize a crucial action. You can make similar changes of pace in objective, factual reporting—of an industrial process, for example, or of a traffic accident—speeding up simpler stages and slowing down complex ones for clarity. Varying the pace is one way you can direct the attention and control the responses of your audience.

3. Distance and point of view. How the reader sees and interprets the events depends largely on the distance you establish between yourself and your subject and between yourself and your reader. Physically, you may be close to your subject, taking part in the action, even causing it; or you may be a remote observer, reporting and analyzing. You can present yourself as a learner and invite the reader to share that perspective, or you can assume the role of an expert—someone who knows much more than the reader does. The prevailing point of view (and it should prevail—that is, be maintained consistently) will help define the tone of what you write. See **Point of view.**

4. The point of the narrative. A good narrative relates a sequence of events in such a way that a point emerges. The reader grasps not only what took place but the significance of what took place. (She doesn't end up thinking "So what?") In an expository narrative the significance may be clearly stated. In other narratives—personal reminiscences, for example—a brief comment on the significance of the action may be justified; but the better the storytelling, the less need there'll be for spelling out the so-what.

nauseous, nauseated

Traditionally, *nauseated* means "sickened, disgusted" (I felt nauseated at the sight), and *nauseous* means "causing sickness or disgust" (The smell was nauseous). But the use of "feeling nauseous" and "getting nauseous" has become so common that dictionaries now record "nauseated" as a second meaning of *nauseous*. Those who grew up observing the distinction find this usage ambiguous. (Was he sick, or was he sickening?)

Negatives and style

When you use both negative and positive words in the same sentence, be sure the combination says clearly what you intend. "The vocational counseling office will try to increase its clients' inability to support themselves" should be rephrased either as "to increase their ability" or as "to remedy their inability."

Poor sentences often result from stating negatively what might better be put positively:

> This mob violence does not reflect the sentiment of an overwhelming majority of the students.

> **Better:** This mob violence reflects the sentiments of only a small minority of the students.

Some writers are fond of tricky negative constructions, including *litotes,* a variety of understatement in which an affirmative is expressed by the negative of its contrary (making it an accepted form of double negative): She was not unfond of him; He was not displeased; "My father was not unmusical" (Ira Gershwin). Litotes can be effective, but when overused it makes the writer sound coy, evasive, or simply tiresome. See **Double negative.**

neither

As a pronoun, *neither* is ordinarily construed as singular and followed by a singular verb. When the verb is separated from *neither* by a prepositional phrase with a plural object, a plural verb is frequently used in informal writing and sometimes in general writing: "Marx and Trotsky, neither of whom were notably gentle or vegetarian" (Dwight Macdonald, *Esquire*). But here, too, grammatical convention calls for a singular verb.

As an adjective, *neither* modifies a singular noun (neither side), and a pronoun referring to the noun should be singular (Neither side achieved *its* goal).

nice

As a word indicating approval (We had a nice time), *nice* is too imprecise for college writing. In formal prose *nice* is usually restricted to meanings like "subtle" or "discriminating": Kirk raises a nice point in his article on Camus.

nobody, no one

The pronouns *nobody* and *no one* take singular verbs, and, strictly speaking, a pronoun referring to either of them should be singular: No one lowered his voice. But *their, they* may be used to avoid a masculine singular; and sometimes meaning demands a plural pronoun: "No one sings; they simply listen reverently" (Ray Jenkins, *New York Times Magazine*). In formal writing the sentence might be recast: No one sings; everyone simply listens reverently.

noisome

Noisome does not mean "noisy." It is a formal work for "stinking."

nom Nominalization

Change the abstract nominalization into a concrete verb.

For most purposes the best writing is direct writing—writing that avoids three words where two will do, writing that represents an action in a verb and the agent of that action as its subject. The difference between indirect and direct writing is illustrated in these two sentences:

> It seems to be the case that certain individuals in attendance at this institution of higher education are in a state of anger over recent announcements on the part of the dean in regard to a necessity for greater restrictions where the consumption of alcoholic beverages is concerned.

> Some students here are angry because the dean announced that he was tightening the rules about drinking on campus.

Probably the most common source of indirect writing is the abstract nominalization, a noun that—according to transformational theory—has been derived from a full subject + verb in the deep structure of a sentence:

> Tom *paid* the money   ⟶ Tom's *payment* of the money
> The monks *reject* wealth   ⟶ The monks' *rejection* of wealth
> The students *are responsible* ⟶ The students' *responsibility*

The direct subject-verb-object or subject-*be*-adjective construction has been made indirect and accordingly less lively and forceful. If this kind of construction occurs often in your writing—say, once every seven or eight words—readers are likely to find your style heavy, abstract, pretentious, and possibly dishonest.

To improve such a style, first look for nouns made out of verbs:

> An investigation is being made of the causes for the decline in wheat production.

When you find them *(investigation, causes, decline, production)*, ask whether the crucial action is in the main verb or in one of these abstract nouns. If it's in a noun *(investigation)*, change the noun to a verb *(are investigating)*, specify who is doing the investigating *(they,* referring to a specific antecedent? *scientists? agricultural chemists?),* and rewrite the sentence around the new subject-verb:

> An investigation is being made of the causes for the decline in wheat production.

> Agricultural chemists are investigating what has caused wheat production to decline.

> Agricultural chemists are investigating why farmers are producing less wheat.

Or, if no specific subject can be stated, make a straight passive: The decline in wheat production is being investigated.

See **Abstract language, Deep structure, Passive voice 2, Subjects, Verbs and style.**

Nominals

A word, phrase, or clause that serves as subject of a verb, as complement of a linking verb, as object of a verb or a preposition, or as an appositive is functioning as a noun and can be called a *nominal.*

Nominative case

A noun or pronoun that is subject of a verb, complement of a linking verb, or an appositive to either is said to be in the nominative (or subjective) case. The form of the nominative singular is the common form of the noun, the form to which the endings for the possessive and the plural are typically added. The pronouns with distinctive nominative forms are the personals—*I, he, she, it, we, you, they*—and the relative *who. (You* is both nominative and accusative.) Though these are the usual forms for the nominative functions, see **it's me; who, whom.** See also **Case 1, Subjects.**

none

The use of *none* with a plural verb is still sometimes condemned, usually on the grounds that *none* means "no one" or "not one" and so must be singular, as in "None of her views, of course, was the slightest threat to slavery" (C. Vann Woodward, *New York Review of Books*). Usage is divided, but when the reference is to countables, *none* has long been used as a plural in the most reputable writing:

> Almost none [of the letters] are either thoughtful in their approach or deliberative in their style.—Louis J. Halle, *New Republic*

None of these documents afford any solid support for those historians who have viewed Pike as a tool or accomplice in the Wilkinson-Burr schemes.—Harvey L. Carter, *American Historical Review*

Nonrestrictive modifiers

A nonrestrictive modifier does not provide essential identification of the word modified and should therefore be set off by commas. See **Restrictive and nonrestrictive modifiers.**

non sequitur

Non sequitur ("it does not follow") is a broad term for all those errors in reasoning in which the stated conclusion is not a logical consequence of the argument. See **Fallacies, Logical thinking, Syllogisms.**

ns Nonstandard English

Change the nonstandard word, form, or idiom to one in standard use.

"Nobody ain't got nothing," "theirself," "he do," "they knowed"—these are examples of nonstandard English. Among the articles that treat nonstandard words or forms are **Adverbs and style; Double negative; lay, lie; learn, teach; Principal parts of verbs.** See also **Dialects, Standard English.**

no place

Although *anyplace, everyplace,* and *someplace* for "anywhere," "everywhere," and "somewhere" have become common in general writing, *no place* for "nowhere" is still mainly informal: An hour of arguing got us no place. It's sometimes spelled as one word.

nor

By itself, *nor* is an emphatic negative conjunction, most commonly used at the beginning of a sentence in the sense "and . . . not": Nor was Paris (And Paris was not) the only place he visited. Before the last member of a negative series, *nor* gives an added distinctness and emphasis: "I did not see him or hear him" is less emphatic than "I did not see him nor hear him."

As a correlative conjunction, *nor* is paired with *neither*. See **Correlative conjunctions.**

not about to

Not about to is not the simple negative of *about to* but an idiom that stresses the remoteness of the suggested possibility: I'm not about to go along with their weird schemes.

not all that, not too

Not all that is heard frequently in conversations and in weather forecasts (Tomorrow will be better but not all that sunny) and is seen increasingly in print. Sometimes *much* completes the phrase: I didn't like the movie all that much. In some cases an antecedent of a sort is provided for *that,* as in "She thought she might graduate with honors, but her grades weren't all that high"—that is, weren't high enough to qualify for honors. More often, as in this opening of a book review, there's no antecedent: "Usually, the tone of a popular novel is not all that important" *(New Yorker)*.

For most college writing, *not all that* is unsatisfactory if only because it invites the question "all what?" So does *that* without *all,* as in "There are not that many windmills left in Iowa" (Michael Martone, *North American Review*).

Somewhat different is the *not too* we use in speaking of ourselves and others. "I'm not feeling too good" means "I'm feeling rather poorly." "Their grades aren't too high" probably means "Their grades are mediocre." This usage, whether intended as understatement or as irony, is well-established idiom and, while hardly precise, would be appropriate in informal writing and in a good deal of general writing, as long as the context made the meaning sufficiently clear.

Both *not all that* and *not too* locutions are too imprecise for formal prose.

Note form

In any paper based on the words of others, the writer has an obligation to acknowledge the sources. This is primarily a matter of honesty and courtesy. In addition, documentation in the form of notes and bibliography invites readers to judge for themselves the evidence an assertion is based on and allows them to turn to the sources for further information.

You must acknowledge your sources not only when you reproduce a paragraph, a sentence, or even a significant phrase exactly but also when you reword or summarize. Whether you use direct quotations or not, you need to give the source of all facts, interpretations, and conclusions that aren't common knowledge and that you haven't arrived at through independent thought, experiment, or investigation. If you name in the text the original source of a quotation that you got from a secondary source, you should cite that secondary source in an endnote or footnote. To neglect to credit the authors and the works that the information and the ideas came from is plagiarism. See **Plagiarism.**

For the note form you should use, consult the manual or style sheet published by the authority for your discipline—the Modern Language Association, for instance, or the American Psychological Association, or the Council of Biology Editors. *The Chicago Manual of Style* offers comprehensive coverage of forms of documentation. See **Research papers.**

not hardly, not scarcely

When *hardly* and *scarcely* mean "almost not," an additional *not* is redundant. See **Double negative.**

Noun clauses

A noun clause is a dependent clause that fills a nominal position: it functions as a noun. Many noun clauses are introduced by *that* or *whether,* some by *what, who, whoever, whatever, why, when,* and other interrogatives.

> *Subject: That anyone could raise his grades by studying* had never occurred to him. *Whether or not she should go* bothered her for days. *Why sociology has been growing so rapidly* is a complicated question. (A noun clause as subject often suggests a formal style.)
>
> *Object of a verb:* He knew [*that*] *it would never happen again.* (When the noun clause is object of the verb, introductory *that* is often omitted in general English.)
>
> *Complement:* His favorites were *whoever flattered him.*
>
> *Object of a preposition:* The cost depends on *where we spend the night.*
>
> *Appositive:* The doctrine *that we must avoid entangling alliances* was first stated by Washington.

See **Relative clauses.**

Nouns

Nouns are best identified by their forms and by the positions they fill in sentences.

1. Forms. Nouns may be inflected by number and case. Many have a plural ending in *-s* or *-es: hats, kindnesses, lecturers.* These and other forms of the plural are discussed in **Plurals of nouns.**

The ending of the possessive singular is written with an apostrophe and an *s: boy's, manufacturer's.* The possessive plural adds an apostrophe to the regular spelling *(boys', manufacturers')* and apostrophe-*s* to plurals not ending in *-s (men's, sheep's).* See **Possessive case.**

Some common distinctive endings make nouns from other parts of speech. They include *-er* (buyer), *-or* (actor), *-ness* (darkness), *-th* (warmth), *-tion* (inflation).

Some nouns in English have different forms for masculine and feminine: *actor-actress, confidant-confidante, executor-executrix.* See **gender, Sexist language.**

Nouns may be single words or compound words written solid, as two words, or hyphenated: *bathroom, bookcase, stickup, high school, go-getter.* See **Group words, Hyphen.**

2. Position and function. *Dog* and *day* are nouns by their forms: they occur with plural and possessive inflections (the dog's leash, two days' work). But since they can occur in positions normally filled by adjectives (*dog* days) and adverbs (He works *days*), they can be called, in context only, adjectivals and adverbials. Thus, if we call them nouns, we define them by formal characteristics; if adjectivals or adverbials, by syntactic function. If they also function as nouns syntactically, as in "The *dog* is man's best friend" or "*Day* will come eventually," then they are nouns in nominal function. See **Nominals.**

Here are examples of the chief uses of noun phrases and therefore of nouns:

Subject of a verb: A high wind from the east blew for three days.
Object of a verb: The wind damaged *the trees, which were loaded with ice.*
Object of a preposition: In *the night,* on *a frozen pond,* fishing is no sport for *a feeble spirit.*
Complement: He has become *president of the firm.*
Attributive: Her *stockbroker* partner had the grace of a *baby* hippo.
Apposition: The first settler, *Thomas Sanborn,* came in 1780.
Modifier of a verb: He arrived *two months ago.*

3. Classes of nouns. In the traditional grouping of nouns that follows, many nouns clearly fall into more than one group:
a. Proper nouns, names of particular people and places, written with capitals and usually without *the* or *a:* Anne, Dale A. Robb, London, Georgia, France, the Bay of Naples. All other nouns are called common.
b. Concrete nouns, names of things that can be perceived by the senses: *leaf, leaves, road, trousers.* Concrete nouns are opposed to abstract nouns—names of qualities, actions, types, ideals, and so on: *goodness, thievery, beauty, heroism.*
c. Mass nouns, names of masses that can be divided but not numbered as aggregates of separate units: *dirt, oxygen, wealth.* They're used with *the* (but not *a* or *an*) or without an article in the singular, and ordinarily they have no plural. Mass nouns are opposed to count nouns, which name what can be counted as separate units. Count nouns are used with both *a(n)* and *the* (but not without an article in the singular), and they have plurals: *a boy, the stick, horses.* Some words, especially abstract nouns, can be either mass or count nouns:

Wood is used in building.	Beauty is only skin-deep.
Mahogany is a valuable wood.	That boat is a beauty.

d. Collective nouns, names of groups of things regarded as units: *fleet, army, committee, trio.* See **Collective nouns.**

nowhere near

Though in general use, *nowhere near* has an informal tone: It was a good score but nowhere near as high as we'd hoped. Formal usage would substitute "not nearly as [*or* so] high as." *Nowheres near* is nonstandard.

Number

Number in English grammar is the singular and plural aspect of nouns and pronouns and verbs. Number in nouns is most important, since it controls the number of verbs and pronouns. In verbs, number is indicated only in the present tense (she sings, they sing) except in the pair *was-were*. See **Plurals of nouns, Reference of pronouns, Subjects.**

number

Number, a collective noun, takes a singular verb when the group as a group is meant and a plural verb when the individual units are the writer's concern. Ordinarily " a number of" takes the plural (A number of tickets have been sold), and "the number of" takes the singular (The number of tickets left unsold is discouraging).

Numbers

1. Figures. Figures are conventionally used in the following:
a. Dates (June 29, 1918, or 29 June 1918), except in formal social correspondence and some ceremonial contexts. See **Dates.**
b. Hours with A.M. or P.M.: 5 P.M. (*but* five o'clock).
c. Street addresses and highway numbers: 2841 Washington Avenue, Route 99.
d. Pages and other references: p. 761; Act III, scene iv, line 28 (III.iv.28) *or* act 3, scene 4, line 28 (3.4.28).
e. Exact sums of money: $4.98, 75¢.
f. Measures expressed in the conventional abbreviations: 15 cc, 3 km, 6″, 10 lbs., 32°F, 0°C.

The plural of a figure is formed by adding either -*s* or, more rarely, apostrophe-*s:* six 5s *or* six 5's; the 1970s *or* the 1970's. For the possessive, the apostrophe is not usual with figures. While "1987's stock market crash" is possible, most writers would prefer "the stock market crash of 1987."

Except in dates, street numbers, ZIP codes, telephone numbers, and a few other regular series, a comma is used to separate thousands, millions, etc., though it may be omitted in four-digit numbers: 2,736 (*or* 2736) bushels; $4,682,981.

2. Figures or words. Words are conventionally used for round numbers and indefinite numbers: ten million, hundreds, a dozen, a score. Words are also customary for numbers that begin sentences—"Nineteen-eighteen did not usher in the millennium'' (Henry Steele Commager, *Saturday Review*)—though the use of figures for a year in that position is not rare. Ordinal numbers like *first, second,* and *third* are normally written out, but larger ones are given in figures: the 142nd Airborne.

As a rule, newspapers use figures for numbers over ten, words for smaller numbers. Magazine and book styles (most general writing) ordinarily use figures only for numbers over one hundred that can't be written in two words: 199 *but* two hundred.

This passage illustrates a typical book style in handling numbers:

> Stage coaches reached new top speeds as their horses galloped over the improved roads. It had taken four and a half days to travel the 160 miles from London to Manchester in 1754; thirty-four years later the journey had been shortened to twenty-eight hours.—T. Walter Wallbank et al., *Civilization Past and Present*

Words and figures shouldn't be mixed in a series of numbers applying to the same units. If one of the numbers is conventionally written in figures, use figures for all: from 9 (*not* nine) to 125 days. But large numbers are increasingly written in a combination of figures and words: "$3 billion" can be grasped more quickly than "$3,000,000,000."

Numbers in two words between twenty-one and ninety-nine are hyphenated: forty-two, ninety-nine. In writing or typing, a hyphen (in print, a short, or en, dash) is used between figures to indicate a range: The prediction was based on 40–50 personal interviews and 200–300 phone calls. *To* should be used instead if the numbers are preceded by *from* or *between:* from 40 to 50 (*not* from 40–50).

3. Arabic and Roman numerals. Arabic numerals (1, 2, 146) are used in almost all places where numbers are not expressed in words. Roman numerals, either lowercase (i, ii, cxlvi) or capitals (I, II, CXLVI), are occasionally used to number units in a rather short series, as in outlines, chapters of books, and acts of plays, though less often now than formerly. Traditionally, lowercase Roman numerals are used for the preliminary pages in a book.

See **Fractions, Hyphen 4, Money.**

Objective case

The object forms of pronouns are said to be in the objective, or accusative, case. See **Accusative case.**

Objects

1. Direct objects. In the simplest kind of sentence, the direct object is a noun phrase that follows a transitive verb: Grammar puzzles *normal people;* Alice saw *the white rabbit;* The man was building *a fence.* Pronouns can replace noun phrases as objects: Jean met *them* earlier. In more complicated sentences a variety of elements can stand as direct objects: Not everybody enjoys *eating steak;* Somebody said *that porpoises are smart.* The objects don't always follow their verbs: *What she meant* I'll never know.

Traditionally, direct objects are said to name what is affected or effected by the actions of their verbs, though this description doesn't apply in a sentence like "He received an injury in the crash" or "They experienced many humiliations."

2. Indirect objects. Indirect objects name the person or thing to which something is given, said, or shown—the person or thing affected, indirectly, by the verbal action: He gave *the church* a memorial window; She showed *him* the snapshot. Like direct objects, indirect objects are noun phrases or their equivalents. They follow a special set of transitive verbs, precede direct objects, and are synonymous, in corresponding sentences, with prepositional phrases introduced by *to* or *for:* He gave a memorial window *to the church.*

3. Objects of prepositions. The noun phrase, or equivalent, that follows a preposition is its object. The preposition indicates what relationship it has to some other element in the sentence (here, "some other element in the sentence" is the object of *to,* and "the sentence" is the object of *in*). When a relative or interrogative pronoun is the object, it may precede the preposition: *What* are you talking *about?*

Obscenity

Though the vulgar terms for the sexual and excretory body parts and functions—the so-called four-letter words—are used much more freely in print, as well as in speech, than they were a generation ago, in most sentences they serve either as mere fillers or as expressions of generalized emotion—most often disgust. In either case, they don't belong in serious writing.

of, off of

The double prepositions *outside of* (just outside of Dallas), *inside of, off of* are in general use in writing, but many formal stylists reject the *of,* particularly with *off.* See **Prepositions and style 1, 2.**

# of course

Of course should be used sparingly and fairly. It should not be used as a substitute for evidence: Of course, we all know that the administration is corrupt.

Nor should it be used to suggest that, for the writer, the esoteric is the everyday. William F. Buckley, Jr., showed awareness of this restriction when he wrote the following:

> I can name my favorite restaurant as glibly as I can name my favorite wife, country, religion, and journal of opinion. It is (I should like to say "of course," but Paone's is not widely known) Nicola Paone.—*Saturday Review*

A sentence that could be an "of course" in *Scientific American* might need a lengthy explanation in *People*. Know your audience.

OK, O.K., okay

OK or *O.K.* or *okay* is informal and general English for "approval" (Harris gave my topic his OK), for "all right, correct" (When I checked the grounds at midnight, everything seemed to be OK), and for "endorse, approve" (If you'll OK my time sheet, I can get paid). The verb forms are *OK, OK'd, OK'ing* and *okay, okayed, okaying*.

one

1. The use of the impersonal *one,* referring to people in general or to an average or typical person, is formal in tone, especially if it's repeated: "the victories and defeats of one's children, the passing of elders, one's own and one's mate's" (Benjamin DeMott, *Atlantic*); One can't be too careful, can one? Because a series of *ones* can seem pretentious, many writers refer back to *one* with forms of *he:* "One can determine his own life" (J.A. Ward, *Journal of English*). But *his* in this context may be regarded as sexist. See **Sexist language.**

A shift from *one* to impersonal *they* should be avoided in writing, and while a shift from *one* to impersonal *you* isn't rare, it would be inappropriate in formal contexts and disapproved by many readers. The *you . . . . you* pattern is most common in general English, with good reason. See **they, you.**

2. *One* is often used to avoid repeating a noun in the second of two compound elements: Fred took the new copy, and I took the old one. The plural *ones* is also used this way, and logically enough, since *one* is not only a number but an indefinite pronoun: She had a yellow poncho and two red ones. But *one* as a noun substitute is often deadwood, taking emphasis away from the adjective that carries the real meaning: The plan was certainly [an] original [one].

one another

The reciprocal pronoun *one another* is used to refer to two as well as to more than two. See **each other, one another; Pronouns 3.**

one of those who

In formal English the clause following *one of those who* and similar locutions is usually plural because the relative pronoun refers to a plural antecedent:

> He is one of those people who believe in the perfectibility of man. (*Who* refers to *people*.)

> That's one of the books that make you change your ideas. (*That* refers to *books*.)

But because there's a strong tendency to regard *one* as the antecedent, a singular verb is common in print as well as in speech:

> Leslie Fiedler is one of those literary personalities who has the effect of polarizing his readers.—Peter Michelson, *New Republic*

> . . . one of those crucial questions that comes up again and again.—David Garnett, *American Scholar*

The more formal your context, the more necessary a plural verb.

on line, in line

On line means "in or into operation": After months of controversy, the power plant went on line. The attraction of technical jargon may be partly responsible for the increasing use of *on line* in quite a different sense—applied to people standing one behind the other, as in "waiting on line at the bus stop." It's also possible that the usage spread from the New York area, where *on line* has had a long history. In majority usage, people continue to stand *in* line, as they have always done.

only

According to the conventions of formal English, a single-word modifier should stand immediately before the element it modifies: I need only six more to have a full hundred. But usage often favors placing *only* before the verb: I only need six more to have a full hundred. The meaning is equally clear, and placing *only* with the verb is an established English idiom.

Even so, precise placement of *only* may be more satisfying to both writer and reader: "In this bicentennial year, let us only praise [*better:* let us praise only] famous men" (Gore Vidal, *New York Review of Books*). And as long as it isn't insisted on where it sound stilted and unnatural, it can at least prevent silly statements like "He only had a face that [*better:* He had a face that only] a mother could love."

In this respect *even, ever, nearly, just, exactly,* and other such limiting adverbs are similar to *only*. Misplaced, they skew the emphasis: I'm tolerant about such things, but his conduct even surprises me (*better:* surprises even me).

Onomatopoeia

By their pronunciations some words suggest particular sounds: *buzz, bang, clank, swish, splash, whir, pop, clatter*. Such imitative words are well established in the English vocabulary. Using sounds that match the sense of a passage in order to intensify its meaning is a stylistic device known as onomatopoeia. Ordinarily the writer works with existing words, sometimes adapting them in the process: "The wire is cut into bullet sizes, the slippery bullets slide from the chopping block on a gangway of grease, they are slithering, skiddering, and slippering into one another" (John Sack, *Esquire*). Onomatopoeia may also inspire outright imitation of sound, as in Tom Wolfe's description of stunting motorcycles: "thraaagggh." Striving for words like *thraaagggh* can produce embarrassing results unless the writer's tongue is visibly in his cheek. See **Alliteration, Assonance, Figurative language, Origin of words 2a.**

on to, onto

When *on* is an adverb and *to* a preposition in a separate phrase, they should be written as two words: The rest of us drove on to the city. The test is that *city* can't be the object of *on*. Used as a preposition, they're written solid: The team trotted onto the floor; The windows looked out onto the park. Both *floor* and *park* are objects of the compound *onto*.

on the part of

On the part of is often wordy for "by," "among," "for," and the like: The new law resulted in less wild driving on the part of (by) young people; There has been a growing awareness of political change on the part of (among) faculty members.

or

According to conventional rules, two subjects joined by the coordinating conjunction *or* take a singular verb if each is singular, a plural verb if both are plural or if the one nearer the verb is plural:

> Cod-liver oil or halibut oil is often prescribed.
>
> Cod-liver oil or cod-liver oil capsules are often prescribed.
>
> Cod-liver capsules or cod-liver oil is often prescribed.

Sometimes writers use a plural verb after singular subjects joined by *or*, suggesting "either and perhaps both" rather than "not both but one or the other": Is there evidence that smoking pot or drinking are affecting grades? The lack of agreement would be condemned by formal stylists. See **Correlative conjunctions.**

oral, verbal

Literally, *verbal* means "pertaining to words," and *oral* means "pertaining to the mouth." Insisting on this distinction, some writers maintain that *oral* is the one true opposite of *written*. But *verbal* is also used in the sense "unwritten" in all varieties of English: "Though written contracts were fairly often produced, a large proportion of the agreements seem to have been verbal" (Robert Sabatino Lopez, *Speculum*).

org Organization

Improve the organization of your essay by arranging the parts in an orderly sequence, or by making the movement clear through the use of appropriate signals and transitions, or both.

A poorly organized paper lacks direction—a logical movement from beginning to end. Or it lacks shape—proportions that do justice to the relative significance of ideas. Or it lacks unity, with irrelevant material diverting attention from the main thread of the discussion. The best way to pinpoint such structural weaknesses is to outline what you've written, reducing it to a skeleton of key statements.

Every paper should have a structure that can be defined and defended. The main cause of poor organization is failure to get clear in your own mind the natural or logical divisions of your subject and the right relation of the parts of your discourse. In writing a paper, arrange the parts in an order that makes sense in terms of your purpose, and as you develop each part, take into account its place and importance in the whole scheme. Then set about reorganizing and rewriting.

If rereading your paper and studying your outline leave you convinced that the organization is basically sound, examine the ways you've introduced topics and linked paragraph sequences. Even though you can justify the order of the parts of the paper, you may find you've neglected to give the reader guidance in seeing the relationships. If this is so, relatively simple repair work—improving connections and supplying transitions—should give the paper the direction, shape, and unity it *seems* to lack. Here the remedy is not drastic reworking of the entire structure but adding or rewriting sentences, particularly those at the structural joints that connect main blocks of material.

See **Coherence, Outline form, Paragraph indention, Transition, Unity.**

Originality

Composing papers in which a good deal of the content is original—that is, based on your own experience—is most useful in improving your writing and most enjoyable for you as a writer. Often, though, you will have to make use of secondary sources like books or magazines. Merely rewriting something you've read in a single source isn't a worthwhile exercise, but putting together ideas taken from several sources and expressing them in your own words calls for selecting, organizing, and rephrasing. And you should try to arrive at an original conclusion. Instead of simply restating what others have written, arrange your materials in a way that reflects your appraisal of them and your own thoughtful judgment of the topic. Original *thought* is a prime virtue in writing. See **Plagiarism.**

Originality in expression, in style, is a different matter. The English language has been used a long time, and absolutely new words and phrases are rare. Trying too hard for originality will produce strained or eccentric expression or "fine" writing, uncomfortable for writer and reader alike. Instead of trying to *sound* original, concentrate on telling the truth as you know it, and then, in revising what you've written, get rid of as many clichés as you can. The result should be straightforward, readable prose that carries some suggestion of your personality. When a style that deserves the label *original* appears, it's usually the by-product of an active and independent mind, not the result of a deliberate search for novelty. See **Figurative language, Figures of speech, "Fine" writing.**

Origin of words

1. The study of the sources of words. Every word has a history. Some words, like *chauffeur, mores, television, parapsychology,* are relatively new in English. Some, like *home, candle, go, kitchen,* have been in the language for centuries. Other have been around for some time but have acquired new meanings, like *satellite* (from a Latin word for "attendant," a term in astronomy which now probably means for most people either a dependent nation or a manmade object that orbits the earth, moon, or other celestial body). Etymology, the study of word origins, traces the changes of forms and combinations of word elements (as in *dis/service, wild/ness, bath/room, room/mate*) and follows the word or its component parts back to Old English, or to the foreign language from which it came into English, and so on to the earliest discoverable forms. Of some words, like *dude, stooge, wimp,* earlier forms are unknown. Of others, like *blizzard,* the sources are debated. But the efforts of generations of scholars have uncovered fairly full histories for most words. These are given briefly in most dictionaries and more fully in the *Oxford English Dictionary* and in special works.

Words have arrived and are still arriving in English through two general processes—the making of new words, by either creating or borrowing them, and the compounding or clipping of words and parts of words that are already in the language. Then the usefulness of this new stock of words is increased as the words undergo changes in form.

2. New words.
a. Creation of words. Coinage, or outright creation, is rare. Even *gas,* first used by Van Helmont, a seventeenth-century Belgian scientist, probably had the Greek *chaos* as well as a Dutch or Flemish word behind it. In the eighteenth

century Horace Walpole got the idea for *serendipity* from a fairy tale, *The Three Princes of Serendip. Kodak* is a coinage, as are a good many other trade names, some familiar from advertising. Informal words like *dud* and *burble* were also creations, good-sounding words that someone made up. Early in this century, F. Gelett Burgess invented *blurb,* defining it as "self-praise; to make a noise like a publisher." Imitative words like *buzz, honk, swish, whiz* are attempts to translate the sounds of nature into the sounds of language. Various exclamations of surprise, pain, scorn may have started as emotional noises— *ow, ouch, fie, phooey*—and later became regular words. Most made-up words don't stick, but new technological developments, like the computer industry, create their own vocabularies by all the different methods of word making. And since World War I, acronyms have become a significant source of new words. See **Acronyms.**

b. Borrowed words. English has always borrowed words freely, from Latin, German, and French and from other languages that English-speaking people have come in contact with. Words of quite un-English form have been assimilated: *khaki* (Hindi), *tycoon* (Japanese), *ski* (Norwegian), *hors d'oeuvres* (French), *borscht* (Russian). The various words for *porch,* itself Norman French but the oldest and most English-seeming of the group, come from various languages: *piazza* (Italian), *stoop* (Dutch), *veranda* (Hindi).

Borrowing is still going on. Some words come into formal English and remain formal words: *intelligentsia, bourgeois, chef d'oeuvre, objet d'art, Zeitgeist,* and many others with political, philosophical, scientific, or literary connotations. *Sphygmograph* and many other scientific words are recent compoundings of Latin and especially Greek words that are not otherwise in English usage, so they may be regarded as borrowings as well as compounds. Others come in as general words, especially when large numbers of people go abroad, as during a war *(camouflage, blitzkrieg)* or when a foreign invention becomes suddenly popular, as in *chauffeur, garage, chassis* in the automobile vocabulary. Some words brought by immigrants have stuck: *sauerkraut, pronto, pizza, kosher, goulash, zombie.*

Many borrowed words are dropped before they gain any general currency. The useful words are more or less adapted to English spelling and pronunciation and become thoroughly assimilated. See **Foreign words in English 2.**

3. Changes in form of words.

a. Word composition. Most new words are made by putting together two or more elements to create a different meaning or function. The elements may be a prefix placed before the root word *(mis-related),* or a suffix added *(foolishness),* or a combining element like *mono- (mono-syllable, mono-rail),* or two independent words built together *(book-case, basket-ball, gentle-man, spacewalk).* Group words like *high school, out of town, couch potato,* though not written as single words, could be included as a type of word composition. Advertisers hitch words together with hyphens to push their wares, as in *userfriendly.*

At first a compound has no more than the meaning to be expected from its elements: *unable* = *not able*. But often it will develop an independent sense that can hardly be guessed at from the meanings of its elements: *cupboard, loudspeaker, meltdown*.

b. Blends. Informal English has a number of words that show the liberties users of language have always taken with their words and always will take. Some of their experiments have been added to the main English vocabulary. One common type is blends, or portmanteau words, made by telescoping two words into one, often making a letter or syllable do double duty. *Squish* is probably a blend of *squirt* and *swish; electrocute,* of *electro-* and *execute; smog,* of *smoke* and *fog*. Blends are common in the names of many firms and products. Other examples include *motel, paratroops,* and a good many folksy efforts, like the old-fashioned *absogoshdarnlutely*.

c. Clipped words. One of the commonest types of word change is clipping—dropping one or more syllables to make a briefer form: *ad* from *advertisement, bus* from *omnibus, taxi* from *taxicab* (earlier, from *taximeter cabriolet*), *limo* from *limousine, quote* from *quotation, hifi* from *high fidelity* (a blend of clips), *stereo* from *stereophonic, auto, movie, plane, phone,* and so on. Shoptalk has many clips like *mike* for *microphone* or *micrometer*. The speech of any closely related group is full of clips; campus vocabulary shows a full line: *econ, home ec, phys ed, grad, alum, dorm, ad building, lab, exam, gym, prof, premed,* and dozens more.

d. Back formations. *Back formation* refers to creating a new word from an older word on the assumption that the latter was derived from the former. Thus *orate* was formed by treating *oration* as if its *-tion* was a suffix that had been added to *orate* in the first place. The new word usually serves as a different part of speech, like *baby-sit* from *babysitter, opt* from *option, peddle* from *peddler, typewrite* from *typewriter*. Some back formations are long established (*beg, diagnose, browse*); some are still avoided by conservative writers (*emote, enthuse, sculpt*); some are mostly for fun (*buttle, revolute*).

e. Common nouns from proper names. Some words have come into general use because of an association with a person or place: *boycott,* from the name of an Irish land agent, Captain Boycott, who was so treated; *macadam,* from the inventor of the road surface, John L. MacAdam; *sandwich,* from the Earl of Sandwich; *jersey,* from the island of Jersey; *pasteurize,* from Louis Pasteur, who developed the process. In many cases the original proper noun has been lost in the common noun: the *jean* in *blue jeans* originally referred to Genoa, the *-nim* of *denim* to the French city of Nîmes.

f. Playful formations. Blends and back formations are likely to have a playful note, and so do other word shifts that can't be classified. Some of these have been quite generally used: *doodad, wingding, jalopy*. Computer talk includes the interjections *quux* and *glork*.

other

In comparing things of the same class, add *other* to *any:* That movie scared me more than any *other* I've seen. See **any 1.**

outl Outline form

Revise the form of your outline to observe the conventions given below.

1. The title. The title of the paper should stand three spaces above the outline. The heads should carry their full meaning and not refer back to the title by pronouns. See **Titles 1.**

2. Thesis statement. An optional practice, but a good one, is to put a sentence stating the subject and scope of the whole paper between title and first main head. See **Thesis statement.**

3. Numbering systems. The most widely used numbering alternates letters and figures, as shown in the example in **7** below. Avoid complicated or confusing schemes of numbering.

4. Indention. Write the main heads flush with the left margin, and indent subheads two or three spaces from the left—enough to place them clearly in a different column.

5. Punctuation and capitalization. Don't use punctuation at the ends of lines in a topic outline, but in a sentence outline punctuate each sentence as you would in ordinary writing. Capitalize only the first word of a head and proper names; an outline head is not a title.

6. Heads.
a. Heads with meaning. Each head should be understandable by itself, especially if the outline is to be shown to someone for criticism or is to be submitted with the paper. The following would do as a scratch outline but wouldn't be satisfactory for other purposes:

My Vocation

    I. The work I am interested in
   II. Why I prefer this type of work
  III. What my responsibilities would be
  IV. The chances for success

b. Heads of equal importance. The main heads of an outline, those usually marked by Roman numerals, should show the main divisions of the material. Similarly, the immediate subdivisions of these heads, usually marked by capital letters, should designate logical divisions of each phase of the subject. The same principle applies to further divisions under any subhead.

Unequal headings	*Equal headings*
Books I Have Enjoyed	**Books I Have Enjoyed**
I. Adventure stories	I. Adventure stories
II. Historical novels	II. Historical novels
III. *Walden*	III. Science fiction
IV. Autobiographies	IV. Autobiographies
V. What I like most	V. Books on mysticism

c. Headings in parallel form. Equivalent heads and subheads are expressed in parallel grammatical form. In a sentence outline, use complete sentences throughout. In a topic outline, use phrase heads only. Make all heads of the same rank parallel; that is, make the heads in one series all nouns or all adjectives or all phrases, or whatever is most appropriate.

Heads not parallel	*Parallel heads*
Hitting a Forehand	**Hitting a Forehand**
I. The stance is fundamental	I. The stance
II. The grip	II. The grip
III. Watch the backswing	III. The backswing
IV. Meeting the ball	IV. The stroke
V. Follow through with care	V. The follow-through

7. Division of main points. Since a topic isn't "divided" unless there are at least two parts, a formal outline should have two or more subheads under any main head—or none at all. For every heading marked *A,* there should be at least a *B;* for every *1,* there should be a *2;* and so on.

Illogical single heads	*Logical subdivision*
The Tripartite System	**The Tripartite System**
I. The executive branch	I. The executive branch
A. President and Cabinet	A. President
	B. Cabinet
II. The legislative branch	II. The legislative branch
A. The House	A. The House of Representatives
B. The Senate	B. The Senate
1. Functions	1. Special functions
	2. Special privileges
III. The judicial branch	III. The judicial branch
A. The Supreme Court	A. The Supreme Court
	B. Lower courts

When a main point can't be divided, include any necessary detail in the head. For an organization in which the president has all the executive power, this heading would be satisfactory:

I. The executive branch (the president)

8. Introduction and conclusion. Ordinarily a paper has a beginning, a middle, and an ending (or an introduction, a body, and a conclusion), but don't use such labels in the outline. They're too general to reflect specific content, and the beginning and ending can rarely be represented by heads that are coordinate with the others. The first and last topics in an outline should be drawn from the main body of material for the paper.

Oxymoron

An oxymoron is a contradiction in terms used as a figure of speech—for example, "sweet bitterness," "loving hate," "mildly fatal," "making haste slowly," Aleksandr Solzhenitsyn's "literary illiterates." See **Figurative language.**

pair

Pairs is now the preferred plural of *pair,* though the older use of *pair* as plural—I lost three pair of mittens in one winter—is not wrong.

Paragraph indention

Indent here for a new paragraph. Or join this paragraph to the preceding one.

1. Indent for a new paragraph. A paragraph symbol in the margin of your paper means that you've failed to meet your readers' expectations. From their experience with good—that is, well-written and well-edited—magazines and books, they expect a paragraph to be a series of related statements, all bearing on the action being narrated, the scene being described, or the point being argued. And they expect to be forewarned by a paragraph break of any shift in focus or any turn in the course of reasoning. When they come to a stretch of writing that drifts or leaps from one topic to another, they're confused and distracted by the lack of unity and coherence.

Your instructor may have other reasons for recommending indention. A single sentence or a short sequence of sentences that makes a significant point may demand the emphasis that setting it apart will provide. Or a brief passage that marks a transition from one stage of the paper to another may be more helpful to the reader if it's detached from the end of a long paragraph to stand on its own. And sometimes, even if the connections in the material are close enough to justify a very long paragraph, you may be advised to break it up simply to give the reader a mental breathing spell.

Though it's not uncommon to find an eight-hundred-word paragraph in a scholarly work where a closely reasoned argument is addressed to interested readers, most expository writing receives nothing like such close attention. Indention helps break a discussion into digestible bites. In using indention this way, be sure to look for a natural subdivision within the long paragraph. Don't divide your subject at a point that will separate sentences that are logically bound together.

In general, the development of your topic should determine the length of your paragraphs. But take into account the kind of writing you're doing: narrative and descriptive paragraphs are likely to be shorter than paragraphs of criticism or analysis. And take into account the probable interest and attention span of your readers.

2. Join separate paragraphs. A succession of very short paragraphs, like a succession of very long ones, makes reading difficult. An unjustified paragraph break throws readers off the track so that they lose the connection between one idea and another. In revising, merge paragraphs in which the details or ideas are so closely related that they form a single stage in the development of the paper. In the process, make sure you provide whatever transitional words and phrases are needed to emphasize the continuity.

While a transitional paragraph that moves a paper from one phase of the topic to another may be very short—perhaps just one sentence—most paragraphs are from four to ten sentences long. If you have more than two or three paragraphs on a typed page of expository prose, be sure you can justify the breaks. A sequence of very short paragraphs may indicate that you're not developing your points adequately, not providing enough examples or details or comparisons. Or it may be that you've failed to recognize the close logical connections that pull your ideas together into larger units. In either case, short, choppy paragraphs suggest a collection of random observations rather than the unified development of a central idea.

See **Coherence, Transition.**

par Paragraphs

Revise or rewrite this unsatisfactory paragraph.

A paragraph is a group of related statements that a writer presents as a unit in the development of her subject. It strikes the eye as a unit because it's physically set off by indention or spacing. It will also strike the mind as a unit if the statements in it are closely related, representing a stage in the flow of the writer's thought.

Here are the most common faults in paragraphs, with suggested remedies:

1. Lack of development. Rewrite the paragraph, including details and illustrations that will lead the reader to understand and accept its central point. See **Details.**

2. Lack of unity. Rewrite, deleting, or perhaps shifting elsewhere, any material that doesn't contribute to the central idea, or core of meaning, of the paragraph. See **Unity 2.**

3. Lack of continuity. Review or rewrite so that the relation between the statements that make up the paragraph is clear. Occasionally you'll find you can improve continuity simply by altering the order of sentences. Sometimes you need to supply a transition between sentences. And sometimes you must rethink and rewrite. See **Coherence, Logical thinking, Transition.**

4. Lack of transition. If adequate transition isn't provided by the end of the preceding paragraph, begin the new one with a word, phrase, or sentence that links it firmly to the material that precedes it. See **Transition.**

5. Lack of a necessary topic sentence. Provide a topic sentence to strengthen the unity of the paragraph or to make clearer to the reader the direction your paper is taking. Not all paragraphs need topic sentences; but some do, either to present the generalization that subsequent details will support, or to pull details together into a generalization, or to introduce or sum up a stage of the discussion. See **Topic sentence.**

Parallelism

When two words or groups of words are alike grammatically and structurally, they are said to be parallel. Parallel constructions range from matching pairs of adjectives *(cold* and *wet)* to series of phrases or clauses—"Some metaphors are harmless, some are useful, some are beautiful, and some are stumbling blocks to clear thinking" (Thomas Middleton, *Saturday Review)*—to sequences of elaborately balanced sentences. The extent to which a writer should deliberately use parallelism depends on the rhetorical situation. The simple parallelism that contributes to clarity and efficiency is appropriate in all varieties of English. The exact, sustained, intricate parallelism of some balanced and periodic sentences is at home only in formal prose. See **Balanced sentence, Cumulative sentence, Parallelism and style, Periodic sentence, Rhetorical situation.**

paral Parallelism and style
//

Use parallel structures for elements that should logically be performing the same grammatical function.

Parallelism is one of the simplest, neatest, and most economical ways of achieving clarity. The sentence you've just read illustrates what it says. The three sentences that follow express the same idea without taking advantage of parallelism:

> Parallelism is one of the simplest ways of achieving clarity. Neatness is a major contribution made by parallelism. A sentence that uses parallel structures is more economical than one that doesn't.

> Parallelism is a mode of coordination. This means that as a general rule *and, but, nor,* and *yet* should match noun (or noun equivalent) to noun, adjective to adjective, infinitive to infinitive, dependent clause to dependent clause, and so on.

1. Put into the same grammatical forms and structures those words, phrases, and clauses that are alike in purpose and related in meaning (complementary or contrasting). "He was *brilliant* but *unstable*" (predicate adjectives modifying *he*) and "He was a *brilliant* but *unstable* person" (adjectives modifying *person*) both make use of parallelism. "He was *brilliant* but an *unstable* person" does not, though the purpose of *brilliant* and *unstable* remains the same: they're still describing the subject of the sentence.

Here are some sentences that use parallelism, followed in each case by a version that doesn't:

> *Parallel nouns:* Rational thought and rational behavior rarely govern either the *formation* or the *operation* of policy.—Barbara Tuchman, *Newsweek*

> *Not parallel (noun mismatched with dependent clause):* Rational thought and rational behavior rarely govern either the *formation* of policy or *how it operates.*

> *Parallel pairs of adjectives:* She satisfies our secret longing to believe that those who are *good and generous* are also *stylish and beautiful.*—A. Walton Litz, *Key Reporter*

> *Not parallel (paired adjectives mismatched with adjective and verb phrase):* She satisfies our secret longing to believe that those who are *good and generous* are also *beautiful and wear the latest styles.*

> *Parallel participles:* The stream negotiated the valley through unshaded fields, farmlands, and residential areas, all the while *slowing* in velocity and *increasing* in temperature and turbidity.—Paul A. Adler, *Natural History*

> *Not parallel (participle mismatched with independent clause):* The stream negotiated the valley through unshaded fields, farmlands, and residential areas, all the while *slowing* in velocity and *its temperature and turbidity were increasing.*

> *Parallel infinitives:* A great writer must feel deeply enough about great issues *to subdue* his talent and *to attempt* heroic feats.—C. W. Griffin, Jr., *Reporter*

> *Not parallel (infinitive mismatched with verbal phrase):* A great writer must feel deeply enough about great issues *to subdue* his talent and *in attempting heroic feats.*

Parallel dependent clauses: He explains *what he likes* and *what he doesn't like, where the book succeeds* and *where it fails.*—John Gardner, *On Becoming a Novelist*

Not parallel (dependent clause mismatched with noun): He explains *what he likes* and *his dislikes, where the book succeeds* and *its failures.*

Failure to use matching grammatical structures is particularly noticeable with the correlative conjunctions *both . . . and, either . . . or, neither . . . nor, not only . . . but (also).* A simple example is given in the first rewritten version above. Here's an equally common type:

The rule is *not only* ignored by those it is directed at *but* those who are supposed to enforce it ignore it too.

It seems clear that the writer wants to emphasize how thoroughly the rule is being ignored. In revising, a good first step would be to put the verb before *not only:* The rule is being ignored. Who's ignoring it? Those who . . . and those who . . . Then, with the correlative conjunctions added, the phrasing falls naturally into parallel form:

The rule is being ignored *not only by those who are supposed to* observe it *but also by those who are supposed to* enforce it.

2. Do *not* make structures parallel unless the relationship of the ideas or details they express justifies parallelism. If parallelism in structure doesn't represent the logic of what's being said, the reader will be misled. The three grammatical elements that end the next sentence are not parallel:

My year abroad taught me a lot about the way Venezuelans earn a living, spend their leisure time, and their attitudes about Americans.

Making the elements parallel (. . . and feel about Americans) would produce a smoother sentence, but as far as *meaning* goes, the change would be a mistake. In the context, the way Venezuelans feel about Americans isn't logically related to the way they earn their living or spend their leisure time. The best revision, then, would be to retain the first two elements in the series but turn the third into a separate sentence. How the new sentence would be phrased would depend on whether the writer was making a casual addition or introducing a major topic:

My year abroad taught me a lot about the way Venezuelans earn a living and spend their leisure time. It also taught me a lot about their attitudes toward Americans. *Or:* More important, I learned a lot about . . .

See **Parallelism, Phrases and style, Shifted constructions.** For further examples of the effective use of parallelism, see **Periodic sentence.**

Paraphrase

A paraphrase is a restatement of another writer's ideas in different words. You paraphrase when you digest the contents of a passage in a book or article in your own words, as in taking notes. Difficulties may arise in the next step— using the paraphrase in a paper of your own. First, you must acknowledge the source of the material. Second, if you include phrases or sentences from the original, you must put them in quotation marks and identify them as the original author's, either in the body of your paper or in a footnote or endnote. But quoting is not paraphrasing. Nor is a paraphrase a précis. While a précis condenses the original, a paraphrase may be just as long or even longer. See **Plagiarism, Précis, Research papers.**

Parentheses

Parentheses may be used to enclose a full, independent sentence that interrupts, or breaks into, the main structure of the paragraph in which it appears. Like commas and dashes, they are also used within a sentence to enclose words and word groups that break away from the main structure. Of the three types of enclosing marks, parentheses indicate the most separation; but the choice of marks may be simply a matter of taste. Of the examples that follow, only the third requires parentheses.

1. For additions. Within sentences, parentheses are used to enclose words and word groups that add facts to a statement without essentially altering its meaning. The additions may be illustrations (as in this book), definitions, or information thrown in for good measure:

> The few verb endings that English now retains *(-s, -ed, -ing)* are being still further reduced in ordinary speech.

> Gresham's Law (that bad money drives out good) applies as usual in this case.

> His concerts were well received in most cities (Cleveland was an exception), but he was still dissatisfied.

When overused, parentheses create clutter. If you've fallen into the habit of using them regularly, look closely at the material they enclose. Unimportant material might better be omitted. Material worth including might better be worked into the structure of the sentence in which it appears or made into a separate sentence.

2. With other marks. When a complete sentence in parentheses comes within a sentence, it needs neither a capital letter nor a period: "Although pasta is not a high calorie food (the tested brands averaged about 350 calories per 10-ounce serving) it has an undeserved reputation for being fattening" *(Consumer Reports)*. Commas and other marks of punctuation in the main sentence always *follow* the closing parenthesis. (A sentence in parentheses, like this one, that does not stand within another sentence has the end punctuation before the closing parenthesis.)

3. To enclose numbers or letters in an enumeration. Parentheses are sometimes used to enclose letters or figures that mark items in an enumeration: The additions may be (1) illustrations, (2) definitions, or (3) information thrown in for good measure.

See **Brackets, Dash.**

Participles

Participles are derived from verbs but can't serve as independent predicates.

1. Forms. The present participle adds *-ing* to the base form of the verb: *asking, singing*. The past participle of a regular verb adds *-ed* to the base *(asked)*, and the perfect participle adds *having* to the past participle *(having asked)*. In "They tried," the verb *tried* is the complete predicate. In "They have tried," the past participle *tried* is part of the verb phrase that forms the predicate. In the passive, the *-ed* form is preceded by *being (being asked)* and *having been (having been asked)*. Many irregular verbs have special past-participle forms: *sung, having sung, being sung, having been sung*. See **Principal parts of verbs.**

2. Functions.
a. In verb phrases. Participles enter into many verb phrases: I am asking, I am being asked, I have been asked. Though referred to as present and past, participles indicate time only in relation to the context in which they're used. See **Tenses of verbs.**
b. As modifiers. When not part of verb phrases, participles function like adjectives in that they modify nouns (a *coming* event, a *frightened* cat), like verbs in that they may take an object (*Following these clues,* he soon found her). Like both, they may be modified by adverbs *(rolling crazily)*.

Compare **Gerunds.**

Participles and style

When a participle functions as an adjectival, it should refer clearly to some particular noun or pronoun: Having opened the envelope, she began reading the letter *(having opened* modifies *she)*. A modifying participle is said to dangle when it seems to refer to a word the writer doesn't mean it to refer to: Kissing his wife good-bye, the door slammed behind him (syntactically, *kissing* modifies *the door)*. Errors like this occur when the subject of the participle and the subject of the main clause aren't the same. In "[*He* was] kissing his wife good-bye, *the door* slammed behind him," *he* and *the door* aren't the same. Compare a correct modifier: [*He* was] kissing his wife good-bye, *he* let the door slam behind him. *He* in "[He was] kissing" and *he* in "he let the door slam" are the same. The first subject can be deleted. See **Dangling modifiers.**
    The participle as adjective shouldn't be confused with the participle in an

absolute phrase—a phrase that's related to the whole sentence rather than to a particular word. Some of these phrases have become formulas: Judging from her looks, she's over fifty. See **Absolute phrases, Formulas.**

Don't use a participle where a subordinate clause would read more smoothly: The train was on time, necessitating our hurrying. *Better:* . . . so we had to hurry. In revising, get rid of clumsy participial phrases like this one: The plane arriving then, we boarded it. *Better:* Then the plane arrived, and we boarded it.

For *very* with participles, see **very 2.**

Parts of speech

Parts of speech are the categories linguists set up in order to describe structures in sentences and finally sentences themselves. They group words into categories and subcategories and then describe the various patterns in which these categories may occur and the ways in which they form larger structures. Linguists working with different grammatical theories create different categories based on different sets of definitions.

Traditional schoolroom grammarians, using a system much like that developed for describing classical languages, cite eight parts of speech: nouns, verbs, adjectives, adverbs, pronouns, prepositions, conjunctions, and interjections. Nouns and verbs are defined semantically, by meaning: a noun is the name of a person, place, or thing; verbs show action. The other parts of speech are defined functionally, by what they do: adjectives modify nouns; adverbs modify verbs, adjectives, and other adverbs; pronouns replace nouns; and prepositions relate a noun or pronoun to some other part of the sentence.

Structural linguists use purely formal definitions. Nouns, they say, are those words that can occur with plural and possessive endings or in positions after *the* and before a verb; verbs are those words that can occur with third-person singular -*s* endings, with past-tense inflections, with perfect inflections, and with progressive -*ing* endings; adjectives are those words that can occur with comparative or superlative endings, after *more* or *most*, and in the position "The (noun) is very ———"; adverbs are those words made up of an adjective and an -*ly* ending. Structural linguists put the residue of words such as *and, in, can, very, the, not, all, therefore, because, please,* and *hello* into a large category of "indeclinable" words, or function words, which is subdivided according to where these words occur in a sentence relative to the parts of speech already identified.

Transformational grammarians are much less concerned than structuralists with devising formal tests to classify parts of speech and more concerned with the most economical and general overall description. The labels for individual words are judged "correct" only if they're necessary to describe how the words behave in the context of a sentence. Transformational grammarians assume that one part of speech may derive from another, as the verb *discover* in a deep structure like "Tom *discovered* gold" becomes, in a surface structure, the noun *discovery,* "Tom's *discovery* of gold." For transformational grammarians, it's impossible to talk about parts of speech without explaining the whole grammar of a language and without distinguishing between deep and surface structures. See **Deep structure.**

With some help from structural and transformational grammars, traditional grammar serves the purposes of this text. For descriptions of the forms and functions of the parts of speech and their stylistic uses and misuses, see the following articles:

Adjectives	**Interjections**
Adjectives and style	**Linking verbs**
Adverbs	**Mass nouns**
Adverbs and style	**Modal auxiliaries**
Articles	**Nominalization**
Auxiliaries	**Nouns**
Collective nouns	**Participles**
Conjunctions	**Participles and style**
Conjunctions and style	**Phrasal verbs**
Conjunctive adverbs	**Plurals of nouns**
Coordinating conjunctions	**Possessive pronouns, possessive**
Correlative conjunctions	**adjectives**
Count nouns	**Prepositions**
Determiners	**Prepositions and style**
Gerunds	**Principal parts of verbs**
Grammar	**Pronouns**
Group words	**Proper adjectives**
Infinitives	**Qualifiers**
Infinitives and style	**Tenses of verbs**
Intensifiers	**Verbs**

Part-whole relationships

We often draw sound inferences based on the axioms "What is true of the whole is true of the part" and "What is true of the part is true of the whole." But many such inferences are unsound, or fallacious. Though Americans *as a whole* may enjoy the highest standard of living in the world, it does not follow that every American lives well. Nor does the malnutrition of the homeless mean that the American people as a whole are ill fed. See **Fallacies, Logical thinking, Stereotyping.**

pass Passive voice

Change the verb or verbs to active voice.

1. Avoiding the passive. Using the passive voice without good reason will tend to make your sentences awkward and wordy, place emphasis where it

doesn't belong, and at times leave your readers wondering who did what.
a. Don't use the passive to avoid using *I*.

> Between Laredo and Austin the driving was done by me.
>
> *Revision:* Between Laredo and Austin I drove. *Or:* . . . I did the driving.

b. Don't use the passive in an attempt to sound weighty or "scientific."

> The proposals that were made by the administration have been received negatively by the student body.
>
> *Revision:* Students disliked the administration's proposals.

c. Don't use the passive to hide or obscure the identity of the source of an action.

> My roommate and I were summoned by the dean because of the water bags that had been dropped from our windows.
>
> *Revision:* The dean summoned my roommate and me for dropping water bags from our windows.

d. Don't use the passive to vary the pattern just for the sake of varying the pattern.

> After finding our way through the woods, we reached the campsite. A half-dozen trips were made to bring in our supplies. By sunset we were more than ready for a hot meal.

The shift from active to passive isn't justified. Revising the second sentence (We had to make . . .) would keep the focus consistent and make the passage easier to read.

2. Appropriate uses of the passive. The passive voice is appropriately used in at least three rhetorical contexts.
a. Passives are appropriate when the agent of the action is either unknown, unimportant, or better left unidentified:

> Entry was not gained, police said, though an attempt had been made to pry open the door.

> Typical diner fare of that period was served on plates. Milkshakes were blended by machines with spindles, then poured into fountain glasses. . . . Place mats describing attractions in the local countryside were slipped under each table setting.—Joseph Monniger, *American Heritage*

> The grammars could not be dismissed as inferior or crude; they were simply different.—J. J. Lamberts, *A Short Introduction to English Usage*

b. Passives can be used (as in this sentence) when the subject under discussion would otherwise be the direct object: *A writer can use passives when . . .* Because passives are what is being discussed in this section, the noun phrase referring to them should be the subject–topic of most of the sentences.

c. Passives allow a writer to focus on the agent of an action by shifting the agent to the end of the sentence, where it will be stressed. This is especially desirable when the agent is represented by a fairly long and complicated noun phrase:

> *Active:* A team bigger and tougher than any you would find outside professional football defeated us.

> *Passive:* We were defeated by a team bigger and tougher than any you would find outside professional football.

Such a shift often makes it possible for the writer to build a tighter transition from one sentence to another. The element ending one sentence leads into the subject of the sentence that follows.

See **Voice.**

Past tense

For past tense, regular verbs add *-ed* to the base form: *ask, asked; answer, answered.* See **Principal parts of verbs, Tenses of verbs.**

people, persons

People has long been used as a collective noun referring to a group, but as recently as the early part of this century, it was regarded as nonstandard when used with numerical quantifiers as the plural of *person,* as in "Six people are here." Though formal usage still tends to prefer *persons* when the number is small and specific, *people* is now thoroughly established in all plural uses. *Person* and *persons* are frequently resorted to by writers who object to using *man* or *men,* alone or in combinations like *businessman* and *policeman,* to represent both sexes, but coinages like *businessperson, chairperson, anchorperson* have met strong resistance. To some, *person* in the singular, as in "Jan is a fine person," is pompous, like *human being* in the same context.

Not surprisingly, *people–persons* is a case of divided usage.

See **Sexist language.**

per

Per (Latin "through, by, among") is most appropriate in phrases that are still close to their Latin originals (per capita, per diem), in commercial expressions ($250 per week, $5.00 per yard), and in some technical phrases (revolutions per minute). In less specialized contexts, use *a* or *every:* a dime a dozen, a thousand words every day.

percent

In informal and general writing (but not in formal) *percent* is commonly used instead of *percentage* or even *proportion:* Only a small percent of the class was (*or* were) present. In such contexts the noun in the *of* phrase determines whether the verb is singular or plural. Here the verb could be either, since *class* is a collective noun.

Use figures with *percent:* 8 percent, *not* eight percent. And write out *percent* (97.6 percent) except in technical and statistical material where the percent sign (97.6%) is appropriate. In some publications, *percent* is printed as two words.

Perfect tense

Tenses formed with *have* and a past participle are traditionally called perfect tenses: present perfect, *has laughed;* past perfect, *had laughed;* future perfect, *will have laughed.* See **Tenses of verbs.**

Period

1. At the end of statements. A period is used to mark the end of every completed sentence except a question or an exclamation. Often, when not really inquiring or exclaiming, a writer will use a period at the end of a sentence in the form of a question or exclamation: Would you be so good as to return the book at your earliest convenience. What a day.

2. Miscellaneous conventional uses.
a. After abbreviations: Oct.; etc.; Mr. W. Fraser, Jr.
b. Between dollars and cents: $5.66; $0.66 (*but* 66 cents *or* 66¢)
c. Before decimals: .6, 3.14159, 44.6 percent

3. With quotation marks. When a quotation ends a sentence, place the period inside the quotation marks whether the quotation is a complete sentence or a single word:

> "The longer you put it off," he said, "the harder it's going to be." He glared at me as he said "harder."

Periodic sentence

A periodic sentence withholds its complete meaning until its last word (as in the first and third sentences below) or until its last clause (as in the second sentence):

> Not so long before he died, still receiving carloads of honors as he always had, and still receiving, as also he always had, from Right and Left in turn, fanatic attacks

on his social views, Mann remarked that he was a "great, unloved name."—John Thompson, *Harper's*

The point is that it is the struggle between the middle-aged and the unpliant young, between parents and children, between teachers and students, with elderly grandparents glooming hopelessly or fulminating angrily in the background at what they see as failures in *all* the generations younger than they, that appears to me to be the busiest proving ground for much of American English usage today.—Kenneth G. Wilson, *Van Winkle's Return*

Anything that ignites the human mind, anything that sets the collective intelligence to racing, anything that creates a new horizon for human hopes, anything that helps to enlarge the vocabulary of common heritage and common destiny—anything that does this is of incalculable value.—Norman Cousins, *Human Options*

A great many short and simple sentences have their base structures at the end and therefore fit the definition of a periodic sentence: "Not long ago a California company selling cassette recordings of books for commuters to listen to in their cars reported that among the most popular selections was none other than *Walden*" (David Shi, *North American Review*). Rhetoricians, however, reserve the term for sentences of some length and complexity. Because a periodic sentence keeps the reader in suspense, its resolution brings a feeling of satisfaction (or, in some cases, relief). A long periodic sentence always gives a passage a distinct touch of formality. It's necessarily a studied production, often using sustained parallelism, as in the examples above. Remaining airborne through clause and phrase as it does, it can achieve unusual dramatic emphasis when it finally returns to earth—or, if poorly done, it can end with the thud of anticlimax. Used sparingly in appropriate contexts, the periodic sentence can give a passage strength and individuality. But a succession of periodic sentences is tiring to read and creates a style too high-flown for everyday topics.

The prime example of the periodic sentence as cliché is the nominating speech. Here, a very long series of clauses beginning "a man who" or "a woman who" precedes the name of the nominee, which usually comes as a surprise to no one at all.

See **Parallelism.** Compare **Cumulative sentence.**

Person

Person as a grammatical term refers to both pronoun classification and verb inflection. Personal pronouns are in the first person, the one(s) speaking *(I, my, me, we, our, us);* second person, the one(s) spoken to *(you, your, yours);* third person, anyone or anything else *(he, his, him, she, her, hers, it, its, they, their, theirs, them).* Nouns are regarded as third person, as are most other pronouns.

Except in the verb *be (I am, you are, he is . . .),* English verbs indicate person only for the third singular of the present and perfect tenses: I see, you see, he *sees;* we see, you see, they see; I have seen, you have seen, he *has* seen; etc.

Personal pronouns

The personal pronouns are *I, we, you, he, she, it,* and *they.* See **Case, Person, Pronouns 1.**

Personification

Personification is a figure of speech in which an object or animal or quality or ideal is given some attributes of a human being. Here the mall of the Smithsonian Institution in Washington, D.C., is personified: "It was a hot summer, but the Mall carried on imperturbably, hosting event after event" (Edward Park, *Smithsonian*). See **Figurative language.**

persons

With numerical quantifiers, *persons* is preferred to *people* in formal usage as long as the number is not large: six persons. See **people, persons.**

phenomenon, phenomena

Phenomenon is the singular and *phenomena* (sometimes *phenomenons*) the plural: phenomena of the mind. Originally *phenomenon* meant "any observable event," but now it also means "something remarkable," and *phenomenal* is almost always used in that sense (Her speed is phenomenal). See **Hyperbole.**

Phrases

A phrase is a group of words that functions as a unit in a sentence, a clause, or another phrase. In these examples the word that determines the classification is in italics:

> **Noun phrase:** the *plumber*
> **Verb phrase:** have *gone* to the store
> **Adjective phrase:** *old* enough to be my father
> **Adverb phrase:** more *quickly* than usual
> **Prepositional phrase:** *in* the house
> **Participle or gerund phrase:** *walking* down the street
> **Infinitive phrase:** *to go* faster

Phrases may be further classified according to their function in a sentence. In the larger noun phrase "my friend the plumber," *the plumber* is an adjectival noun phrase. In "Walking down the street, she saw the accident," *walking down the street* is a participle phrase because its function is adjectival. In "Walking down the street is dangerous," *Walking down the street* is a gerund phrase because its function is nominal. *In the morning* is an adverbial prepositional phrase in "He left in the morning," an adjectival prepositional phrase in

"Breakfast in the morning," a nominal prepositional phrase in "In the morning will be soon enough."

Phrases and style

The style of a passage depends in part on how the writer combines and coordinates phrases:

His ideas
　　　　about the need
　　　　　　　　for intellectual renewal
　　　　　　　　　　and
　　　　　　　　spiritual reform
　　indicate the crisis
　　　　　　faced not only
　　　　　　　　　by those
　　　　　　　　　　　in places
　　　　　　　　　　　　　of power
　　　but
　　　　　　　by those
　　　　　　　　　in all walks
　　　　　　　　　　of life.

In the preceding sentence the phrases are balanced and coordinated to create a rhythm that carries the reader along smoothly to the end. In the next sentence the phrases are merely strung out one after the other, creating a heavy, bumping kind of movement that interferes with the reader's understanding of the writer's idea:

Our situation
　　　　　in this century
　　　　　　　of turmoil
　　　　　　　　　in the cities
　　can only be alleviated
　　　　　by improving the living conditions
　　　　　　　in ghettos
　　　　　　　　　in the central cities
　　which have decayed
　　　　　beyond the endurance
　　　　　　　of most people
　　　　　　to live
　　　　　　　in them.

When you pile phrase on phrase, make sure you also establish enough parallelism to give your sentence shape and smooth movement.

See **Absolute phrases, Gerunds, Infinitives, Participles, Prepositional phrases.** See also **Dangling modifiers, Parallelism.**

Plagiarism

Plagiarize is defined in *Webster's New Collegiate Dictionary* as "to steal and pass off (the ideas or words of another) as one's own." Students in college courses commit plagiarism for several different reasons, including panic, dishonesty, and ignorance of what plagiarism is. Sometimes students plagiarize when they drift unconsciously from paraphrasing into copying. Whatever the cause, the penalty—a failing mark on the paper and, if the cheating is chronic or flagrant, a failing mark in the course—is justified. Copying someone else's work is the most complete failure possible.

If you haven't learned how to handle material obtained from your reading, you need guidance in the fundamentals of scholarship. When you use published material, you have a twofold responsibility: first, to make the ideas part of your own thinking and, second, to give credit to the sources you've consulted. You are not *composing* when you're copying.

Digest the material you read so that you can present it in your own words (except for the brief passages you intend to quote directly). Be able to talk about what you've read before you write about it, and when you do write, name the sources of your ideas and facts, including ideas and facts you've paraphrased or summarized. This is not only courtesy but a sign of good workmanship, part of the ethics of writing. It's also part of the legality of writing, since the plagiarist who uses copyrighted material is liable to prosecution.

In an informal paper you can give credit informally, perhaps in a preliminary note: "This essay is based on . . . ." Or you can acknowledge a source in the body of the paper: "Professor Hudspeth said in a lecture . . . ." or "According to an editorial in . . . ." or "Here is Jackson's position as presented in last night's debate." Or you can give credit more formally in the endnotes or footnotes that are a customary part of a research paper.

Plagiarism is stealing. And besides being dishonest, it's unnecessary and unproductive. By giving credit where credit is due, you gain free and legitimate access to everything in print (though if what you write is to be printed, you must get permission to quote copyrighted material directly). And you learn to integrate the ideas of others with your own ideas. Finally, when you express what you have to say in your own words, you're not copying but composing. See **Documentation, Originality, Paraphrase, Research papers.**

plenty

As a qualifier (I was plenty worried; That car is plenty fast) *plenty* is chiefly informal. In formal and general styles such established adverbs as *very (much)* and *extremely* are preferred. An *of* is expected between *plenty* and a following noun: We had plenty of time (*not* plenty time).

plurality, majority

In an election a plurality is the largest number of votes received by any one candidate but less than a majority, which is more than half of all the votes cast. See **majority, plurality.**

Plurals of nouns

The plurals of the great majority of English nouns are made by adding -*s*. Some exceptions and special cases follow.

1. Special groups in -*s* or -*es*.
a. Some plurals can be pronounced only by adding a full syllable. The spelling is -*s* if the noun already ends in a silent -*e* (*edges, mazes*), otherwise -*es*: *birches, misses, dishes*.
b. With a few exceptions, common nouns ending in -*y* preceded by a consonant or *qu* change *y* to *i* and add -*es*: *beauties, bodies, soliloquies*. Words ending in -*y* preceded by a vowel add -*s*: *bays, boys, honeys*.
c. Nouns ending in -*o* preceded by a vowel make regular plurals with -*s*: *radios, studios*. Some words ending in -*o* preceded by a consonant always or nearly always take -*s*: *Filipinos, pianos, solos*. Some always or nearly always take -*es*: *echoes, potatoes, vetoes*. Some take either: *cargoes, cargos; dominoes, dominos*.
d. Some common nouns ending in -*f* or -*fe* (*calf, wife, half, knife, self*) use -*ves* (*calves, wives, halves, knives, selves*). Some have two plurals: *hoof, hoofs/hooves; scarf, scarfs/scarves*. But many nouns ending in -*f* and -*fe* form regular plurals with -*s*: *beliefs, fifes*.

2. Same form for both singular and plural. Nouns with the same form for singular and plural include names for some living creatures (*fowl, sheep*), words ending in -*ics* (*athletics, politics*), and some common measurements (*foot, pair, ton*—although these also have different plural forms).

3. Survivals of older forms. Survivals include plurals in -*en* (*brethren, children, oxen*) and plurals with changed vowels (*feet, geese, men, teeth, women*).

4. Foreign-language plurals. Many nouns taken into English from other languages keep their foreign plurals, at least for a time. Words chiefly in scientific or foreign use keep the foreign plural longer. *Antenna*, for example, has the plural *antennae* in biology, though it's *antennas* for TV and radio. Some common words have two plurals, the foreign (*appendices, media, nuclei*) and the English (*appendixes, mediums, nucleuses*).

5. Compound and group words. Most compound words and group words add -*s* to the end of the group, whether written as one word or as several: *high* *schools, cross-examinations, bookcases.* In a few the *-s* is added to the first element: *daughters-in-law* (and other *in-law* words), *passersby, courts-martial* (also *court-martials*).

6. Plurals of figures, words, letters. Usually the plural of a letter of the alphabet, of a word as a word, or of a figure is written with *-'s*: There are two *c*'s and two *m*'s in *accommodate*. But usage is divided: the plural of figures especially is often made with *-s*: three 2s.

See **Apostrophe 3; -ful, full; Possessive case 1a.**

plus

Though *plus* can be used as preposition, conjunctive adverb, adjective, and noun, writers would do well to restrict the term to arithmetical contexts.

P.M.

This abbreviation for *post meridiem,* "afternoon," should not be used as a noun. See A.M. and P.M.

Poetry

When verse is quoted, it should be lined off (as well as capitalized and punctuated) exactly as written. If possible, the quoted lines should be centered on the page, indented according to the scheme of the original. When so spaced, lines of verse quoted in a prose passage needn't be enclosed in quotation marks. Slashes, or virgules, are used to indicate line breaks when a short passage of poetry is run into the text: It was Frost who wrote, "But I have promises to keep/And miles to go before I sleep."

℘ Point of view

The shift in point of view in the passage marked is illogical or unjustified.

Your point of view in a paper is the position from which you view your subject. The position may be physical—your location in space and time—or psychological—your attitude toward your subject. The correction symbol *pv* indicates that, in the context, your change in point of view doesn't work.

1. Don't make unjustified shifts in physical point of view. When you write a description of an object, a place, a process, or an incident, readers see it through your eyes; and if they are to understand what they're looking *at,* they must have a clear idea of where they're looking *from.* In describing a building on campus, for example, you may begin with a head-on view and then lead your readers full circle, using such phrases as "looked at from the left," "from the rear," "on the Main Street side." Or you may begin with a view from far across campus or even a bird's-eye view—how the building would look if it was approached in a helicopter. The important thing is to keep readers oriented. A description that jumps from front steps to basement lab to clock tower to classrooms is bound to befuddle.

2. Don't make unmotivated shifts in attitude. If you set out to describe your dormitory, what you show your readers, what you show in greatest detail, and what you don't show at all will depend on your feelings about the place. Thus psychological point of view may determine physical point of view. And attitude may also lead to some role-playing. Suppose you hate your dorm and want to convince your readers that it deserves hating. Can you best accomplish your purpose by stating your attitude in the opening sentence? By being sarcastic throughout? Or by adopting an objective, analytical tone and counting on the examples and details you present to win readers to your side? The strategy is yours to chose; but once you've made your choice, stick to it. Like an erratic change in physical point of view, a switch in tone from sympathetic to contemptuous or from hostile to nostalgic will confuse and irritate your readers.

3. Don't make confusing changes in the distance between you and your readers. Point of view—physical or psychological or both—influences your choice of a *personal* mode of narration, description, or argument, in which your presence is clearly felt, or an *impersonal* mode, in which you don't seem to be present at all. The pronouns, if any, that you use to refer to yourself will signal to readers something about the relationship that you want to establish. Heavy reliance on the pronoun *I* (or *we*) may suggest casual intimacy or restricted but personal knowledge of the subject or real authority. Use of *you* may give the impression that you hope to engage your readers in a dialog. The third person ("If one should . . .") may lend objectivity or imply remoteness. A completely impersonal approach focuses on what's being discussed without calling attention to either the writer or the audience. Once you've established yourself in one relation to your readers, it's unwise to adopt another without good reason.

Many problems in word choice and syntax stem from failure to maintain a consistent point of view. For related grammatical problems, see **Passive voice, Reference of pronouns, Shifted constructions, Tense, you.** See also **Description, Details.**

politics

Politics in the usual sense is treated as a singular: In almost any group, politics *is* a controversial subject. But when used in the sense of "principles," "activities," or "tactics," it may be treated as a plural: Republican politics *were* offensive to the Federalists. Avoid treating the word both ways in the same passage.

position, job

Position is the formal word for *job*. See **job, position.**

Positive degree

The positive degree of adjectives and adverbs is the base, or root, form of the adjective *(poor, high, golden)* or adverb *(slow, slowly, bitterly)*. See **Comparison of adjectives and adverbs.**

Possessive adjectives

My, your, her, his, our, their are sometimes called possessive adjectives. See **Possessive pronouns, possessive adjectives.**

Possessive case

1. Signs of the possessive. The possessive, or genitive, function in English is shown in four ways:

a. Apostrophe-*s* or apostrophe alone. Singular nouns that don't end in the sound of *s* as in *chess* or *z* as in *breeze* and plural nouns that don't end in the letter *s* add apostrophe-*s: boy's, one's, England's, men's, children's, freshmen's.* After plural nouns ending in -*s*, only an apostrophe is used: *workers' incomes, dogs' teeth, coaches' rules.*

The general rule is to use an apostrophe-*s* after singular nouns ending in the *s* or *z* sound, but *The Chicago Manual of Style* follows tradition in calling for an apostrophe without *s* after *Jesus, Moses,* classical names ending in -*es (Socrates, Xerxes),* and words like *conscience* and *appearance* before *sake.* These exceptions take an apostrophe only.

To indicate joint possession, the apostrophe is added only to the second of two coordinate nouns: Martha and George's son. In "Mary's and Tom's bicycles," separate objects are possessed, and an apostrophe-*s* is needed for each noun.

b. The *of* possessive. Most possessives formed with an apostrophe or apostrophe-*s* can also be formed with an *of* phrase: the dancer's performance, the performance of the dancer. (Exceptions include such idioms as "a day's work," "an hour's time.") The choice between the two will usually depend on considerations of rhythm, idiom, and what fits best with neighboring phrases and clauses. Idiom calls for "the roof of the house," not "the house's roof." The *of* possessive is easier to work with when the noun in the possessive is modified by clauses or by other possessives. For example, both "the car's tires" and "the tires of the car" are acceptable, but if *car* is modified by the clause "that John wants to buy," the *of* possessive is clearer: the tires of the car that John wants to buy (*not* the car that John wants to buy's tires). If we want to indicate that the car is John's, the *of* possessive avoids a succession of apostrophes: the tires of John's car (*not* John's car's tires). *Of* may also be chosen to avoid a hissing of *s* or *z* sounds, as in "James's sister's seizures."

In some contexts there's a possible difference in meaning between the two forms. "Jane's picture" probably means a picture belonging to Jane, but it might mean a picture of Jane. "A picture of Jane" can only mean that Jane is represented in the picture. (The possessive doesn't always indicate possession. A picture of Jane may be owned by someone else. See **2** below.)

c. Double possessive. Using the *of* possessive and apostrophe-*s* together is an English idiom of long and respectable standing. It's especially common in locutions beginning with *this* and *that* and usually has an informal flavor: that boy of Helen's; friends of my father's; hobbies of Anne's. The double possessive is useful in avoiding the ambiguities mentioned above: the meaning of "Jane's picture" is made clear either as "that picture of Jane" or as "that picture of Jane's."

d. Possessive of personal pronouns. The personal and relative pronouns have possessive forms without an apostrophe: *my, your, his, her, its, our, their, whose*. It's as important not to put an apostrophe in these pronouns (and in the forms used without nouns: *ours, yours, theirs, hers*) as it is to put one in a noun in the possessive. See **its, it's; Pronouns 1; which 2.**

2. Uses of the possessive. The most common function of the possessive is to indicate possession: the professor's house, Al's dog, my daughter. It also indicates a number of other relationships:

> *Description:* a writer's responsibility, children's toys, suit of wool
>
> *Doer of an act:* the wind's force, the force of the wind; the author's second novel, the second novel of the author; with the dean's permission, with the permission of the dean; the doctor's arrival, the arrival of the doctor
>
> *Recipient of an act:* the police officer's murderer, the murderer of the police officer; the bill's defeat, the defeat of the bill

> See **Case, Gerunds 2.**

Possessive pronouns, possessive adjectives

The personal pronouns have the following possessive forms: *my, mine; your, yours; his; her, hers; our, ours; their, theirs*. The relative *who* has *whose*. *Its* is the only one that regularly tempts writers to use an apostrophe, through confusion with *it's*, the contraction for "it is."

My, your, her, his, our, their are used as adjectives (and sometimes called possessive adjectives) before a noun: my car. *Mine, yours, his, hers, its, ours, theirs* are used without a following noun: Ours is better than yours.

post hoc

Post hoc, ergo propter hoc ("after this, therefore because of this") is the logical fallacy of assuming that because *B* follows *A*, *A* caused *B*. A president may have no responsibility for an economic recession that occurs near the beginning of his administration. See **Cause and effect 2, Fallacies.**

precedence, precedents

Don't confuse these words. *Precedence* means "priority" or "preference": The graduating class was granted precedence when seats were assigned. Precedents are actions or decisions that can be used to justify similar moves: The graduating class established precedents for succeeding classes by setting up a scholarship fund and planting saplings along the mall.

Précis

A précis condenses the original piece of writing but retains its information, emphasis, and point of view. Rules for the formal précis prohibit direct quotation and call for a final version that's between one-third and one-fifth the length of the original. The writer condenses the original by substituting appositives, verbals, and series for more expansive statement and by eliminating nonessential material. To produce a précis that accomplishes all this and is also well written calls for practice, hard work, and considerable skill. See **Paraphrase.**

Predicate

Almost all English sentences divide into two main elements—subject and predicate. The predicate of a clause or sentence is the verb with its modifiers and objects or complements. The predicate may be a single verb (The bell *tolled*), a transitive verb and its object (She *landed the big fish*), or a linking verb and its complement (The oldest member of the family *is usually the first to go*). Two verbs depending on one subject form a compound predicate: The men *washed* and *wiped* the dishes in fifteen minutes.

p adj Predicate adjectives

Use an adjective here, because the verb is a linking verb.

The error of using an adverb instead of a predicate adjective (The stereo sounds loudly) results from the habit of putting adverbs after verbs. When the verb is a linking verb, adjectives, not adverbs, fill that position: The stereo sounds loud. In addition to *be*, about sixty verbs (*become, feel, turn, look, taste,* and so on) can perform this linking function. What follows the verb relates to or qualifies the subject, not the verb. Accordingly, an adjective—known as a predicate adjective or an adjective in the predicate position—is required, even though in its other functions the same verb is followed by an adverb. Compare "He felt *tired*" (adjective, relates to subject) and "He felt the edge of the knife *carefully*" (adverb, relates to the verb).

> *Adjective:* She acts *tired*.   *Adverb:* She acts *brilliantly*.
>
> *Adjective:* She looked *cold*.   *Adverb:* She looked at him *coldly*.

The test for a linking verb is that the appropriate form of *be* can replace it: "The story rings true" is structurally the same as "The story is true." When you've identified a verb as linking, use an adjective after it.

See **bad, badly; Linking verbs; look.** See also **Adjectives 1.**

Predicate nominative

Words and word groups that follow linking verbs and function as nouns are called predicate nominatives or complements. They include nouns, pronouns, phrases, and clauses. See **Linking verbs.**

predominant(ly)

Predominant is an adjective: a predominant sentiment, a sentiment predominant in the state. *Predominantly* is an adverb: The population is predominantly Muslim. But the verb is *predominate:* The Muslims predominate there. Not surprisingly, the spellings *predominate* and *predominately* for adjective and adverb have become common enough to be recognized by some dictionaries. To avoid criticism, stick with *predominant* and *predominantly.*

prefer

To is ordinarily used with *prefer:* I prefer Ireland to Spain; She preferred going by train to flying. But when an infinitive is used instead of a noun or gerund, *to* is impossible, and *than* or *rather than* is used: She preferred to take the train rather than to fly (*or* rather than a plane).

Prefix

A prefix is a letter or letters that can be placed before a word or root to change its meaning or function: *un*tie, *im*mobilize. A combining of prefixes produces *hemidemisemiquaver,* a sixty-fourth note in music. See **Origin of words 3a.** See also **Hyphen 4, Long variants.**

Prepositional phrases

A prepositional phrase consists of a preposition and its object: without hope, in a hurry, toward a better life. In sentences, prepositional phrases are used chiefly in the functions of adverbs (She arrived *at just the right time*) or adjectives (The man *in the black coat* was gone). See **Phrases.**

Prepositions

A preposition connects a noun phrase or a pronoun or a clause to some other part of the sentence. The whole phrase is usually adverbial or adjectival in function: He showed her *to her room;* He was old *in experience;* She was surprised *at what she saw;* the click *of flying wheels.* What follows a preposition is called its object. Prepositions may be word groups (in regard to, according to) as well as single words. And many words that serve as prepositions, such as *after, but, since,* also serve as adverbs and conjunctions. See **Objects 3, Prepositions and style.**

prep Prepositions and style

Change the preposition to one that is idiomatic or less conspicuous; or supply the missing preposition.

1. Use prepositions that are exact or idiomatic. A number of words are accompanied by particular prepositions: we say "contented *with* conditions," "*in* my estimation." Some words take on different meanings with different prepositions: agree *with* (a person), agree *to* (a suggestion), agree *in* (principle).

Choosing the right preposition presents no problem with words you use often, because you learn the words by hearing or seeing them in their typical combinations. When you learn new words, learn how they're used as well as what they mean: *acquiesce in* (acquiesce in a decision) rather than just *acquiesce.* Dictionaries give the preposition appropriate to some words. This book has entries for a few idioms in which prepositions occasionally cause trouble: **ability to; agree to, agree with; all of; compare, contrast; different from, different than.** See also **Idiom.**

When coordinating two words that take different prepositions, include both prepositions: The first lesson he learned was obedience *to* and respect *for* his elders (*not* obedience and respect for his elders). When both words take the same preposition, there's no need to use it twice: The box office refused to make any allowance [ ] or refund *for* tickets purchased from an agent.

2. Avoid wordy group prepositions. English has a number of group prepositions that take up too much space for the work they do. A reference to "recent complaints on the part of dissatisfied students" is weighed down by *on the part of* where *by* would do the job. Sometimes we carry over from speech the habit of using double prepositions: *(in) back of, off (of).* And there is a tendency to tack unnecessary prepositions onto verbs. *Beat* grew to *beat up* and then to *beat up on. Up* was added to *free* and to *listen, out* to *punch.* In each case the goal seemed to be greater emphasis, but such add-ons should be omitted in writing of any formality. See **as to; of, off of; on to, onto; prior to.**

3. Don't omit prepositions indiscriminately. Prepositions aren't dropped in formal writing. Some can be dropped in general writing as well as in informal: ". . . one of the best pieces written about the United States [in] this century" (Arthur Schlesinger, *New Republic*). But expressions like "a couple [of] days later," "a different type [of] girl," and "outside [of] his interest in boxing" remain decidedly informal. The dropping of prepositions in airline lingo—depart [from], arrive [at]—should be left at the terminal.

4. When a preposition falls naturally at the end of a sentence, leave it there. There's an old "rule" that a preposition shouldn't end a sentence (She is the one I did it for). But postponing the preposition has long been a characteristic English idiom, and rhythm often demands placing the preposition at the end: "What Fay Weldon seems to have found out in the process of mastering the art of the English novel is that storytelling is power—a kind of power that she might be all too willing to be corrupted by, and that her readers are far too eager to submit to" (Terrence Rafferty, *New Yorker*). Putting the preposition at the end comes so naturally that if you place it earlier in the sentence, you may end up having it in both places: He brightened the life of everyone with whom he came in contact [with].

Present tense

The base form of a verb *(ask, answer, buy, say)* is its present tense. In most verbs *-s* is added in the third-person singular. See **Tenses of verbs.**

pretty

Pretty for *rather* or *fairly* gives a sentence an informal tone: "[Archibald Cox] sets pretty straight . . . the real impact of the great case of Marbury v. Madison" (Charles L. Black, Jr., *New York Times Book Review*). The usage is standard.

preventive, preventative

Unless you're being paid by the letter, *preventive* is preferable.

Prewriting

Prewriting is the stage of thinking, worrying, and doodling that you go through before you set down even the rough form of a paper. The process is related to what's known in classical rhetoric as invention and discovery—finding out what you have to say about your subject.

People prewrite in different ways. Some scribble, apparently aimlessly, trying to find their way to a lead-in idea. Some think through the subject again and again, doing their prewriting entirely in their heads. And some look into promising sources, jot down facts, thoughts, and impressions, and try various ways of ordering their ideas to discover the points that need most emphasis.

Whether or not your exploration of your subject involves hunting up information and finding out what others have said, the end product of prewriting is not a collection of notes. It's a sure sense that you've made the subject your own. Making the subject your own means that whatever you write will be motivated by personal concern. Writing that lacks personal concern—intellectual commitment or emotional commitment or both—is very likely to be dull writing, trite and mechanical in both thought and expression. Writing that grows out of personal concern is just as likely to have some drive and freshness. It's the kind of writing that quickly wins and holds the attention of a reader.

Though there are no rules that will guarantee successful prewriting, or pump priming, one practice that helps many writers is keeping a daily journal—entering sentences and paragraphs that capture thoughts and opinions, making notes of images that match half-formed ideas. Because his journal proved so rich a source for his public writing, one author called it his savings bank. Certainly keeping a journal is worth a try. You may find that, like other prewriting techniques, it will give you a running start on writing your papers.

principal, principle

Principal is either a noun or it is an adjective, spelled like other adjectives ending in *-al: historical, political, musical. Principle* is a noun only.

Principal as a noun is probably an abbreviation of a phrase in which it was originally an adjective. The principal that draws interest was once the principal sum; the principal of a school, the principal teacher; the principal in a legal action, the principal party; the principals in a play, the principal actors. These are the only common uses of *principal* as a noun.

The noun meaning "a general truth or rule of conduct" is *principle:* the principles of science, a matter of principle.

pp Principal parts of verbs

Change the verb form to one in standard use.

1. The principal parts of a verb. The principal parts are the base form or infinitive *(ask),* the past-tense form *(asked),* the past participle *(asked).* Most English verbs are "regular"—that is, their past tense and past participle are formed by adding *-ed* to the base form. A number of the most common change a vowel *(sing, sang, sung)* in making their past-tense and past-participle forms. Some *(let, cost)* remain unchanged. Some *(bend, make)* change the final consonant. And some have less common irregularities (past forms of *teach: taught, taught*).

The trend has been toward regularity. A few verbs *(broadcast, shine, speed)* have acquired regular forms in addition to their old ones: *broadcasted, shined, speeded.* A few others *(dive, fit, prove, sew)* have reversed the trend, acquiring irregularities that are either new or revivals of archaic forms: *dove, fit* (past tense), *proven, sewn.* For some verbs *(dream, plead, show, strive, thrive)* variant pairs have long existed side by side: *dreamed, dreamt; pleaded, pled; showed, shown* (as past participle); *strived, strove; thrived, throve.*

The following list includes a number of verbs with irregular past-tense and part-participle forms. The forms labeled *NS* (nonstandard) and *D* (dialect) would not ordinarily be written. When you're in doubt, consult a recent dictionary for verbs not listed here. Usage is by no means uniform, even among speakers and writers of standard English, and neither this list nor the dictionaries record all variations.

Infinitive	Past tense	Past participle
arise	arose	arisen
bear	bore	borne
bear	bore	born (given birth to)
begin	began (D: begun)	begun
bite	bit	bitten, bit
blow	blew (D: blowed)	blown (D: blowed)
break	broke	broken (NS: broke)
bring	brought (NS: brung)	brought (NS: brung)
catch	caught (chiefly D: catched)	caught (chiefly D: catched)
choose	chose	chosen
come	came (NS: come)	come
dig	dug	dug
dive	dived, dove	dived
do	did (NS: done)	done
drag	dragged (D: drug)	dragged (D: drug)
draw	drew (NS: drawed)	drawn
dream	dreamed, dreamt	dreamed, dreamt
drink	drank (D: drunk)	drunk
eat	ate (D: pronounced *et*)	eaten (D: pronounced *et*)
fall	fell	fallen
fly	flew	flown
forget	forgot	forgotten, forgot
freeze	froze (D: friz)	frozen (chiefly D: froze)
get	got	got, gotten
give	gave (NS: give)	given (NS: give)
go	went (D: goed)	gone (NS: went)
grow	grew (D: growed)	grown (D: growed)
hang	hung	hung
hang (execute)	hung, hanged	hung, hanged
hear	heard	heard
know	knew (D: knowed)	known (D: knowed)
lay	laid	laid
lead	led	led
lean	leaned	leaned
lend (loan)	lent	lent
lie (see **lay**)	lay	lain
lose	lost	lost
prove	proved	proved, proven
ride	rode (D: rid)	ridden (D: rid)
ring	rang, rung	rung
run	ran (NS: run)	run
see	saw (NS: seed)	seen (NS: seed, saw)
shake	shook (chiefly D: shaked)	shaken (chiefly D: shaked)
shine	shone, shined	shone, shined
show	showed	showed, shown

Infinitive	Past tense	Past participle
shrink	shrank, shrunk	shrunk
sing	sang, sung	sung
sink	sank, sunk	sunk, sunken
sit	sat (D: set)	sat (D: set)
slide	slid	slid
sneak	sneaked (chiefly D: snuck)	sneaked (chiefly D: snuck)
speak	spoke	spoken
spring	sprang, sprung	sprung
stand	stood	stood
steal	stole	stolen (chiefly D: stole)
swim	swam	swum
swing	swung	swung
take	took (D: taken)	taken (D: took)
tear	tore	torn
throw	threw (D: throwed)	thrown (D: throwed)
wear	wore	worn
write	wrote (D: writ)	written (D: wrote)

2. Black English verbs. Linguists investigating the patterns of some Black English dialects have found a structure that is predictable and therefore grammatical in sentences that have traditionally been called ungrammatical. An example: The teacher gone right now, but she be back soon. The lack of a *be* form in the first clause—"The teacher [is] gone"—and the apparently incorrect form of *be* in the second—"she [will] be back"—result from what grammarians call a deletion transformation. It regularly and predictably omits a form of *be* and other auxiliary verbs such as *will, would,* and *have* where standard English speakers contract their form of *be*. (An exception is *'m,* as in "I'm going.") This sequence represents the process:

The teacher is   gone right now, but she will be back soon.
The teacher's   gone right now, but she'll   be back soon.
The teacher[ ]   gone right now, but she [ ] be back soon.

Where speakers of standard English can't contract a form of *be*, speakers of some dialects of Black English can't omit it:

Standard English: I don't know who he is. *Not* I don't know who's.
Black English: I don't know who he be. *Not* I don't know who he.

See **born, borne; do; got, gotten; grammatical, ungrammatical 1; hanged, hung; lay, lie; proved, proven; set, sit.**

prior to

Prior to, a rather formal preposition, is most appropriate when it adds to the notion of "before" the notion of "in anticipation of": "He urged reform leaders to work prior to the convention so as to minimize the influence of Greeley's supporters'' (Matthew T. Downey, *Journal of American History*). In most contexts, particularly in general styles, *before* is the better choice.

professor

Write: Professor Moore; Prof. E. W. Moore; E. W. Moore, a professor of chemistry; *or* E. W. Moore, Professor of Chemistry.

Strictly speaking, the title *Professor* should be given only to assistant professors, associate professors, and full professors, and not to those who haven't achieved professorial rank. When the title follows the name in an *of* phrase, exact rank is usually indicated: Professor A. B. Plant, *but* A. B. Plant, Assistant Professor of English.

The informal *prof* (my math prof) is a clipped word, not an abbreviation, and is written without a period.

Pronouns

A pronoun is commonly defined as a word that replaces a noun or another word or group of words used as a noun. The word or phrase or clause that it substitutes for, as *it* substitutes for *a pronoun* in the sentence you're reading, is called its antecedent: *it* is said to refer to *a pronoun; a pronoun* is the antecedent of *it*. Not all pronouns have antecedents. What *I* and *you* refer to depends on the identity of the writer or speaker and the audience being addressed, not on the verbal context in which *I* and *you* appear.

Like nouns, pronouns can serve as subjects and objects (though not all pronouns can serve as both). Many have a possessive form, and a few have a separate plural form. Unlike nouns, pronouns are a small, closed class of words— that is, no new pronouns are being added to the language.

The traditional subclasses of pronouns are listed below.

1. Personal pronouns. The personal pronouns are those words that specifically indicate person (first, second, or third), number, and, in the third-person singular, gender.

		Nominative	*Possessive*	*Accusative*
1st-person	*singular*	I	my, mine	me
	plural	we	our, ours	us
2nd-person	*singular*	you	your, yours	you
	plural	you	your, yours	you
3rd-person	*singular*			
	masculine	he	his, his	him
	feminine	she	her, hers	her
	neuter	it	its, its	it
	genderless	one	one's, one's	one
	plural	they	their, theirs	them

Except for the relative pronoun *who (whose, whom)*, only the personal pronouns—and not all of them—have different forms for the three cases. Some of the most common grammatical mistakes occur because, unlike nouns, *I, we, she, they,* and *who* have different forms in subject and object position. See **between you and me; Case; it's me; who, whom.**

In some traditional grammars, personal pronouns in the possessive case are classified separately as possessive pronouns.

2. Reflexive pronouns. The reflexives are formed by adding *-self* or *-selves* to the possessive case of personal pronouns in the first and second persons *(myself, yourself, ourselves, yourselves)* and to the accusative case in the third person *(himself, herself, itself, themselves)*. They are used when an object or a subjective complement refers to the same thing or concept or event as the preceding noun or noun phrase:

Direct object	She hurt *herself.*
Object of preposition:	The road twisted back on *itself.*
Indirect object:	They made *themselves* caftans.
Subjective complement:	Ben isn't *himself* today.
Object of infinitive:	Jane wanted Betty to help *herself.*

As intensives, the reflexive forms are considered to be pronouns in apposition: The owner *himself* sold the car; The owner sold the car *himself;* I *myself* saw the crash. See **Apposition, appositives; myself.**

3. Reciprocal pronouns. The reciprocals *each other* and *one another* substitute in object position for a compound or plural subject when the action of the verb is directed by each member of the subject toward the other members: Tom and Bill looked at *each other;* The losers kidded *one another.* Like the personal pronouns, the reciprocals are freely used in the possessive: They borrowed *one another's* clothes.

4. Relative pronouns. *Who, which,* and *that* are relatives. (*Who* and *which* are also interrogatives.) Like the personal pronouns, *who* has different forms for the possessive *(whose)* and the accusative *(whom)*. *Which* and *that* are not inflected for case.

Relative pronouns introduce dependent clauses:

The student *who* submitted this paper has dropped out.
The paper *that* she submitted won an award.
His decision to leave school, *which* caused some excitement, was never explained.

When no specific referent for the pronoun is intended, the indefinite, or expanded, form of the relative is used: *whoever, whomever, whichever, whatever.* Unexpanded *what* is also an indefinite relative pronoun:

Whoever receives this will be pleased.
I will support *whomever* you nominate.
They will believe *whatever* he says.
They will believe *what* he says.

See **Relative clauses.**

5. Interrogative pronouns. The interrogatives *who, whose, whom, which,* and *what* are used to introduce direct and indirect questions: *What* happened? He asked me *what* happened.

6. Demonstrative pronouns. *This, that, these,* and *those* are considered adjectives when they modify nouns (*this* hat, *these* books), pronouns when they function as nouns: *This* will fix it; *Those* are too large; I prefer *these.* The demonstratives discriminate between referents close at hand *(this, these)* and referents that are more remote *(that, those).*

7. Indefinite pronouns. *Some, any, every,* and *no* compounded with *one (someone), thing (everything),* and *body (nobody),* and other words like *all, any, some, each,* and *either,* have traditionally been called indefinite pronouns. When used as subjects, the compounds take singular verbs, and pronouns referring to them are usually in the singular: Everyone is expected to do his part.
    Informally, *they* is also used for indefinite reference: They ought to do something about these roads. See **they.**

See **Antecedent, Determiners, gender, Reference of pronouns.**

Proofreading

Check the final, clean copy of your paper against the last draft to be sure that you have omitted nothing and introduced no errors in the copying. See **Careless mistakes, Caret, Manuscript form, Typewritten copy.**

Proper adjectives

Proper nouns that are used like adjectives are capitalized, and so are adjectives that are directly derived from proper names if they still refer to the place or person. After proper adjectives lose the reference to their origins, they become simple adjectives and are no longer capitalized: the Indian service, india ink; the Roman forum, roman type. See **Capital letters.**

proved, proven

Prove is a regular verb, forming a past tense and past participle with *-ed: proved. Proven* has been used for centuries as an alternative past participle of *prove* and is now established in all varieties of usage.

provided, providing

Both *provided* and *providing* are in standard use as connectives:

> You can't even argue, much, with the picture, providing you look at it only as a clever Western.—David R. Slavitt, *Yale Review*

> Anyone who can get into M.S.U. can get into Justin Morrill, provided he is willing to work.—Duncan Norton, *Fortune*

When *if* can be used in place of either form, it probably should be.

psychologese

Psychologese, a jargon made up of words with specialized meanings in psychology, is used enthusiastically if inexactly by many outsiders: *instinctual* for *instinctive, operant* for *operating, motorical* for *motor.* A great many other terms from psychology—*compulsive, empathy, motivational, neurotic, paranoid, relate, traumatic*—have entered the language, become vogue words, and lost much of their technical meaning.

public

Meaning "the people as a whole," *public* is a collective noun and can be treated as either singular or plural. A plural construction is more common: The public depend on TV newscasts for most of their information. But in the sense "a group of people with a common interest," *public* is more often singular: "There is a foreign policy public that is considerably smaller than the general public" (Carl N. Degler, *American Historical Review*).

pn Punctuation

Insert necessary punctuation. Or change your punctuation to conform to standard usage.

The basic purpose of punctuation is to mark off sentences and to link, separate, and set off elements within sentences in ways that will make the meaning clear to readers. A good rule to follow is to use all punctuation required by current convention and then to add whatever optional punctuation you may need to help your reader. Don't use unnecessary punctuation, which can make reading more difficult. And don't rely on punctuation to bail out badly constructed sentences. Instead, rewrite.

1. To end sentences. Use periods to end statements. Use question marks to end sentences that ask direct questions. Use exclamation marks to end sentences (or to follow words or phrases) that express strong emotion and demand special emphasis. See **Exclamation mark, Period, Question mark.**

2. To separate.
1. Use a comma before the conjunction to separate independent clauses joined by *and, but, for, or, nor, so, yet.* For exceptions, see **Comma 1.** You can also use a comma before the other coordinating conjunctions in compound sentences. To indicate a stronger separation, use a semicolon. See **Semicolon 1c.**
b. Use a comma after a long introductory phrase or dependent clause to separate it from the main clause. It's not incorrect to use a comma after all introductory phrases and clauses. Don't use a comma after introductory *but, and,* or other conjunction. See **Comma 2a.**
c. Use a comma before a nonrestrictive dependent clause or phrase that follows the main clause. Don't use a comma before a restrictive modifier that follows the main clause. See **Comma 2b.**
d. Use commas to separate the units in a series and to separate adjectives modifying the same noun. To separate the units in a series that already includes commas, use semicolons. See **Comma 5, Semicolon 2.**
e. Don't use a comma between subject and verb, between verb and object or complement, or, in most cases, between the verbs in a compound predicate. See **Comma 8.**

3. To set off.
a. Use paired commas to set off nonrestrictive modifiers.
b. Use paired commas, paired dashes, or parentheses to set off interrupting elements. Commas mark the least separation, parentheses the most. Setting off short interrupters is optional. See **Comma 4a.**

4. To link.
a. Use a semicolon to link independent clauses that are closely related in thought and expression. See **Semicolon 1.**
b. Use a colon (*not* a semicolon) to link a series, a quotation, or other material to the sentence element that introduces it. See **Colon 1.**
c. Use a dash to link to the end of a sentence a word, phrase, or clause you want to emphasize. See **Dash 1.**
d. Use a hyphen to link syllables and words. See **Hyphen.**

5. Other uses.
a. Use quotation marks to identify direct quotations. See **Quotation marks 2.**
b. Use ellipsis to indicate omission of words. See **Ellipsis.**
c. Use apostrophes to indicate possession and to indicate the omission of letters in contractions. See **Apostrophe 1, 2.**

Puns

A pun is a figure of speech in which a word is simultaneously used in two different senses (the nut that holds the wheel) or substituted for another word of similar sound but different meaning (effluent society). Deliberate punning may serve serious purposes as well as humorous ones. Unintentional puns, which may get laughs you don't want, should be weeded out in revising.

Qualifiers

Qualifiers are words used not to convey meaning in themselves but to qualify—usually by intensifying—the meaning of adjectives. They include the first words in the phrases "much older," "very quiet," "too young," "somewhat sick," "rather careless," and "quite intelligent" and adverbs of degree like *slightly*. Excessive use of qualifiers will weaken writing instead of strengthening it.

Question mark

The chief conventions governing the use of the question mark are these:

1. As an end stop. The principal use of the question mark is as the end stop of a direct question: What was the real reason?

A question mark is not used after an indirect question: He wanted to know what the real reason was.

As a rule, a request that's phrased as a question is not followed by a question mark: Will you kindly reply at once. See **Period 1.**

2. With quotation marks. When a sentence ends with a question mark and closing quotation marks, the question mark belongs outside the quotation marks if the sentence that encloses the quotation is the question (Did you really say, "I thought you were older than that"?), inside if the quotation is the question (He asked, "Did you really say that?"). If both are questions, only the inside question mark is used: Did she ask, "How many are coming?"

3. Within sentences. Usage is divided over a question built into a sentence: Should I quit school now[ ] I ask myself. A question mark after *now* would emphasize the question; a comma would make it less emphatic. If quotation marks were used around the question, a question mark would be appropriate: "Should I quit school now?" I ask myself. "I'm trying to decide whether I should quit school now" avoids the problem.

Questions

1. Direct and indirect questions. A direct question is a question as actually asked, not just reported. It begins with a capital and ends with a question mark: Who killed Cock Robin?

An indirect question isn't a question as actually asked but a question as reported in another sentence. An indirect question doesn't begin with a capital or end with a question mark, and it's not set off by quotation marks.

> *Direct:* He asked, "Do you really understand what you have read?"
> *Indirect:* He asked us *if we really understood what we had read.*
> *Indirect:* He always asks us *whether we understand what we have read.*

2. Leading questions. A leading question is one that's phrased so as to suggest the desired answer: "You'd like to go, wouldn't you?" "You don't want to go, do you?" (*Compare* "Do you want to go?") Leading questions may, in fact, be statements and, when written, can be followed by periods rather than question marks.

quot Quotation marks

" / " Make the quotation marks conform to conventional usage.

1. Methods of indicating quotations.
a. Double quotes, not single, are the usual marks in the United States.
b. For quotations within quotations, alternate double and single quotes. Use single quotes inside double quotes and so on: " 'Perry's instinct,' he says, 'soundly chose the point at which to halt the extension of the term "formula" ' " (Joseph Russo, *Yale Classical Studies*).
c. When a quotation is longer than one paragraph, use quotation marks at the beginning of each paragraph but at the end of the last paragraph only.
d. When you include a long quotation in a paper, make it a block quotation. Omit beginning and ending quotation marks and indent the entire quotation five spaces. To begin the quotation and to indicate the paragraphing of the original, you have two choices: follow the practice of indenting the first line of each paragraph or substitute for every indention an extra line between paragraphs, as in **Business letters 7.**

2. Principal uses of quotation marks.
a. Except when the quotation is indented, quotation marks are used to indicate all passages taken from another writer, whether a phrase or a page or more. Any change within the quotation should be indicated—omissions by ellipses, additions and corrections by brackets. The quoted matter may stand by itself or may be worked into your own sentence. Both methods are shown in this passage, the more formal first:

> Mathews acknowledged the power of usage in deciding linguistic correctness. "They that will fight custom with grammar are fools," he remarked, quoting Montaigne's aphorism; they are even more foolish "who triumphantly appeal against custom to the dictionary."—Edward Finegan, *Attitudes toward English Usage*

When brief passages of conversation are introduced not for their own sake but to illustrate a point, they are usually incorporated in the paragraph:

Her name was Erika Bayer, like the aspirin, she said. "I like it living here," she said. "I'm at the end of the line, and I don't have to worry about anybody except intruders." She agreed to pose in front of her lighthouse, and she wore a reluctant smile.—Thatcher Freund, *New England Monthly*

b. There are no half-quotes. A sentence is either an exact quotation and therefore in quotation marks, or else it is not an exact quotation and so is not quoted. Don't present as a direct quote material containing pronouns and verb tenses that are appropriate only to indirect statements: He boasted that he "could do twice as much work as I could." The boast must have been, "I can do twice as much work as you can." The choice is between direct and indirect quotation: He boasted, "I can do twice as much work as you can"; *or* He boasted that he could do twice as much work as I could. In the second alternative, the words *do twice as much work as* could be quoted.

3. Miscellaneous uses of quotation marks.
a. Quotation marks enclose titles of poems, articles, stories, and chapters of books, and, in most newspapers and many magazines, the titles of books. See **Titles 2a.**
b. Words that are used as words rather than for their meaning usually appear in italics in formal writing, in quotes in general writing. But usage is divided:

There is the ugly and almost universal use of "like" for "as."—Douglas Bush, *American Scholar*

The word *buff* is old in the English language.—Webb Garrison, *American Legion Magazine*

c. A word from a conspicuously different variety of English is sometimes put in quotation marks, but this only calls attention to it. If you decide that such a word suits your needs, use it without apology and without quotes:

He spurns aspirants not of his clique, thereby creating a tyranny of taste that soon will have every center of imaginative expression . . . under its cheesy [*not* "cheesy"] thrall.—Benjamin DeMott, *New American Review*

d. A word may be put in quotation marks to show that the writer is not accepting its conventional sense in the context:

In numerous cases it is impossible to maintain on any solid ground that one pronunciation is "better" than another, as, for example, that one pronunciation of *swamp* is better than the others given.—John S. Kenyon and Thomas A. Knott, *A Pronouncing Dictionary of American English*

But putting a word in quotation marks to signal sarcasm or ridicule (The "cute" Great Dane had eaten my sweater) is on a par with putting a question mark in parentheses to get a laugh. Irony should work without visual aids.
e. It is standard practice to omit quotation marks when directly quoted *yes* and

no (sometimes capitalized, sometimes not) are built into the sentence: ''Michael Dukakis says no; George Bush says yes'' (James J. Kilpatrick, syndicated columnist).

4. Quotation marks with other marks.
a. When a question mark or an exclamation mark ends a quotation, it's placed inside the quotes:

> ''Don't go near that wire!'' he shouted.
> Later he said, ''Aren't you wondering what would have happened?''

When a question mark or exclamation mark belongs to the construction that includes the quotation, it's placed after the quotes: What is an ordinary citizen to do when he hears the words, ''This is a stick-up''? See **Question mark 2.**
b. American practice is to put periods and commas within closing quotation marks, colons and semicolons after them.
c. *He said* and all its variations are normally set off by commas from the quotations they introduce:

> ''History,'' it is said, ''does not repeat itself. The historians repeat one another.''
> —Max Beerbohm, *Works*

But the quoted phrase may be so closely built into the sentence that no comma is wanted:

> Any moron can say ''I don't know who done it.''—Francis Christensen, *Notes toward a New Rhetoric*

raise, rear

Raise in the sense of bringing up a child is suitable in all varieties of usage. *Rear* is somewhat formal. See **bring up.**

reaction

Reaction has drifted from the scientific vocabulary and is now used for nearly any response, whether emotional or mental, general or specific. Try to find a more precise term or at least a different one—*response,* for instance.

real, really

Ordinarily, *real* is the adjective (a real difficulty, in real life), and *really* is the adverb (a really significant improvement; I really thought so). Both are overused as intensifiers; TV commercials and talk shows could barely exist without them, and "in a real sense" and "the real world" are among the most tiresome of current clichés. Adverbial *real,* as in sentences like "Write real soon" and "It's real pretty," is informal.

reason is because

In formal writing there's a strong preference for *reason is that,* on the grounds that *reason is because* is redundant. Even in general writing, *that* is much more common when there are no intervening words after *reason* (My only reason is that I have to work tonight) or when the intervening words aren't a clause with a subject of its own (The only reason usually given for such failures in sports is that there was inadequate concentration). But when many words or a clause with a separate subject intervenes, *reason . . . is because* often occurs in both formal and general prose:

> One reason why music can stand repetition so much more sturdily than correspondingly good prose is because music, of all the arts, is by its nature least suited to the psychology of information, and has remained closer to the psychology of form. —Kenneth Burke, *Psychology and Form*

> And the reason the press isn't a menace, Reston says, is because it has divested itself of so much of its power.—*Newsweek*

Even though *reason is because* has a long history in literature and is regularly used by educated speakers, keep in mind that to some readers it's a hobgoblin. (So is *reason why,* as used in the first example above, though this locution too is an established idiom.)

Reciprocal pronouns

Each other and *one another* are called reciprocal pronouns. See **each other, Pronouns 3.**

Redundancy

In writing, words and phrases that are repetitive or simply unnecessary are redundant. See **Repetition, Wordiness.**

 ## Reference of pronouns

Change the pronoun marked (or revise the sentence) so that the reference will be clear and the pronoun appropriate to the context.

In the sentence "Because my brother loves to ski, he spent Christmas vacation in Colorado," the pronoun *he* replaces the nominal *my brother. My brother* is called the antecedent of *he; he* refers to the same person as *my brother.* In "He got so frostbitten I scarcely recognized him,'' the pronoun *I* has a referent (the speaker) but doesn't have an antecedent. Both categories of pronouns—those that have antecedents and those that don't—create some problems for writers.

1. Clear reference. If the meaning of a pronoun is completed by reference to an antecedent, the reference should be unmistakable. The reader shouldn't have to figure it out. Here are situations in which reference lacks the precision that college writing demands.

a. When the pronoun seems to refer to a nearby noun that it can't sensibly refer to:

> The next year he had an attack of appendicitis. *It* burst before the doctor had a chance to operate.
>
> *Revision:* . . . His appendix burst . . . (*It* can't sensibly refer to *appendicitis*. Such slips in reference are common when the pronoun is in one sentence and the antecedent in another.)

b. When there's no noun nearby:

> He isn't married yet and doesn't plan on *it*.
>
> *Revision:* . . . and doesn't plan to marry.

c. When the pronoun refers to a noun used as a possessive or as an adjective:

> Bill was skipping stones across the swimming hole. One cut open a young girl's head *who* was swimming under water.
>
> *Revision:* . . . One cut open the head of a young girl who . . .
>
> Nancy longed for a chinchilla coat, though she wouldn't have dreamed of killing *one*.
>
> *Revision:* . . . of killing a chinchilla.

d. When pronouns are used in such a way that exactly what is referred to can't be readily determined:

> Businessmen without regard for anyone else have exploited the mass of workers at every point, not caring whether *they* were earning a decent living but only whether *they* were making big profits.
>
> *Revision:* . . . not caring whether they paid a decent wage but only whether they were making big profits. (The sentence needs complete rewriting, but this revision at least makes both *they*'s refer to the same antecedent.)

2. Broad reference. General English uses *which, that, this,* and sometimes *it* to refer not to a specific word or phrase but to the idea of a preceding clause. Formal English avoids broad reference.

General: Her friend was jealous of her clothes and money and had taken this way of showing *it*.

Formal: . . . and had taken this way of showing her feeling.

General: The recent price jumps, then, are not primarily the middleman's fault, *which* is why he is happy no longer to be fingered in the [Consumer Price] index. —William Safire, *New York Times Magazine*

Formal: . . . the middleman's fault, and this fact explains why he . . . (More formal: . . . the fault of the middleman, and this fact explains why he . . .)

3. Indefinite reference. Often you'll use the pronouns *one, you, we, he, they* in your papers to refer to your readers or to people in general instead of specifically mentioned individuals. Which of these pronouns to use is a matter of style, not of grammar. Once you've settled on one of them, use it consistently: When *you* have worked a day here, *you* have earned *your* money.

With *one,* a shift to *he* is standard: When *one* has worked a day here, *he* has earned *his* money. But *not:* When *one* has worked a day here, *you* have earned *your* money. See **one.**

Don't substitute indefinite *one, you, he, we* or *they* for a definite personal pronoun:

For *me* there is no fun in reading unless *you* can put *yourself* in the position of the characters and feel that *you* are really in the scene.

Revision: . . . unless I can put myself in the position of the characters and feel that I am . . .

As a common-gender pronoun meaning "he or she," *he* is traditional in formal English, *they* in informal. General usage is divided. *He* is more conventional, *they* often more practical. See **Agreement 2, Sexist language.**

4. Avoiding and misusing pronouns. Writers who are uncertain about the reference or agreement of pronouns sometimes try to avoid them by repeating nouns. The result is usually unidiomatic or clumsy: Arrest of the woman yesterday followed several days of observation of the woman's (her) activities by the agents.

Referent

The referent of a word is the person or thing or event or concept the word refers to. In a specific context, "Carolyn Robb" and "the love of my life," referring to the same person, would have the same referent.

Reflexive pronouns

Myself, yourself, himself, herself, itself, ourselves, yourselves, and *themselves* are reflexive pronouns. See **myself, Pronouns 2.**

relate

In the shoptalk of psychology the verb *relate* is a convenient term meaning to "have a realistic social or intimate relationship," as in "the patient's inability to relate." This sense of *relate* has passed into everyday usage, but the relationship is usually—and preferably—specified by a *to* phrase: They find it almost impossible to relate to adults. *Relate* became a vogue word in the 1960s. See **Jargon.**

Relative clauses

Relative clauses are introduced by relative pronouns *(that, which,* or *who)* or by relative adverbs *(where, when, why).* Those introduced by relative pronouns are often referred to as adjective clauses. A relative clause stands after the noun it modifies:

> The rain *that began in the morning* kept on all night.
> The coach was abused by the alumni *who two years before had cheered him.*
> The road to the left, *which looked almost impassable,* was ours.
> The first place *where they camped* turned out to be a swamp.

When the clause is restrictive, an introductory adverb may be omitted in informal-to-general styles:

> He will never forget the time *you tried to cheat him.*
>
> *More formal:* . . . the time *when you tried to cheat him.*

An introductory pronoun may also be omitted if it is not the subject of the clause:

> The man *I met that afternoon* became my closest friend.
>
> *More formal:* The man *whom I met* . . .

When relative clauses are introduced by indefinite relative pronouns *(who, what,* and the compounds with *-ever),* the clauses function as nouns or as adjectives:

> The stranger at the door wasn't *who we thought she was.*
> *What actually happened* was very different from *what the newspapers reported.*
> The stranger at the door was the woman *who had moved in downstairs.*

Several relative clauses in succession make for an awkward house-that-Jack-built sentence: People who buy houses *that* have been built in times *which* had conspicuous traits of architecture *which* have since been abandoned often find *that* they have to remodel their purchases completely. See **Subordination 1.**

See **Pronouns 4; Restrictive and nonrestrictive modifiers; that; which; who, whom.** Compare **Noun clauses.**

Relative pronouns

The relative pronouns are *who (whose, whom), which (of which, whose), that, what, whatever,* and *whoever (whomever):*

> Somebody *who* was sitting on the other side shouted, "Put 'em out!"
> The senator, *whose* term expires next year, is already worrying.
> I haven't read the same book *that* you have.

That refers to persons and things, *who* to persons. *Which* refers to animals or objects or situations and also to collective nouns, including those for groups of persons:

> The house *that* stands on the corner . . .
> The Board of Directors, *which* met on Saturday . . .
> The Board of Directors, *who* are all bankers . . .

See **Pronouns 4; Restrictive and nonrestrictive modifiers; that; which; who, whom.**

rep Repetition

Get rid of the ineffective repetition of word, meaning, sound, or sentence pattern.

Repeating words, meanings, sounds, or sentence patterns is often effective in writing, giving prose clarity and emphasis. This article reviews some kinds of repetition that call for revision.

1. Of words and phrases. You're bound to repeat nouns unnecessarily if you don't use pronouns:

> Ann accepted the boy's challenge and proceeded to teach the boy [him] a lesson. When the boy [he] stayed at the base line, Ann [she] ran the boy [him] from one side of the court to the other.

If you write hurriedly and don't take the time to read over what you've written, you're likely to end up with careless repetition:

> I'm having financial difficulties and need to *get* out of housing. So the hassle I *got* when I tried to *get* released from my dorm contract upset me.

When you use the same word in two different senses, the result may be worse:

> After I fell only a few feet, my left foot found footing.

> I would like to find a job with a concern that shows some concern for the environment.

In cases like these, the repetition is obvious enough to be caught and corrected with little trouble—either by omitting the unnecessary repetition or by substituting synonyms. But it does call for that little trouble.

Harder for writers to spot but equally conspicuous to readers is the pet word or phrase that pops up three or four times in the course of a paper. If it's a cliché or a vogue expression, as it's likely to be, it may bother some readers on its first appearance and become increasingly irritating thereafter. (*Really* as an intensifier is a prime example.) In going over a first draft, then, keep an eye out for expressions that recur. Some of the repeated words and phrases will be unavoidable, some desirable. But you may also spot some pets that you've repeated simply because they're pets. Abandon them.

2. Of meaning. In reviewing what you've written, watch for words and phrases that unnecessarily repeat what you've already said. For example, a gift is free and a fact true by definition, so drop the adjective from "free gift" and from "true fact." If the setting of many TV plays is Los Angeles, then Los Angeles must frequently be the setting of TV plays. Writing "In many TV plays the setting very often is Los Angeles" adds words but subtracts sense. So does "at 8 A.M. in the morning."

2. Of sounds. Jingles and rhyming words (hesitate to take the bait, a glance askance at the dance) are distracting in papers because they draw attention from sense to sound. So are noticeable repetitions of unstressed syllables, especially the *-ly* of adverbs and noun endings like *-tion*. Reading first drafts aloud is the best way to catch such unintentional repetition of sound as "Reliance on science has led to compliance." See **Adverbs and style, Alliteration, Assonance.**

4. Of sentence patterns. If you unintentionally use the same pattern in one sentence after another—beginning three sentences in a row with a dependent clause, for example, or writing three successive compound sentences, or using the same coordinating conjunction in a series of sentences for no rhetorical purpose—your readers are likely to begin nodding. Sometimes this sort of repetition sets up a rhythm even more distracting than the repetition of sound within sentences. Sometimes it simply begins to bore the readers; they feel that they're being led over the same route again and again. Deliberate varying of sentence patterns isn't often called for, but if you find yourself recycling a pattern, make an effort to get untracked.

A major exception to this rule is repetition in oratory. From Shakespeare's Mark Antony to the Reverend Martin Luther King, Jr., great speeches have frequently been marked by deliberate repetition. So if you write a speech, you may choose repetition as a device to stir your listeners. It will succeed only if you use it with skill and care.

See **Parallelism.**

Requests

Requests in the form of questions that are disguised orders (Will you please cooperate) normally end with a period rather than a question mark. See **Commands and requests, Question mark 1.**

Research papers

The research paper—sometimes called the reference paper, library paper, investigative paper, source paper, or term paper—is the culminating assignment in many college courses. Done well, it serves as a valuable introduction to scholarship: preparing a good paper requires resourcefulness in using the library, ingenuity in following up leads, judgment in analyzing data, and skill in organizing, writing, and documenting an essay of some length and complexity. Because a research project is an ambitious undertaking, often extending over several weeks, it should be planned carefully and worked at methodically.

1. Choosing a topic. The best topic is one that you know something about but want to learn much more about. The motivation to learn more gives point and direction to your research. And the motivation to learn more about *something in particular* will help keep you from taking on an impossibly broad topic. "Robert E. Lee and the Civil War" is too big. "Lee at Gettysburg" is manageable. But neither title tells what kind of reading, thinking, and writing you'll need to do. Decide early whether what you write is to be primarily a report or a thesis paper. A report assembles the material available on the subject, digging out the information and perhaps presenting it from a fresh perspective. A thesis paper shapes evidence into support for a hypothesis; it argues a point. The decision to make the paper primarily expository (a report) or primarily argumentative (a thesis paper) has some bearing on the sources you'll investigate and more on the use you'll make of what you find.

2. Preparing a working bibliography. In your initial canvassing of sources, move systematically from the card catalog to indexes of periodicals to appropriate reference books and special encyclopedias. For information about reference books in your field of interest, consult the latest edition of the *Guide to Reference Books*. For each source that looks promising, make out a bibliography card. Copy accurately on a $3'' \times 5''$ or $4'' \times 6''$ filing card the facts of publication as well as author and title, and note where the source is located in the library. (You're bound to find that some of the publications you want aren't available, and the frustration will strain your patience and your temper. But that's part of research.) Keep your working bibliography flexible. As you begin your reading, you'll discard items that looked promising but turned out to be dead ends, and you'll add items from the new sources that keep coming to your attention.

3. Taking notes on sources. In addition to making out bibliography cards that identify your sources, you'll need to take notes on what the sources have to say. Record these notes on 4″×6″ or 5″×8″ cards, which are easy to sort, discard, or rearrange. Restrict yourself to one note—fact, opinion, quotation, or summary—per card, with the author's name and the source written in the upper right corner and, in the upper left corner, an identifying word or phrase to indicate the specific subject the note is about. Before writing the note, set down the exact page on which the material was found.

As you make notes, be sure to distinguish clearly between an author's facts and his opinions, between direct quotation and summary, between what you're taking *from* the source (see **Paraphrase**) and what you're saying *about* the source. You'll find it helpful to keep a separate running log of notes to yourself—comments, questions, hunches that will remind you, when you begin to sift through and arrange your notes, of leads to be followed up, conflicting sources to be weighed, puzzles to be solved, and hypotheses to be tested.

4. Developing an outline. Early in the note-taking stage, sketch a tentative outline for your paper. Keep it fluid. Let it give direction to your thinking, but don't let it channel your ideas too early. Try to divide your material into logical blocks—from five to eight, perhaps—and then keep shifting these units around until you have them in the right order. Once you have the shape of the whole paper clear in your mind, you can write (and rewrite) a section at a time.

5. Writing drafts. Much of a research paper consists of a digest of sources that lead to, support, or elaborate on the researcher's findings or generalizations. In summarizing, interpreting, and analyzing your sources, it's important to represent them accurately and to do so in your own words. But you won't be able to free yourself of the original phrasing until you fully understand the ideas. If you merely tie together a succession of direct quotations from a source, you don't show that you've mastered the material. If you use phrases and clauses from a source without putting them in quotation marks, you leave yourself open to the charge of plagiarism (see **Plagiarism**).

As you write, keep a close check on the sources you're consulting and summarizing, so that you can give accurate and adequate credit. Be meticulous in reproducing direct quotations (see **Quotation marks 2b**). And when you quote, make sure that the passage bears directly on the point you're discussing, that you present it so that its relevance is immediately clear, and that you fit it smoothly into your text.

The style of a research paper should be comparatively formal and impersonal. This doesn't mean that it should be stilted or dull. Nor does it mean that you need to avoid using *I;* in some published research *I* appears regularly. It does mean that you should keep the focus on the subject and what you've managed to find out about it—not on your feelings about it. But since all good research papers reveal the writers' interest in their topics, communicating your own interest will be a natural consequence of engaging yourself fully in your subject.

6. Documenting the paper. Your readers' chief interest will be in the substance of your paper—what you've found out about your subject—and the clarity and force with which you present it. They'll also examine the documentation, the notes and the bibliography that record your journey of exploration. Check and recheck details of bibliographical form and note form for accuracy and consistency.

rest Restrictive and nonrestrictive modifiers

If the modifier marked is restrictive, don't separate it from the word it modifies by a comma. If it is nonrestrictive, set it off by a comma or by two commas.

"Lemmon, who isn't Jewish, plays Jews who aren't Jewish either" (Pauline Kael, *New Yorker*). The first *who* clause in the quoted sentence tells us something about Jack Lemmon, but it doesn't set him apart. It can be dropped from the sentence without destroying the meaning: Lemmon plays Jews who aren't Jewish. But the *who* clause modifying *Jews* is essential to Kael's point: the Jewishness of the characters Lemmon plays is superficial and trivial. Dropping that clause would leave us with "Lemmon plays Jews," which isn't what Kael is saying. Separating the second clause from the main clause with a comma would give us "Lemmon plays Jews, who aren't Jewish," which is nonsense. The first *who* clause is nonrestrictive. The second *who* clause is restrictive.

1. Restrictive modifiers. An adjective (or relative) clause or an adjective phrase is a restrictive modifier when the information it provides about something in the main clause is essential to the meaning the writer intends.

If you speak a sentence before you write it, or read it aloud after you've written it, you can usually tell whether a clause or phrase is restrictive:

> The girl *whose book I borrowed* has dropped the course.
> The books *stolen from the library* were found in that locker.

When the modifier is restrictive, you don't pause between the word modified and the clause or phrase that modifies it.

You can be quite sure a clause is restrictive if you can begin it with *that:* The year *that I dropped out* is one *that I'd be glad to forget.* And a clause is restrictive if you can omit the relative pronoun: The year [*that*] *I dropped out* is one [*that*] *I'd be glad to forget;* The people [*whom*] *we met;* The plan [*which*] *they came up with.*

2. Nonrestrictive modifiers. An adjective (or relative) clause or adjective phrase that can be dropped from a sentence without changing or blurring the meaning is nonrestrictive and should be set off by a comma or commas. The importance of the information the modifier provides is not the deciding factor. If you write, "The bullet *which came within an inch of my head* smashed my mother's favorite teacup," the content of your adjective clause would seem to be a lot more important than the destruction of the teacup. But unless you're using the clause to specify *this* bullet among a number of bullets—unless the information in the clause is essential to the meaning of *this* sentence—you should set it off with commas.

If *which* were used to launch only nonrestrictive clauses, as *that* is used to launch restrictive clauses, *which* and *that* clauses would cause few problems. But there are times when *which* seems a better choice for starting a restrictive clause: In "That was the bad news *which we had been given every reason to expect*," *which* avoids the repetition of *that* (see **that 1**). And some clauses are restrictive in one context, nonrestrictive in another. In a different context, the clause *whose book I borrowed,* used as an example of a restrictive clause in the preceding section, can be nonrestrictive: The girl, whose book I borrowed, left soon afterward with an older woman. So can the example of a restrictive phrase: The books, stolen from the library, later turned up in a secondhand store.

Your job, then, is to know what you mean. In the modifying clause or phrase, do you mean to say something that the sentence requires for its basic meaning, or do you mean to offer information which—no matter how important—can be omitted from that sentence without detracting from its central message? If the former, the modifier is restrictive—no commas. If the latter, the modifier is nonrestrictive—commas. Say the sentence out loud. Do you make a definite pause before the modifier? Then it's nonrestrictive—commas.

You may find the same advice useful in punctuating other modifiers. Traditionally, the restrictive/nonrestrictive distinction has applied to a dependent clause introduced by a relative pronoun and functioning as an adjective. Some grammarians extend the principle to all adjectival modifiers, to appositives (see **Apposition, appositives**), and to some adverbial modifiers, including final adverbial clauses (see **Comma 2b**).

rhetoric

To the ancient Greeks and Romans, rhetoric was the art of persuasion as applied to public speaking. With the invention of printing, the term was broadened to include written argument, and some modern theoreticians broaden it still further—to something like "the art of expression." What modern rhetorics have in common with classical ones is the idea of influencing an audience: the speaker or writer of rhetorical discourse aims to bring about a change in the attitudes, beliefs, habits, or actions of the audience.

Perhaps because skill in persuasion can serve bad purposes as well as good ones, in general usage *rhetoric* has acquired connotations of manipulation, deceit, trickery, flamboyant insincerity, or empty verbiage—"just words." Currently a writer must assume that most readers other than those who are studying, or have studied, the principles of rhetoric will regard *rhetoric* as a term of abuse.

The suggestion of empty verbiage is equally strong in most current uses of *rhetorical:* "It will be interesting to see how many men are prepared to give more than rhetorical support today to the sex from which they have, for centuries, demanded and accepted so much" (Adrienne Rich, *Chronicle of Higher Education*).

In this book the connotations of the term *rhetoric* are entirely favorable. To be skilled in rhetoric is to write well, and the good writer never writes "just words." The use of language for dishonest purposes is, of course, condemned.

Rhetorical questions

Rhetorical questions are really statements in the form of questions, since no direct answer is expected: "Who of us born before 1950 went to college burdened with the psycho-babble of the self which recurs in all three of these memoirs—'creating a supportive community' with 'people who feel comfortable with each other's needs'?" (Francine du Plessix Gray, *New York Review of Books*). As a stylistic device the rhetorical question has its dangers: the reader may reject the answer the writer intends—in the preceding example, "None of us."

Rhetorical situation

Whenever a writer asks anything of her readers—agreement, understanding, belief, action, even just a laugh—she's engaging in the art of persuasion, or rhetoric. As she writes a paper, every decision she makes, from the selection of material to the choice of a particular word, should be guided by her sense of the rhetorical situation. The chief elements in that situation are the writer, her subject, her purpose, and her audience. Each of these elements is influenced by the other three; each offers opportunities and imposes limits.

As you plan a paper, and especially as you revise it, asking yourself questions like the following will sharpen your sense of the rhetorical situation:

> What do I want to say about this subject?
>
> Do I have enough information and evidence now, or do I need to dig for more?
>
> Who are my readers? How much do they know about this subject, and what is their attitude toward it? What are their tastes, values, fears, hopes, prejudices?
>
> What common ground do we have? What assumptions do we share? What can I take for granted, and what do I have to explain or argue for?
>
> How can I make my readers see what I want them to see, think the way I want them to think, do what I want them to do? Should I start by declaring what my purpose is, or would they be more responsive if I invited them to take part in an inquiry with me, if I raised problems that we would try to solve together?

How can I make my readers identify with me, share my feelings about my subject? How can I make them understand and adopt my point of view?

Will this detail, this bit of evidence, have more weight than that one? If so, should it come first or last? How can I phrase this idea so that it will be both clear and compelling? How can I make this sentence say precisely what I mean?

Will *this* word, *this* image, *this* mark of punctuation work with *this* audience? Do I need to make my style simpler, more relaxed, or does my relationship with my readers call for increased distance, greater objectivity, a style that is altogether more formal?

Which side of my personality do I want to come through in this paper? How do I want my readers to see me?

As these questions suggest, you can assess the appropriateness of what you're saying and how you're saying it only in a specific rhetorical situation. The arguments you advance, the evidence you offer, the organization you adopt, the language you select—you should test all these as you revise your paper, for their fitness in communicating to the particular audience your thoughts and feelings about your subject.

right

The use of *right* in the senses "directly" and "immediately" before phrases of place and time (right across the street, right after the show) is avoided in most formal writing but is established in general usage. Phrases like *right here, right there, right now,* and *right then,* though similarly avoided in formal contexts, are commonplace in general ones. Idioms like *right away* and *right off* ("at once" or "now") and *right along* ("continuously" or "all the time") are slightly more informal.

rise

Rise is somewhat less formal than *arise,* more formal than *get up.* See **arise, rise, get up.**

rob

A person or place is robbed. What's taken in the robbery is stolen. *Rob* for *steal* (They're the ones who robbed the money) is an old usage considered nonstandard today. See **burglar, robber, thief.**

Roman numerals

Roman numerals may be either lowercase (iii, v, x) or capitals (III, V, X). See **Numbers 3.**

round, around

Round is a preposition and adverb in its own right, often interchangeable with the much more common *around:* ''an easy irony, good for a laugh the first two or three times round'' (Stanley Kaufmann, *New Republic*). It should not be written with an initial apostrophe ('round).

Around for ''approximately'' (around 1920; a cast of around forty) is now found in all varieties of usage.

The general adjectives *all-round* and *all-around* are overused, particularly with *athlete*.

Run-on sentence

The label *run-on sentence* is applied variously to a sentence in which two independent clauses are run together with no punctuation between, to a sentence in which two independent clauses are joined with only a comma between, and to a sentence in which a series of independent clauses are joined with coordinating conjunctions. Unless a particular meaning is specified, *run-on* is more confusing than useful. See **Comma splice, Fused sentence.**

said

As a modifier (the said person, the said idea) *said* is legalese. In general writing, *that* or *this* or just *the* is the right choice. See **legalese.**

saint

The abbreviation *St.* is commonly used in names of places (St. Albans, St. Louis) and often before the names of saints (St. Francis, St. Anthony of Padua). The plural of the abbreviation is *SS.* (SS. Peter and Paul). Occasionally the French feminine form *Sainte* is used (Sault Sainte Marie); the abbreviation is *Ste.* Spanish forms are common in the American West: San Diego, Santa Barbara. In writing a personal name beginning with *Saint* (Camille Saint-Saens) or *St.* (Louis St. Laurent), use the spelling the bearer uses or did use.

say

Say is the usual word for ''speaking'' and can also be used for what's written: In his journal, Gide says . . . . In dialog, repetition of ''he said,'' ''she said'' is almost always better than strained alternatives like *expostulated, muttered, babbled, hissed. State,* which implies a formal ''saying,'' is a poor substitute for *say,* whether in dialog or in ordinary text: ''To be able to state this of the new work of an American poet of 50 is, to state the least, unusual'' (Aram Saroyan, *New York Times Book Review*). *Assert* and similar substitutes are also unsatisfactory in most contexts. The use of *go* for *say* (So she goes, ''Well, what band's playing?'') has no place in serious writing. See **claim.**

Say in the sense of ''approximately,'' ''for instance,'' ''let us say,'' is used in all varieties of writing: ''the specialist in the literature of, say, the English eighteenth century'' (Howard Mumford Jones, *Journal of the History of Ideas*).

scarcely

When *scarcely* means ''almost not,'' adding a *not* as in ''can't scarcely'' is redundant. See **Double negative.**

scenario

Scenario became a vogue word in the 1970s and took on meanings having little connection with ''script'' or ''synopsis.'' When you mean *plan, prediction,* or *possibility,* use that word, instead of relying on *scenario* and forcing the reader to decide which is meant. Some readers who associate *scenario* with Hollywood make-believe and *game plan* with sports dislike the application of these terms to matters of vital importance, but both appear in all styles: ''In this scenario the war would most likely continue'' (Roseanne Klass, *Foreign Affairs*).

seem

Seem is often used to qualify a statement unnecessarily: They [seem to] run with a gang that can't [seem to] keep out of trouble. Limit your use of *seem* to situations in which you must be tentative. Don't say something *seems to be* when you know it *is.* See **can't help but, can't seem to.**

self

Self as a suffix forms the reflexive and intensive pronouns *myself, yourself, himself, herself, itself, oneself, ourselves, yourselves, themselves.* These are used chiefly for emphasis (I can do that myself) or as objects identical to the subjects of their verbs (I couldn't help myself). See **himself, herself; myself; Pronouns 2.**

As a prefix, *self* is joined to the root word by a hyphen: *self-control, self-explanatory, self-made, self-respect.* When *self* is the root word, there is no hyphen: *selfhood, selfish, selfless.*

semi-

Semi- is a prefix meaning ''half or approximately half'' *(semicylindrical),* ''twice within a certain period'' *(semiweekly, semiannual),* or ''partially, imperfectly'' *(semicivilized, semiprofessional). Semi-* is a live element in forming new words.

Semicolon

Use a semicolon as the link between these sentence elements.

1. To link coordinate clauses.
a. Between clauses without connectives. Use a semicolon, especially in a rather formal context, to link two independent clauses whose relatedness you want to emphasize:

> Goya was never an outcast; he loved society.—Robert Wernick, *Smithsonian*

> Some years ago, a learned colleague who was old and ill complained to me that he could no longer read German; it made his legs feel queer. I know that feeling well; I have had it while trying to read Henry James.—P. B. Ballard, *Thought and Language*

b. With conjunctive adverbs. Use a semicolon to link clauses connected by a conjunctive adverb such as *however, moreover, therefore* at the beginning of the second clause:

> His popularity was undiminished; however, he no longer enjoyed the work.

> Finally, despite the hopes and prophecies described before, we do not really agree on philosophical and political values; therefore the conference, moved by the same desire for survival and development as the world at large, carefully avoided exposing the ideological differences that remain.—Stanley Hoffman, *Daedalus*

A comma before *however* or *therefore* in these sentences would produce a comma splice. See **Conjunctive adverbs.**

c. With coodinating conjunctions. Consider using a semicolon between clauses connected by a coordinating conjunction *(and, but, for, or . . .)* if the clauses are long, if they contain commas, or if for some reason—perhaps for contrast— you want to indicate a more definite break than you would show with a comma:

> The War on Poverty was a *policy* that purported to cure America's gravest social ills; but while Johnson was raising millennial expectations, federal *spending* programs in fact were making inner-city problems worse.—T. D. Allman, *Harper's*

> Newton's admirers assumed that he had; but it was an illusion.—Stephen Toulmin, *American Scholar*

2. To separate units with internal commas.
The units may consist of listed figures or words: *himself, herself; myself; yourself.* They may be phrases or clauses. The sentences may be long or short:

> Americans hated death, denied death, and spent lavishly on funerals; but they had not been gripped by today's frantic illusion that diet and exercise will make death go away.—Robert MacNeil, *The Way We Were*

The debates affect the Minnesota Valley National Wildlife Refuge. One concerns the preservation of fens; the other, the control of mosquitoes.—Suzanne Winckler, *Audubon*

In the second example the comma after *other* makes the semicolon after *fens* necessary.

3. Semicolon and colon. Do not confuse the semicolon with the colon. Don't use a semicolon to introduce a quotation or a listing or to perform other conventional functions of the colon (see **Colon 3**). The one occasion when you have a choice between colon and semicolon is when you're punctuating independent clauses. The semicolon is the usual link. The colon is more formal and suggests that the second clause will explain or illustrate the first. Often the choice is a matter of style.

4. Semicolons and style. Semicolons are usually more suitable in the longer, more complicated sentences of formal styles than in general and informal writing, except when other punctuation makes them necessary (see **2** above). In general styles, commas are often used where semicolons might appear in formal writing, or else clauses that could be linked by semicolons are written as separate sentences. But this doesn't mean that, when writing general English, you should deny your prose the effects that semicolons can give it. The use of a semicolon is often as much a matter of personal choice as of correct punctuation.

Compare **Colon, Comma.**

sensual, sensuous

Both *sensual* and *sensuous* refer to the senses, but the connotations of *sensual* are more physical, of *sensuous* more aesthetic. According to this distinction (which is frequently blurred), sensual music and sensuous music affect listeners differently.

Sentence fragment

A sentence fragment is a part of a sentence punctuated as a complete sentence. See **Fragment.**

Sentences

1. Classifying sentences grammatically. On the basis of their clause structure, sentences are classified grammatically as simple, complex, compound, and compound-complex. Each kind of sentence can be expanded by making its subjects, verbs, and objects compound and by adding appositives and modifiers. See **Absolute phrases, Clauses.**

2. Analyzing sentences rhetorically. A sentence is not only a grammatical unit but also a rhetorical unit. Rhetorical analysis of a sentence takes into account the order of elements, the repetition of grammatical structures, and the appropriateness of such ordering and repeating to the idea expressed and to the rhetorical situation. See **Balanced sentence, Cumulative sentence, Parallelism, Periodic sentence, Phrases and style.**

3. Building good sentences. In your writing, build your sentences so as to bring out the natural and logical relationships in your material. When properly used, subordination and parallelism clarify such relationships. Misused, they blur or distort them. If reducing clauses to phrases or single words is a way of packing more meaning into a sentence, reversing the process—converting some elements into separate sentences—can lighten an overloaded sentence and improve its unity and clarity. See **Coordination, Shifted constructions, Subordination.**

Although some structures that lack an independent subject-verb combination are rhetorically effective, most sentences have at least one such combination. Generally, faults in sentence construction result from failure to recognize the difference between a dependent clause and an independent clause or from failure to show the relation between a modifier and what it modifies. See **Comma splice, Dangling modifiers, Fragment, Fused sentence.**

Sequence of tenses

In some sentences the tense of a verb in one clause is determined by the tense of a verb in another. See **Tense 3.**

Series

A succession of words, phrases, or clauses that are grammatically coordinate makes a series. Sometimes the units are simply separated by commas (apples, pears, persimmons), but usually the last unit is joined to the rest by a coordinating conjunction. Usage is divided over putting a comma before the conjunction:

> He worked in an ad agency, trained polo ponies, and did landscape gardening on a Long Island estate.—Sanford J. Smoller, *Adrift among Genuises*

> Another patron . . . came to see the go-go boys with her mother, her sister[ ] and her Kodak movie camera.—Jeannette Smith, *Washington Post*

Though many writers, especially in general and informal styles, omit the comma before the conjunction, using it helps to indicate that the units are equivalent and in some instances prevents misunderstanding (see **Comma 5**). If the units are long or have internal commas, they can be separated by semicolons (see **Semicolon 2**).

For the rhetorical effects of a series, see **Parallelism, Parallelism and style, Phrases and style.**

set, sit

In standard English, people and things *sit* (past: *sat*) or they are *set* (past: *set*)—that is "placed":

> I like to sit in a hotel lobby.
> I have sat in this same seat for three semesters.
> She set the casserole down with a flourish.
> The post was set three feet in the ground.

A hen, however, sets (on her eggs), cement sets, and the sun sets. A large dining-room table sits eight, and most of us don't know how to sit a horse.

Sexist language

Since the revival of the movement for equality of the sexes, there has been much criticism of discrimination against women—that is, sexism—both in current usage and in the grammar of formal English. Examples of usage that patronizes or denigrates women include labels like *working girls, coed, the little woman, the weaker sex, boss lady, woman driver*, and *lady doctor* and use of the suffixes *-ess* and *-ette: poetess, Jewess, suffragette, usherette*. Similarly offensive to many is the use of first names for women where men's full names or last names are used: Before Robert Browning came to know her, Elizabeth [Barrett] was already considered a rival of Tennyson.

Then there are the words for certain occupations and offices that seem to imply that women are excluded: *policeman, businessman, chairman, congressman*. And most galling of all to many is the use of *man* and *men* to stand for *men and women (manpower, the common man, man-made, free men)* and for the whole human race *(prehistoric man, mankind,* "all men are created equal," "the brotherhood of man") and the use of *he (him, his)* as the pronoun referring to a noun that doesn't specify gender or to an indefinite pronoun *(student, citizen, spectator, person, anyone, no one).*

Though some feminists attach relatively little importance to such usage, others see it as a subtle but powerful conditioner of attitudes toward the sexes from very early childhood. For them, the substitution of *-woman* for *-man* in the words for occupations and offices *(policewoman, businesswoman, chairwoman, congresswoman)* is no solution to the problem. Like *lady driver* and *woman doctor*, it calls attention to sex where sex is not, or should not be, of any significance. (*Male nurse* belongs in the same category. Logically, opponents of sexist language should deplore terms that stereotype either men or women.)

Person(s), people, and *humans* or (better) *human beings* are common substitutes for *man, men, mankind* when both sexes are intended. Many writers now avoid the traditional use of *he* to stand for *he or she* by using the latter in its various forms (Everyone must turn in his or her theme . . .). But because the wordiness is easily compounded and awkwardness is almost inevitable (. . . if he or she wants a passing grade), there's a growing tendency to write in the plural (All students must turn in their themes . . .) or to treat *they (them, their)* as an indefinite common-gender singular (Everyone must turn in their theme . . .). Another device, which may be confusing to readers, is to alternate *he* and *she,* using *she* in one passage, *he* in another. See **Agreement 2, he or she, they.**

If you consider sexism in language an issue of overriding importance, then in your writing you'll try to avoid all the usages you look on as sexist, including the use of *man* for an individual of either sex and any age and the use of *he* for *he or she.* If you don't believe that sexism exists in the language, or don't care if it does, or applaud the masculine bias, you'll ignore the whole matter when you write. But if you belong to neither of these extremes, you have choices to make. Even if you're mainly satisfied with the language as it is, you should be aware that your readers may not be. You can easily avoid the more obtrusive sexist usages, such as descriptive terms that classify women physically when their looks have no relevance (the blonde defense attorney) or that suggest a general lack of intelligence and competence (a cute little premed student). You may also decide to find substitutes for the *-man* words (*police officer* for *policeman,* for example) and to cut down on your use of generic *he* in sentences like "When a young person says he is interested in helping people, his counselor tells him to become a psychiatrist."

How far you go will depend in part on your own sensitivities as a writer. If your sense of style makes you wince at *he or she* (or *he/she*), if the connotations of *artificial* prevent you from accepting it as a substitute for *man-made,* if *persons* and *humans* bother you at least as much as generic *man,* then you face some difficult choices. For those truly torn between the demands of feminist ideology and the demands of stylistic grace and flow, the only solution is to write and revise and rewrite until at last the conflicts are resolved and both ideological and aesthetic demands are satisfied.

In this book, in order to avoid *he or she* and the constant use of plural forms *(writers . . . they), she* is used to refer to *writer* or *reader* in some entries, *he* in others. Unfortunately, in most pieces of writing, such shifts from *she* to *he* and back again would cause confusion.

shall, will

Since the eighteenth century some grammarians have insisted that in expressing determination in statements about the future, *will* should be used with first-person subjects (I will pass the course) and *shall* with second- and third-person (They shall do as they're told). But practice has never been uniform. In current American usage, *will* is much more common with all three persons.

The same grammarians have tried to keep the single function of indicating the future distinct by urging that *shall* be used with first-person subjects (I shall be at a meeting that night) and *will* with second- and third-person (You will arrive about Thursday, Joan says). But again, in standard usage *will* is much more common than *shall* in all persons.

Shall occurs most frequently in legal language and is usually the natural choice in first-person requests for instructions: Shall I close the door?

See **should, would.**

shift Shifted constructions

Avoid the unnecessary shift in construction.

Shifted constructions are needless changes in grammatical form or point of view within a sentence. In speech and in much informal writing, shifted constructions are common, but in general and formal prose they're avoided because they trouble the reader. The many types of needless shifting include the following:

1. Between adjective and noun: This book is interesting and an informative piece of work. *Revised:* . . . interesting and informative.

2. Between noun and clause: The most important factors are time and temperature, careful control at every point, and the mechanical equipment must be efficient. *Revised:* . . . and efficient mechanical equipment.

3. Between adverb phrase and adjective phrase: Along these walks are the cottages, some of which have stood since the founding but others quite recent. *Revised:* . . . but others for only a short time.

4. Between gerund and infinitive: Carrying four courses and to hold down a job at the same time will either develop my character or kill me. *Revised:* Carrying four courses and holding down a job . . .

5. Between gerund and finite verb: I have heard complaints about the plot being weak and that the setting is played up too much. *Revised:* . . . and the setting being played up . . .

6. Between participle and finite verb: You often see a fisherman trying to get quietly to his favorite spot but instead he broadcasts warnings with his rhythmical squeak-splash, squeak-splash. *Revised:* . . . but instead broadcasting warnings . . .

7. Between transitive verb and linking verb: Anyone who has persistence or is desperate enough can get a job on a ship. *Revised:* . . . who is persistent or who is desperate enough . . .

8. Between past and present: The tanks bulled their way through the make-shift barricades and fan out across the enormous plaza. *Revised:* . . . and fanned out . . .

9. Between active and passive: The committee members disliked each other heartily, and their time was wasted in wrangling. *Revised:* . . . heartily and wasted their time in wrangling.

10. Between personal and impersonal: When one is sick, you make few plans. *Revised:* When one is sick, one (*or* he) makes . . . *Or:* When you're sick, you make . . .

No enumeration of shifted constructions could be complete: there are too many constructions to shift.

See **Parallelism and style; Point of view; Reference of pronouns; Tense 2, 3; when, where.**

Shoptalk

Shoptalk is the words that people in the same occupation use among themselves to refer to the things they regularly concern themselves with in their work: the noun *mud* among bricklayers to mean "mortar," the verb *docket* among lawyers to mean "make an abstract."

No occupation gets along without shoptalk. All have everyday terms that may be meaningless to outsiders but are indispensable to those who practice the trade or profession. Especially convenient are short, informal substitutes for long technical terms. A *mike* may be a microphone in a broadcasting studio, a microscope in a laboratory, a micrometer in a shop. A *hypo* is a fixing bath to a photographer, a hypodermic injection to a nurse. Many such words are metaphoric (the television *ghost*) or imitative (the radar *blip*.) Much shoptalk is so specialized or colorless that it never spreads to the general vocabulary—such printshop words as *chase, em, pi, quoins,* for example.

So long as the terms from shoptalk remain narrowly specialized, they should be used only in certain contexts or in technical writing. They are inappropriate in prose intended for general audiences.

See **Jargon.** See also **educationese, gobbledygook, journalese, legalese, psychologese, Slang.**

should, would

In indirect discourse, *should* and *would* can function as the past tenses of *shall* and *will.* "We will go" can be reported as "He announced that we would go," and "We shall go" as "He announced that we should [*or* would] go." Because *should* has a connotation of propriety or obligation (ought to) that may not be intended, *would* is preferable and is majority usage. See **shall, will**.

sic

Sic, the Latin word meaning "thus," is used to indicate that what precedes it has been quoted correctly. See **Brackets.**

sick, ill

Ill is the more formal, less common word. In the United States *ill* and *sick* mean the same thing. In British usage *sick* is usually restricted to mean "nauseated": "The mere touch of the thing would make me sick or ill, or both" (Richard Jones, *The Three Suitors.*) In American usage *sick* in that sense is made clear by adding a phrase: It made me sick to (*or* at, *or* in) my stomach. Saying that something or someone "makes me sick" is normally figurative, meaning "disgusts me," "nauseates me." See **nauseous, nauseated.**

Simile

A simile compares with *like* or *as:* He swims like a winded walrus; straight as a lodgepole pine; "Where a mountain lion hisses, a leopard would snarl like a truck stuck in the snow" (Edward Hoagland, "Hailing the Elusory Mountain Lion"). See **Figurative language.**

Simple sentence

A simple sentence consists of one independent subject-predicate combination. See **Clauses.**

simplistic

Don't use *simplistic,* which means "oversimplified," as a fancy form of *simple.* A simple explanation and a simplistic explanation are quite different. When you mean "oversimplified," *oversimplified* is a better choice than the voguish *simplistic.*

since

As a subordinating conjunction, *since* can have the meaning "because": Since we were already late, we didn't rush. See **because.**

sit, set

People and things *sit* or *are set.* See **set, sit.**

-size

Size is typical of a class of nouns *(age, color, height, shape, width, weight
. . .)* that also function as apparent modifiers: *medium-size, standard-size, life-
size, outsize, oversize.* The *-size* words are redundant in compound modifiers
with adjectives that should modify the head nouns directly: not "small-size
box" but "small box," and similarly with "round-shape table," "younger-age
students," "dark-color hair," and so on. See **Wordiness 1.**

Slang

Drawing a line between slang and other kinds of informal English is difficult.
Many people use the term *slang* too broadly, applying it to almost any informal
word, and dictionaries have been too generous with the label, marking as slang
many words that simply suggest spoken rather than written style. In fact, there
is no fully accepted criterion for marking off the segment of the vocabulary
that constitutes slang, as disagreement among and between dictionaries and
handbooks makes clear.

   Though some of the words labeled slang in current dictionaries—*lulu, puss*
for "face," *fin* for "$5 bill"—have been around for generations, the central
characteristic of slang comes from the motive for using it: a desire for novelty,
for vivid emphasis, for being up with the times or a little ahead, for belonging—either to a particular social group or, more broadly, to an age group or,
more broadly still, to the in-group that uses the current slang. These are essentially qualities of style, and the tone and connotation are as important as the
meaning of the words. Other varieties of language have ways of expressing the
ideas of slang words, but their tone is more conventional. Young people like
novelty, and so do grown-ups with youthful ideas. Entertainers need it in their
trade. In-groups, both legal and illegal, have their slang vocabularies, which
often spill over into general English. Some of the slang of drug users *(fix,
snort, hit)* has wide circulation among nonusers.

   Slang is made by natural linguistic processes. It's full of clipped words
(porn, natch, hood, vibes, pecs and *delts)* and compounds and derivatives of
ordinary words *(screwball, sourpuss, cockeyed, put-on, rip-off).* Many slang
terms are borrowed from the shoptalk of sports and the popular arts, especially
jazz and rock. And a great many are figurative extensions of general words:
nut, dope, egg (applied to people), *heavy, hung up, turned on, plugged in,
spaced out.* Sound often contributes a good deal, as in *barf, booboo, ding-a-
ling, goof, geek, goober, grimbo, nerd, wonk, zap, zip, zonk.* Something about
the sound of *wimp* gave it national currency and political significance.

   Because most slang words have short lives, any discussion of slang in print
is bound to be out of date. *Skidoo, vamoose, beat it, scram, hit the trail, take
a powder, drag out, shag out, cut out, split* succeeded each other within a
short lifetime. Words for being drunk *(soused, plastered, bombed, hammered)*
and words of approval *(tops, neat, the most, chill, groovy, out of sight, bad-
dest, dynamite, intense, froody, rad)* and disapproval *(all wet, lousy, cruddy,*

gross, downer, bummer, shuck, turkey) change from year to year—though some survive and some recur. *(Groovy* recurred with its meaning reversed.) Many slang words prove permanently useful and become a part of the informal vocabulary *(blind date, boyfriend)* or the general vocabulary *(highbrow, lemon).* Many others—particularly students' vogue words—never spread beyond a single campus and are quickly forgotten.

The chief objection to slang in writing, aside from its conspicuousness, is that it elbows out more exact expressions. A slang cliché is at least as boring as a cliché in standard English, and slang that names general impressions instead of specific ones is in no way better than comparable words in the general vocabulary, such as *nice* and *good.* If slang expressions are appropriate to the subject matter and the audience and if they come naturally to the writer, they should be used without apology (that is, without quotation marks). If they're not appropriate—or if they've become tiresome vogue expressions, as slang words and phrases often do—they should not be used, with or without quotation marks.

Slash

Until the late 1980s the slash, also called the slant or virgule or solidus, lived in quiet obscurity in *and/or* and *c/o* ("care of"); in ratios, including the P/E, or price-earnings, ratio of stock-market listings; in some mathematical settings for fractions; to mark the line breaks in poetry set as running copy; and in a few other specialized ones. Now it often appears in print where a comma or a dash or a hyphen would be expected. Public television advertises the "Mac-Neil/Lehrer NewsHour." Logicians write of the either/or fallacy and grammarians of the restrictive/nonrestrictive distinction. Newspapers report car/pole accidents. Anne Fausto-Sterling writes in *Daedalus* of "one other etymological/scientific issue."

The trouble with a voguish profusion of slashes is that the reader often has difficulty interpreting them. Is the slash the equivalent of *or,* of *and,* or of some other relationship between the terms it separates? If you use the slash, make sure it helps rather than hinders your readers. And be aware that some may find it as unpleasant to the eye as its name is to the ear.

slow, slowly

Slow is widely used in speech and in informal writing in place of *slowly.* In general writing its use is restricted to only a few contexts: Go *slow; but* He drove away *slowly.* See **Adverbs and style 1, Divided usage.** Compare **bad, badly.**

so

1. *So* and *so that.* To introduce clauses of purpose, *so that* is ordinarily expected in formal contexts, but *so* by itself is respectable in general use:

> [The ghost of] Patroclus comes to ask Achilles to bury him quickly so that he may pass into the realm of Hades.—Anne Amory, *Yale Classical Studies*

> I might have tried . . . to give a clearer idea of the rest of the contents, so readers could gather some notion of whether or not this kind of material might interest them.—John Thompson, *New York Review of Books*

To express consequence or result, both *so* alone and *so that* are found in all varieties of usage. *Speculum: A Journal of Medieval Studies* had these two passages in the same issue:

> The old bishop was better known as a fighter than as a churchman, so we may reasonably assume that it was prudence and not cowardice which prompted him. —Herbert L. Oerter

> He quotes frequently from the Old French, so that the reader gains a very good appreciation of the style.—Alfred Foulet

2. *So* as substitute. *So* can substitute for a whole clause: I think *I will win;* at least I hope *so.*

3. *So* as an intensifier. As an intensifier, *so* is informal: They're so rich!

so . . . as

So . . . as is a somewhat formal alternative to *as . . . as* in negative comparisons: Hers was not so unlikely a prediction as many considered it to be. See **as . . . as 3.**

so-called

If you have to use *so-called,* don't duplicate the idea by putting the name of the so-called object in quotes: the so-called champion, *not* the so-called ''champion.''

some

1. As a subject. *Some* as a subject takes either a singular verb *(Some of the material is difficult)* or a plural verb *(Some of the tests are easy),* depending on the context.

2. As an adverb. *Some* as a qualifier is informal: He's some older than she is. More formal usage would have *somewhat.* Informally, *some* is also used to modify verbs: The springs were squeaking some.

3. As one word or two. The compounds *somebody, somehow, something, someway, somewhat, somewhere* are written as one word. *Someone* is one word (Someone is coming) unless *one* is stressed (some one of them). *Someday* is written as either one word or two. *Sometime* in "Drop in sometime" means "at some time [two words] in the future."

somebody, someone

Like *anybody* and *anyone, somebody* and *someone* are singular and take singular verbs. In formal writing they too are referred to by a singular pronoun— *he (him, his)*. In informal and general styles, both words are often referred to by *they (them, their)* in the sense "he or she" ("him or her," "his or her"): If somebody dents my car in the parking lot, I expect them to leave their name. But conservative prejudice against this usage is strong.

somewhere, someplace

Though both *somewhere* and *someplace* are standard English, *somewhere* is the better choice for writers unless the style is informal.

Spelling

Correct the spelling of the word marked, referring to a dictionary if necessary.

Use your dictionary, and when alternative spellings are listed, choose the one that introduces the entry. See **Apostrophe, Capital letters, Foreign words in English, Hyphen, Plurals of nouns, Principal parts of verbs.** See also **British English, Divided usage.**

Split infinitive

An infinitive is said to be split when an adverb or an adverbial element splits the *to* from its following verb: The receptionist asked them to *kindly* sit down.

The rule that infinitives should not be split makes good sense when the interruption is lengthy, as in "They were eager to *freely, without restriction of any kind,* take on the privileges and responsibilities of adulthood." But few writers would produce such an unwieldy construction. In the great majority of cases, infinitives are separated by single adverbs: They were eager to freely take on . . .

Formal stylists avoid even those:

> We must have sufficient foresight and vision patiently to guide the peoples of the world along the road they have chosen to follow.—Bernard Kiernan, *American Scholar*

> The Chinese model . . . never eclipsed the local differences that made Japan always and Korea sometimes so distinct from China as properly to constitute a separate civilization.—William H. McNeill, *The Rise of the West*

In both examples, the adverb is placed before the infinitive—"patiently to guide" and "properly to constitute." In the first sentence *patiently* could be placed after *world,* but in the second the only alternatives are to split the infinitive or to rework the sentence.

Adverbs that modify the infinitive often fit smoothly and clearly between the *to* and the verb; and while a writer may reject "to properly constitute" for reasons of personal taste, split infinitives of this sort appear frequently in good writing. Sometimes they provide a way to keep a sentence out of trouble. Here the sentence would be ambiguous if "really" were placed before "to" and unidiomatic if it were placed after "hate": "To really hate the old ruling class we would have to live under it in its days of decay" (John K. Fairbank, *New Republic*).

If the sentence "No one expected those who have been campaigning for a greater role for women in the Catholic Church in the U.S. to meekly drop their efforts" *(Newsweek)* ended instead with "to drop their efforts meekly," *meekly* would receive greater stress. When concern about splitting an infinitive makes a writer bend over backward to avoid it, meaning is often bent as well.

Your main goal as a writer should be to express your meaning as clearly and naturally as possible. When placing an adverb after *to* and immediately before the verb it modifies serves that purpose, place it there.

See **Infinitives and style 4.**

Spoken and written English

Though talking and writing are related, overlapping skills, they differ in several respects. Speech is peppered with expressions that seldom appear in writing other than dialog: "y'know," "y'see," "right?" and all the grunts and murmurs that ask for and provide feedback in conversation. When we talk, we pay far less attention to the shape of our sentences than when we write. We're more casual about pronoun reference and agreement; we let *and* and *so* do most of the work of joining statements; we rarely make the effort to build phrases and clauses in parallel series; and we hardly ever use the nonrestrictive clause. (We might write, "Picasso, who was born in Spain, never lost his fondness for Barcelona," but we'd probably say, "Picasso was born in Spain, and he always loved Barcelona.")

The number of significantly different sounds that all of us use in speech is much larger than the number of symbols in our writing system. In talk, words are always part of a pattern involving pitch, stress, and pause, about which the marks of punctuation provide only the barest hints. Writing blurs or fails to suggest a great many speech signals, including body language—the stance, the gesture, even the slight rise of an eyebrow that may reinforce or modify the message. Whether "more" modifies "competent" or "competent men" in "more competent men" would be shown in speech by stress (heavier stress on the "more" that modifies "competent men"). To make the distinction in writing, rewording might be necessary: more men who are competent; more truly competent men.

But if we can communicate some things more directly in speech than in writing, the reverse is also true. Punctuation indicates quotations efficiently, including quotations within quotations. Spelling distinguishes between some words that are generally pronounced the same way: We'll have it; We'll halve it. Capital letters identify proper nouns and proper adjectives. Because writing can be reread, it's a surer means of communicating difficult material—detailed, complicated instructions, for example. And because writing can be repeatedly revised, it can be more precise, better organized, and more economical than talk.

In spite of their differences, written English and spoken English have a close relationship. When we say someone "talks like a book," we mean that his talk is uncomfortably elaborate or stiff. It's more often a compliment to say that someone "writes the way he talks." For most purposes we value writing that has the flavor of good talk. But having the flavor of talk and being just like talk—even good talk—are by no means the same. Even informal written English, the written English that comes closest to casual speech, has to be far more coherent, far more selective, and far less casual than casual speech if it's to be read with ease and comprehension.

See **Colloquial English.**

spoonful, spoonfuls

Spoonfuls is the plural of *spoonful.* See **-ful, full.**

Squinting modifier

A squinting modifier looks in two directions; that is, it may refer to the word or phrase that precedes it or to the word or phrase that follows it: Getting out of bed *often* is a nuisance; The secretary I spoke to *reluctantly* gave me an appointment.

Standard English

Standard American English is the social dialect used by educated Americans according to the lexicographers who compile our dictionaries. Both spoken standard English and written standard English can be divided into formal, general, and informal, as in this book, or into different and more numerous categories. But when used appropriately, all the locutions called standard are supposed to be acceptable to all educated users of the language. In fact, there's disagreement, in dictionaries, English texts, and books on language etiquette, about a good many usages. But there's agreement on the great majority, and the chief purpose of this book is to call attention to the areas of agreement and to encourage the intelligent use of standard English in writing. See **Nonstandard English, Usage.**

state

When you mean no more than "said," don't use *stated*. See **say.**

Stereotyping

Stereotyping is one version of the *part-whole* fallacy. To stereotype is to apply group labels that ignore individual differences and may also ignore significant characteristics of the group. There are popular stereotypes for almost any group—bird watchers, scientists, South Africans, Texans, "the enemy," schoolteachers, and so on—including college students and young people generally. Stereotypes in your own thinking may reflect unexamined assumptions that weaken your entire argument. See **Fallacies, Logical thinking, Part-whole relationships.**

strata

In formal usage *stratum* is singular and *strata* plural. In general English *strata* is sometimes treated as a singular (that strata of society), but readers who know Latin, and some who don't, condemn the usage.

Style

Style is choice. Style consists of the choices a writer makes—choice of words, choice of sentence patterns, even choice among optional ways of punctuating. If there weren't many different ways of expressing ideas, there would be no such thing as style.

Style is character. Or, in a nonsexist version of a famous aphorism, "Style is the writer." How writers attack a problem, how they arrange their material, the manner in which they make their assertions, the "voices" they speak in—all these reveal something about their personalities, their characters, their values.

There needn't be any contradiction between these two views of style if we think of style as the sum of the choices, *conscious or unconscious,* that a writer makes among the options the language offers. Such matters as basic word order in sentences and ways of forming plurals and indicating verb tenses are part of the structure of English and therefore not stylistic. But other matters—the ways sentences are linked, their relative length and complexity, the placing of those elements that are movable, the words used and their connotations and figurative values—give a passage the distinctive features we call style. Some of these features are the result of unconscious choice, reflecting linguistic habits and ways of thought that the writer isn't aware of. Some of them are the product of deliberate calculation. To the extent that style is the result of such conscious choice, it can be improved.

A style is good or bad, effective or ineffective, to the extent that it achieves or fails to achieve the writer's purpose, wins or fails to win the response he wants from his readers. One of the best ways of improving your own style is to analyze the prose of writers you admire and try to determine how, in choosing words and shaping sentences, they won your response. The more you know about the choices the language offers, the more likely you are to write with clarity, force, and grace, qualities that are the foundation of all good styles. And if you have something to say, you will—through constant writing and rewriting—find your own style, your own voice as a writer.

Because syntax, usage, rhetoric, and style are all interrelated, the great majority of the articles in this *Index* have a bearing on style.

Subjective case

A noun or pronoun that's the subject of a verb or the complement of a linking verb is in the subjective, or nominative, case.

Subjects

1. Definition. The subject of a sentence can be defined in a number of ways. Here are three:

a. The subject performs an action (The dog bit the mailman) or is in a particular state of being (The mailman was unhappy). But this doesn't explain such sentences as "These socks wear out too quickly" or "He received the condemnation of millions." Neither *socks* nor *he* is the performer of any action. Instead, both are the objects of actions.

b. The subject is the person, place, or thing that a sentence is about. This definition doesn't explain "I just heard that a car hit the mayor." The sentence is quite clearly not "about" the speaker or a car. It's about the mayor or the mayor's being hit by a car.

Both these definitions could be correct for some sentences. "The mayor defeated his opponents in three elections" is "about" the mayor, the performer of the action—defeating.

c. The subject is the word, phrase, or clause that usually stands before the verb and determines whether the verb will be singular or plural. Where the first two definitions are based on meaning, this one is based on position in the sentence or on the relationships between inflections for number in the subject and verb: The *woman is* here; The *women are* here. In a sentence in which *there* is an expletive—adding nothing to the meaning—the subject is the noun following the *be* verb that the number of the verb agrees with: There *is a woman* outside; There *are women* outside.

2. Subjects and style. In direct, vigorous writing, the subject and predicate usually express the central action in a sentence, and the subject is often the topic of a paragraph. Continuing the same grammatical subject from sentence to sentence, using pronouns and synonyms for variety, helps keep the focus of a paragraph clear. See **Nominalization, Passive voice.**

See **Agreement 1, Comma 8, Compound subject, Deep structure.** For subjects of gerunds and infinitives, see **Gerunds 2, Infinitives 2.**

Subjunctive mood

Traditionally, English grammar recognizes three moods of verbs: indicative, imperative, and subjunctive. In modern English very few forms can be surely identified as subjunctives, and the use of those few is so inconsistent that definite criteria are hard to set. Generally, the subjunctive is optional. It is one means writers use, consciously or unconsciously, to set their language a little apart from everyday expression. Though not always a trait of formal style, the subjunctive is used regularly in some formal contexts, such as resolutions.

1. Form of the simple subjunctive. The identifiable forms of the subjunctive are *be* throughout the present tense of that verb ("be they young or old" instead of "whether they are young or old"), *were* in its past-tense singular ("If she were here" instead of "if she was here"), and *s*-less forms of the third-person singular of the present tense of other verbs that normally have an -*s* ("that he see" instead of "that he sees"). Some past-tense forms with present or future reference are also subjunctives.

2. Uses of the subjunctive.
a. Formulas. The subjunctive is found in many formulas, survivals from a time when it was used freely. Here are a few:

Suffice it to say	Heaven forbid	As it were
Long live the king	God bless you	Be that as it may

Some of the formulas are used in all varieties of the language. Some, like "Come what may," are rather formal.
b. *That* clauses. The subjunctive is relatively common in demands, resolutions, recommendations, and the like, usually in formal contexts. Ordinarily, alternative expressions without the subjunctive are available.

Formal: I ask that the interested citizen *watch* closely the movement of these troops.
General: I ask the interested citizen to watch the movement of these troops closely.

Formal: Who gave the order that he *be* dropped?
General: Who gave the order to drop him?

Formal: It is necessary that every member *inform* himself of these rules.
General: It is necessary that every member should inform himself . . . *Or:* . . . for every member to inform himself . . . *Or:* Every member must (should) inform himself . . .

c. Conditions. The subjunctive may be used in *if* clauses when the fulfillment of the condition is doubtful or impossible: "If one good were really as good as another, no good would be any good" (Irwin Edman, *Four Ways of Philoso-*

phy). In that example the subjunctive *were* isn't necessary to convey the meaning, which the past indicative *was* would convey just as well by its contrast between past form and present or future sense. *Were,* however, makes the tone a little different.

A large proportion of the conditions the subjunctive is used to express are real or open conditions, not contrary to fact:

> We set up standards and then proceed to measure each judge against these standards whether he be a sixteenth or nineteenth or twentieth century judge—Louis L. Jaffe, *Harvard Law Review*

> Stunkard recorded each subject's stomach contractions for four hours, and at 15-minute intervals asked him if he were hungry.—Stanley Schachter, *Psychology Today*

In conditions like these the writer has a choice between the subjunctive and another verb form. There's no special virtue in using the subjunctive, and it shouldn't be used when it gets in the way of natural, idiomatic expression. See **Conditional clauses.**

Subordinate clauses

A dependent, or subordinate, clause (when day is done) has a subject and verb but can't stand as a sentence. See **Clauses, Comma 2.**

Subordinating conjunctions

The most common subordinating conjunctions—words that relate dependent clauses to independent clauses—are these:

after	before	since	until
although	how	so that	when (whenever)
as	if	that	where (wherever)
as . . . as	in order that	though	whether
as if, as though	once	till	while
because	provided	unless	why

The relative and interrogative pronouns *who, which,* and *what* and the relative *that* also function as subordinating conjunctions. See also **for.**

sub Subordination

Correct the faulty subordination.

Faulty subordination is the mishandling of dependent clauses—clauses introduced by subordinating conjunctions or by relative pronouns and used in the grammatical functions of nouns, adjectives, and adverbs. Three types of faulty subordination are commonly distinguished:

1. Tandem, or excessive, subordination occurs when you write a string of dependent clauses, each modifying an element in the clause before it. The weakness is in style, not grammar:

> *Tandem:* For his teachers, he had carefully selected those who taught classes that had a slant that was specifically directed toward students who intended to go into business.

> *Revised:* . . . those who slanted their courses toward students intending to go into business.

2. Thwarted subordination occurs when you add *and* or *but* to a dependent clause that's already connected to the independent clause by its subordinating conjunction or relative pronoun. This is a grammatical lapse, most commonly found in the form of *and which* or *but which* (see **which 3**):

> *Thwarted:* In the spring, after a long search, they bought a very expensive condominium and which was a financial burden for many years.

> *Revised:* . . . condominium, which was a financial burden . . .

Compare the appropriate use of a coordinating conjunction to join two dependent clauses that are parallel: Tolerance is a virtue [which] all of us praise but [which] few of us practice.

3. Upside-down, or inverted, subordination occurs when you use subordination in such a way as to make the relationship between statements seem illogical. Since it's not a blunder in grammar or style, upside-down subordination is hard to illustrate in isolated sentences. Often only the context determines whether subordination is logical or upside down. In one paper, ''Pearl Harbor was attacked when Roosevelt was president'' would be all right. In another, ''When Pearl Harbor was attacked, Roosevelt was president'' might be much better. Without a context, we can't be sure which statement should be put into the independent clause and which in the dependent clause.

But the nature of some statements makes the choice relatively easy. In most contexts this sentence would sound odd: While I received a salary increase that solved my financial problems, I had to report for work five minutes earlier on Mondays. Some such statement as this would be more likely to make sense: Though I had to report for work five minutes earlier on Mondays, the salary increase solved my financial problems. Ordinarily, upside-down subordination is corrected by turning the dependent clause into an independent clause and vice versa. Often, as in the example just given, some rewriting is advisable.

See **Coordination.**

such

As an intensifier, *such* is somewhat informal (It was such a hot day; I had never seen such energetic people). In formal and most general writing   the construction would usually be completed by a *that* or an *as* clause (It was such a hot day that the tar melted; I had never seen such energetic people as the fishermen of Ballydavid), or the basis of the comparison would be indicated elsewhere in the passage:

> In spite of high winds and raging seas, they were all out in their boats before dawn. I had never seen such energetic people.

Formal usage often introduces examples with *such as,* where general usage would have *like. Such as* is preferable when the example is only loosely or nonrestrictively connected to the preceding noun: ''A number of big processors, such as Campbell and Heinz, still make their own cans'' *(Fortune).*

Suffix

An element that can be placed after a word or root to make a new word of different meaning or function is called a suffix: *-ize (criticize), -ish (foolish), -ful (playful), -th (warmth).* See **Origin of words 3a.**

Superlative degree

Hottest, most pleasant, quickest, and *most surely* are examples of adjectives and adverbs in the superlative degree. See **Comparison of adjectives and adverbs 3.**

sure

Sure in standard written English is primarily an adjective (sure footing; as sure as fate; Are you sure?). As an adverb meaning ''certainly,'' *sure* is informal to general, while *surely* is general to formal:

> It's a novel interpretation, but it sure saves oranges.—Horace Sutton, *Saturday Review.*

> The Art Commission said it surely did want to honor this splendid son of Italy.— Donovan Bess, *Harper's*

The idiom *sure* (never *surely) enough* is in general use: ''And sure enough, in all the fearful discussions about computers, the question that inevitably comes up . . .'' (Robert Langbaum, *Yale Review).*

Syllabication

When you're not sure where to break a word that comes at the end of a line, consult a dictionary. For general rules, see **Division of words.**

Syllogisms

A syllogism represents deductive reasoning reduced to a pattern consisting of a major premise, a minor premise, and a conclusion. If the rules of inference (after each example below) are followed, the reasoning will be valid. Good arguments must satisfy another condition as well: the premises must be true. The rules of inference are concerned only with validity.

1. Common patterns for syllogisms.
a. Hypothetical syllogisms:

Major premise:	If P, then Q	*or*	If P, then Q
Minor premise:	P		Not Q
Conclusion:	Therefore Q		Therefore not P

Arguments that follow this pattern will not be valid if the minor premise is "not P" and the conclusion is "Therefore not Q," or if the minor premise is "Q" and the conclusion is "Therefore not P." The major premise gives no grounds for either of these inferences.

b. *Either-or* syllogisms:

	Disjunctive	*Alternative*
Major premise:	Either A or B but not both	Either A or B
Minor premise:	A	Not A
Conclusion:	Therefore not B	Therefore B

Arguments that follow the pattern of the alternative syllogism will not be valid if the minor premise is positive—that is, "A" or "B." The major premise does not exclude the possibility of both A and B. It simply requires one of the two.

c. Categorical syllogisms:

Major premise:	All M are P
Minor premise:	S is an M
Conclusion:	Therefore S is a P

Arguments that follow this pattern will be invalid if they introduce a fourth term (in addition to M, P, and S); if they shift the meaning of a term; if the middle term (M) is not distributed (that is, if one or more of the premises in which it appears fails to affirm or deny something about the whole class the term stands for); or if a term that has not been distributed in a premise is distributed in a conclusion.

2. Testing arguments. Although a syllogism or, more likely, a series of interlocking syllogisms is the underpinning of most solid arguments, writers don't normally construct arguments by first formulating a syllogism and then looking for evidence to support the premises. Nor does a writer present her ideas in statements that fall naturally into the pattern of syllogisms. Even so, an elementary acquaintance with the rules of inference can help a writer in at least two ways.

First, it can make them aware of the premises that underlie their argument.

In "It's not a poem; it doesn't rhyme," the first clause is the conclusion and the second clause the minor premise of an incomplete syllogism that has as its major premise a proposition something like "If the lines of the passage don't rhyme, the passage is not a poem" or, to put it another way, "All poems rhyme." That unstated assertion, or hidden premise, is too controversial to be allowed to go unsupported. The writer who intends to base an argument on it had better argue for it.

Acquaintance with the rules of inference can also help writers check the validity of their line of reasoning:

> Why do colleges waste time teaching students material they can understand or skills they can learn on their own? Instead of giving courses in science fiction, they should teach double-entry bookkeeping. *That's* a skill students can't pick up on their own.

The reasoning here might be spelled out as three syllogisms, each of which invites the reader to raise questions about the validity of the reasoning as well as about the truth of the premises. To take just one of the syllogisms:

> If students can learn a skill on their own, a college shouldn't teach it.
> (If P, then Q)
>
> Students can't learn double-entry bookkeeping on their own. (Not P)
>
> Therefore colleges should teach double-entry bookkeeping. (Not Q)

Quite aside from questions of truth, the reasoning is invalid. The major premise does not assert that a college should teach *all* the skills students can't learn on their own.

See **Deduction, Fallacies, Logical thinking.**

Synecdoche

Synecdoche is a figure of speech in which the whole stands for the part (a nation adopts a policy) or a part stands for the whole (a baseball player's bat wins a game). See **Figurative language.**

Synonyms

Broadly, synonyms are words that mean the same thing. More strictly, they are words that share at least one meaning. Very few words are completely interchangeable, because no two are likely to share all their meanings and have the same connotations. At the very least, they'll differ in sound and therefore represent different stylistic choices.

In choosing among synonyms, you need to consider both sense—connotations as well as denotations—and sound. The meaning and suggestions of the word you want must express as precisely as possible what you have to say, and the word must fit the sound pattern of your sentence.

See **Connotation.**

Syntax

Syntax refers in general to the order and relationships of the elements of sentences. That the subject of a sentence ordinarily comes before the predicate, for example, is a feature of English syntax. Words, phrases, and clauses are all syntactic elements.

Tandem subordination

Tying a succession of dependent clauses together produces tandem subordination. See **Subordination 1.**

teach, learn

A teaches *B,* who is taught by *A. B* learns from *A.* See **learn, teach.**

Technical writing

Good expository writing conveys information accurately, clearly, and concisely. When such writing is about specialized subject matter—in engineering, for example, or physics or chemistry—it's called technical writing. More particularly, technical writing appears in reports, articles, and manuals produced by professionals in science and technology.

Whatever the subject matter or the nature of the communication, the first obligation of technical writers is to present their information so clearly that it can't be misunderstood by their audience. In addition to presenting information, they must often analyze data, weigh alternative solutions to problems, make predictions, argue for a course of action. In every case, they need to take into account what their readers already know and what they want to find out.

1. Technical writers and their audience. When addressing their peers—professional associates at a convention, for example—technical writers will naturally use the specialized terms of their profession. But when writing reports for their superiors or giving directions to subordinates, they have to gauge the readers' probable familiarity with this specialized vocabulary. (The president of a potash firm may have been chosen for his managerial ability rather than his knowledge of potash. In reporting to him, the technical writer may have to work as hard at translating shoptalk as she would if she were addressing a general reader.) Even students in aerospace engineering might have trouble understanding this announcement of a lecture by an expert in the field:

He will talk about flow visualization experiments of a turbulent water jet in a confined tank modeled to simulate certain flow conditions expected in the Anechoic Chamber/Jet Noise Facility.

Though the gap between general English and technical vocabularies is often large, what makes technical writing difficult for the reader, either layman or professional, may not be so much the terminology as the tangled syntax that results when the writer relies heavily on nominalization, passive verbs, and strings of prepositional phrases (four in the sentence quoted above). Some industrial firms, financial institutions, and professional societies have recognized this problem. The American Chemical Society, for one, gives short courses in communication skills for chemists and chemical engineers. Notes on a recent course stress the need for directness, simplicity, and brevity and recommend the use of the active voice and, on occasion, the first-person pronoun.

2. Technical reports. The merit of any technical report lies in its efficiency in communicating its content to its intended audience. Its format should therefore be carefully planned.

Technical reports differ visually from other expository writing. They're divided into sections, which are often numbered. They have no long stretches of consecutive sentences. They use subheads, tables, charts, diagrams. Many, though not all, present at the beginning a summary (or abstract) of the findings, results, or recommendations. In this format, everything vital is in the summary. No crucial new information is introduced as the report proceeds through its next three or four or dozen sections. Subsequent headings depend on the nature of the report, and the order in which they appear depends on the nature of the audience. One adaptable format follows:

I. Summary—important results, conclusions, recommendations
II. Introduction—background, purpose, problem being addressed, scope
III. Review of previous work—if short, a part of the Introduction
IV. Description of present study—details of apparatus used, if the investigation is experimental; derivation of equations; procedures followed
V. Presentation (in table or graph form) and discussion of results—comment on salient features of the data
VI. Conclusions and recommendations—interpretation of results; inferences; recommendation of a solution, action, or future investigation
VII. Appendices—supporting data, usually highly specialized

Technical writers who are preparing a report for several different audiences will choose a format that permits them to move from the simple to the complex in content and vocabulary. They will begin with a summary phrased in nontechnical language and an introduction that's as uncomplicated as they can make it. They will then proceed directly to conclusions and recommendations, again presenting them so that the least informed readers can follow them. The experimental section, the discussion of results, and subsequent sections will be increasingly technical, and the final sections will supply data likely to be understandable only to specialists. The advantage of this format, with its progression from simple to complex, is that readers can continue until they have satisfied their interest or reached the limit of their understanding. Even the reader who is ignorant of the technicalities of procedures, operations, or calculations will be able to grasp the general purpose, scope, and results of the study.

See **Abstract language, Nominalization, Passive voice, Phrases and style, Shoptalk.**

tense Tense

Make the tense of the verb conventional in form, or make it consistent with, or in logical sequence with, other verbs in the passage.

1. Use the standard form. In general English, avoid nonstandard forms such as *drawed* and *had went* and dialectal forms like *drug* for *dragged* and *throwed* for *threw*. See **Principal parts of verbs.**

2. Make the verb consistent with others that refer to the same time. Consistency doesn't demand that you use the same tense for verbs throughout a sentence or a paragraph or a paper. Choose the verb form or verbal phrase that expresses the distinction of time you intend. In a single sentence you may refer to past, present, and future time: When I *was* ten, I *planned* to be a veterinary surgeon, but now I *know* I *will spend* my working life as an accountant. Through skillful use of verbs, you can interweave particular events with habitual action:

> Summers we generally *follow* a simple routine. Every day we *travel* the fifteen miles to our lakeside cabin. We *start off* at dawn, Mother driving and the kids rubbing sleep from their eyes, and we seldom *get* home before dark. Then we *fall* into bed, tired from a day outdoors. One night last July our simple routine *was wrecked*. Just before we *turned* into the driveway, we *saw* that the lights *were* on all over the house. Since we *knew* we *had left* the lights off and the doors locked, we *were* puzzled and a little frightened. My brother *offered* to reconnoiter. When he *came* back to the car, he *said* he *had seen* . . .

But though it's natural and easy to shift tense, don't make a shift unless it serves a purpose—normally, to mark a change in time. Careless shifts like the following are distracting for the reader:

> The observers unobtrusively *slipped* in the back door while the children *were* still getting settled at their desks. The class *begins* with the teacher reading a short passage from a book about Columbus, at the end of which she *asked* for comments.

To keep the tenses consistent, *begins* should be *began*. Or, if there's a reason for doing so, you might put all the verbs in the historical present: *slip, are, begins, asks*. See **may, might; Tenses of verbs 3a.**

3. Observe the conventional sequence of tenses. In certain contexts actual time takes second place to the conventions of tense sequence.
a. Between independent and dependent clauses. A dependent clause that's the object of a verb in the past tense is usually put in the past tense even though it refers to an existing state of affairs:

> What did you say your name *was?*
> They didn't tell me you *were looking* for an apartment.

But when the dependent clause describes a timeless state of affairs, the present tense is often used: He told me that I always *remind* him of my father. And when the point of the sentence is the current existence of the state of affairs reported in the dependent clause, the present tense is common:

> Simply observing the people and comparing them with those I had seen three decades ago, I was convinced that they are a lot better off materially than their predecessors.—Robert Shaplen, *New Yorker*

b. From direct discourse to indirect discourse. When a dependent clause reports something said, its verb is ordinarily shifted from present to past (He said, "I *am* leaving" *becomes* He said he *was* leaving) or from past to past perfect (He said, "I *did* it" *becomes* He said he *had done* it). But this formal sequence can sometimes be misleading. To report the statement "I'm optimistic about the outcome of the election" as "He said that he was optimistic . . ." doesn't make clear whether the optimism persists. "He said that he is optimistic about the outcome of the election" leaves no doubt in the reader's mind.
c. With infinitives and participles. Infinitives and participles express time in relation to the time of the main verb. Use the present infinitive to indicate time that's the same as the time of the main verb or later than the time of the main verb:

> I plan *to go* to Washington, and I expect *to see* her there.
> I planned *to go* last week and expected *to see* her today.
> I would have liked *to see* her on her last trip.

Use the perfect infinitive for action prior to the action of the main verb:

> I would like *to have seen* her on her last trip.

Use the perfect form of the participle to express time prior to the time of the main verb, the present form to express the same time as the time of the main verb:

> *Having driven* safely through the worst blizzard in local history, he slid off the edge of his own driveway and, *jamming on* the brakes too fast, overturned the car.

See **Tenses of verbs.**

Tenses of verbs

1. Time and tense. In English there is no simple correspondence between tense and time. The term *tense* refers to inflection, or change in form. English verbs have only two tenses: present (he leaves) and past (he left). There is no single-word verb, no inflection, that applies only to the future. But we do have various ways of referring to future time. We use the present tense accompanied by an adverb (He leaves tomorrow) or an auxiliary before the uninflected verb (He will leave tomorrow). Or we say "He will be leaving" or "He is going to leave" or "By this time tomorrow he will have left." Some grammarians call *will leave, will be leaving,* and so on, the future tense.

2. Tense and auxiliaries. If we use no auxiliaries, the only tenses we can form are present and past. But auxiliaries enable us to refer to times in the future as well as in the past extending into the present, the past not extending into the present, and the past of a certain time already past. So some grammarians speak of six tenses, which roughly translate into the six of Latin:

Present:	He eats	*Present perfect:*	He has eaten
Past:	He ate	*Past perfect:*	He had eaten
Future:	He will eat	*Future perfect:*	He will have eaten

Still more tenses emerge if we consider the uses of *do* (emphatic tense: does eat, did eat) and *be* (progressive tense: *is eating, was eating*). If the past of *shall* and *will* is also taken into account, we can speak of a past future *(would eat)* and even a past future perfect *(would have eaten).*

3. Special uses of simple present and past.
a. In addition to its basic function of referring to something going on now, the present tense is used to refer to a state of affairs that is generally true, without reference to time (Oil *floats* on water); to habitual action that continues into the present (He *writes* in his journal every day); and, when accompanied by an adverbial, to a time in the future (She *goes* to college in the fall). Other special uses of the present tense are illustrated in the following:

I *hear* you are going to Europe.
He'll come if you *ask* him.
Thoreau *urges* us to do without luxuries.
In the 1950s all *is* buttoned down; in the 1960s there *are* rumblings of discontent.

The third example is sometimes known as the *literary present* (Thoreau died in 1862), the fourth as the *historical present.*
b. The simple past tense is normally used to refer to something that took place in the past, either a single occurrence (He *broke* his leg) or a repeated occurrence (She studied every weekend). But the past tense does not refer to past time in sentences like these: I heard that you *were* in town; If you *knew* him, you wouldn't be surprised; *Would* you send me the catalog.

See **Auxiliaries, Tense, Verbs.**

than

At its simplest level, the choice of the case of a pronoun after *than* can be illustrated by the sentences "He is taller than I" and "He is taller than me." Both are used in general writing. Formal stylists favor the nominative after an intransitive or linking verb, but many writers use the objective.

When the verb before *than* takes an object, the nominative and objective cases after *than* may have different meanings: She likes him more than I [do]; She likes him more than [she likes] me. So in standard English the case of the pronoun used with *than* after a transitive verb is the case that would be used if the dependent clause were written out. Use of the nominative case where the objective case is called for, as in the following example, is hypercorrect—that is, wrong: Though the jury said we were both guilty, the judge gave my partner a lighter sentence than [he gave] I. See **Hypercorrectness.**

that

1. *That* **or** *which*. Writers are often urged to use *that* to introduce restrictive clauses and *which* to introduce nonrestrictive clauses, and the advice can be helpful for those who use *which* everywhere, perhaps in the belief that it's more elegant than *that*. In practice, the choice between *which* and *that* in restrictive clauses is likely to depend on rhythm, sound, emphasis, and personal taste. If *that* has already been used in the sentence, writers may shift to *which* to avoid repetition. On the other hand, when the restrictive clause is compound, *which* may be chosen as a clearer signal to the reader that the construction is being repeated: "He had an exploratory operation for cancer which the doctors were reluctant to undertake but which he was convinced he needed" (David Halberstam, *Atlantic*). *Which* normally introduces nonrestrictive clauses in all varieties of usage.

2. **Redundant** *that*. When *that* introduces a noun clause in which a modifying phrase precedes the subject, there's a temptation to repeat *that* after the modifier: It seems probable that if they had worked as hard on the project as they did on finding excuses for neglecting it [that] they would have completed it on schedule. Don't do it.

3. **Clauses without** *that*. A complex sentence like "The work [that] he does shows [that] he has talent" is perfectly correct without either *that*. The dependent clauses "he does" and "he has talent" are related to the rest of the sentence clearly enough to need no explicit signs of subordination. Don't handicap yourself by thinking a *that* must be inserted wherever it will fit. *That*-less clauses are common, and many professional writers prefer them:

> He thinks that the Italians neither approved of Fascist terror nor were really terrorized by it. He thinks [ ] they became numb, resigned, apathetic, and cynical.—Naomi Bliven, *New Yorker*

The convention [ ] we accept unthinkingly had not as yet established itself.—William Nelson, *Journal of English Literary History*

Using *that* to stress the subordination of short clauses often robs them of their force: He knows [that] I'm sorry; I'm glad [that] you're here; Take anything [that] you want.

That is necessary when the clause comes first (That she might be hurt never occurred to us) and when a clause has no other subject (There is a moral standard that has long been accepted). When a modifier stands between two clauses, *that* is sometimes necessary to show which clause is being modified: Mr. Wrenn said [ ] after the guests were gone [ ] Mrs. Wrenn should pack her bags. Depending on the intended meaning, *that* is needed either after *said* or after *gone*.

See **this.**

that is

That is is a rather formal connective that introduces the equivalent of, or the explanation of, what precedes it. When it both follows and introduces a complete statement, it may be linked to the preceding independent clause with a semicolon: The men worked continuously for three whole weeks to complete the dam; that is, they worked twenty-four hours a day in three shifts, seven days a week. Or it may begin a new sentence. In briefer constructions a comma or dash before *that is* is adequate: They used the safest explosive for the purpose—that is, dynamite. Better yet, *that is* could be omitted: They used the safest explosive for the purpose—dynamite. See **namely.**

their

Their is the possessive of *they*. *Theirs* is the absolute form: This table is exactly like theirs. Except in formal usage, *their* is often used as a common-gender singular to refer to words like *somebody, anybody, everyone:* "Almost nobody has the words to really talk about their lives" *(Time)*. See **Agreement 2.**

then

Then is an adverb of time frequently used as a connective (conjunctive adverb): The next three hours we spent in sightseeing; then we settled down to the business of being delegates to a convention.

then, than

Don't confuse *then*, the adverb of time, with *than*, the conjunction in clauses of comparison: *Then* the whole crowd went to Louie's; It was better as a movie *than* as a novel.

there is, there are

When *there* is used as an anticipatory subject, the verb ordinarily agrees in number with the "real" subject, which follows it: "There is still occasional sniping at the 'supersquad' and there are still lazy, indifferent homicide detectives" (Barbara Gelb, *New York Times Magazine*). When the subject is compound and the first element is singular, usage is divided. Some writers follow the rules of formal agreement and use a plural verb, while others find a plural verb awkward before a singular noun:

> There are much good history, intelligent analysis of social problems, and good writing.—David Fellman, *American Historical Review*

> There is no jargon, few footnotes, some repetition, few insights and little analysis.—Lewis A. Froman, *American Political Science Review*

Like repeated use of *it is,* repeated use of *there is* and *there are* constructions robs sentences of strong subject-verb combinations.

Thesis statement

A thesis statement is the most explicit statement you can make of your purpose—what you want to assert or prove. Whether or not it appears in the essay itself, the thesis statement must be firmly fixed in your mind, at least by the time you prepare your final draft. If you can't state your purpose, it's doubtful that you will achieve it. See **Outline form 2, Topic sentence 3.**

they

They occurs in all varieties of usage with no specific antecedent: "One thinks of Tolstoy, and the story that all day long they had to be beating omelets for him in the kitchen" (Louis Kronenberger, *New York Times Book Review*). The indefinite reference is troublesome, however, when there's a second *they* in the same sentence: Around campus *they* were saying that *they* had a plan to boycott classes. Often impersonal *there* is preferable: There were reports around campus that they had a plan to boycott classes. *Or:* Around campus they were saying that there was a plan . . . See **Agreement 2, he or she.**

thing

Thing often encourages the accumulation of deadwood in writing: [The] first [thing] you [do is to] dry out your sleeping bag.

this

Though often criticized as a sign of lazy writing, *this,* like *that,* is regularly used to refer to the idea of the preceding clause or sentence: He had always had his own way at home, and this made him a poor roommate. Confusion is caused when *this* refers only to some part of the idea of a clause or sentence or to an antecedent that's not actually expressed. See **Reference of pronouns 2.**

though

Though in the sense "however," "nevertheless," "for all that" appears in all varieties of writing: Two facts are clear, though. So used, it often lacks the bite of other choices: But two facts are clear; two facts are clear, however.

thus

Thus at the beginning of participial phrases tends to encourage loose modifiers. In sentences like this one there's no noun or pronoun for the participle to modify: "D. Eldred Rinehart's term on the racing commission also is expiring, thus opening up the chairmanship" *(Washington Post).* See **Dangling modifiers.**

Thwarted subordination

Subordination is said to be thwarted when a coordinating conjunction precedes the subordinating conjunction: By the end of the summer he had completed three reports, [and] which were accepted for publication. See **Subordination 2.**

till, until

In all varieties of writing, *till* and *until* are interchangeable both as prepositions (Wait till/until tomorrow) and as conjunctions (Wait till/until they get here). *Till* is less formal. Most dictionaries don't recognize the spelling *'til.*

Titles

1. Choosing a title. Although a title that captures the reader's interest is an advantage for a paper, trying too hard for originality or impact is a mistake. If no striking title comes to mind, just name the subject of your paper as precisely as you can in a few words. Because the title is considered a separate part of the paper, it shouldn't be referred to by a pronoun in the opening sentence: not "This is an important issue today" but "The parking problem [or whatever you're writing about] is an important issue today."

2. Referring to titles.
a. Italics or quotation marks. For most purposes, there's a simple rule of thumb: Italicize titles of long works (by underlining them) and quote titles of short works. Italics are traditional for titles of books, magazines, pamphlets, long poems, plays, movies, television series, paintings, pieces of sculpture, symphonies, and operas. Quotation marks are usual for the titles of short stories, essays, short poems, songs, chapters of books, and lectures.

b. Capitalizing. A good rule to follow is to capitalize the first and last words of titles (and the first word after a colon) and all intervening nouns, pronouns, verbs, adjectives, and adverbs. Do not capitalize intervening articles or prepositions. Examples: *Wit and Its Relation to the Unconscious; Peace through Meditation;* "Letter from Birmingham Jail"; "Nobody Knows You When You're Down and Out." Capitals are similarly used, without italics or quotation marks, in titles of unpublished works, book series, and books of the Bible.

The is capitalized and italicized or set within quotation marks only if it's part of the recognized title: *The Yale Law Review* but the *Harvard Law Review; The American Historical Review* but the *American Sociological Review; The New York Times* but the *Los Angeles Times.* In some styles initial *the* is never treated as part of the title of a newspaper or periodical. In the pamphlet entitled *The MLA Style Sheet,* that publication is referred to as "the *MLA Style Sheet.*"

c. Consistency. Many newspapers and magazines have their own rules for handling titles. Some use quotation marks around book titles and merely capitalize the names of periodicals. A writer should choose an accepted style for handling titles and stick to it. For example, the name of the city in a newspaper title may be either italicized or not italicized: the *Los Angeles Times,* the Los Angeles *Times.* Similarly, while strict formality may demand that a title be given in full each time it appears, current styles permit the use of short forms and the omission of initial articles when they would cause awkwardness: Hemingway's [*A*] *Moveable Feast* provides background for his [*The*] *Sun Also Rises.*

too

In the sense "also," *too* is sometimes set off by commas, sometimes not. At times, commas are necessary for clarity. Without them, the sentence "Bob, too, frequently interrupted rehearsals to give advice" could be taken to mean that Bob interrupted too often. Stylists warn against beginning a sentence with *too:* Too, she wrote a book that year.

Though *too* is used to modify past participles after linking verbs in all varieties of usage (She was too excited; They were too concerned), conservative stylists prefer another adverb of degree between *too* and the participle: too greatly excited, too much concerned. Objection is strongest when the participle couldn't be placed before the noun or pronoun as a modifier: He is too identified with the opposition; Priests are too removed from real life. In such cases, many writers would use intervening adverbs—"too closely identified," "too far removed"—particularly in formal contexts. Some formal stylists would continue to criticize both examples, on the grounds that the constructions are incomplete—"too closely identified" for what? "too far removed" for what?

See **not all that, not too.**

Topic sentence

Normally, the topic sentence is the broadest, most general statement in a paragraph, the one that expresses most directly the idea that the paragraph as a whole conveys. The other sentences in the paragraph develop the idea, particularize it, illustrate it, or qualify it.

1. Position. The topic sentence has no fixed position in a paragraph. Most often it's the first sentence, as it is in this paragraph, or the second sentence, coming immediately after a sentence that provides transition from the preceding paragraph. But the topic sentence sometimes stands at the end of a paragraph, pulling details and observations together into an inclusive statement. And occasionally it occurs midway through a paragraph, introduced by particulars that lead up to it and followed by further particulars that support or qualify it. In textbooks and in other types of explanation and instruction where it's vital that the reader have a firm grasp of each stage of the discussion, the writer sometimes sets forth the central idea at the start of a paragraph and restates it in a somewhat different way at the end.

2. Rhetorical use. Topic sentences keep a reader fully informed of the chief points being made. Phrasing topic sentences keeps the writer on track, too, encouraging him to stick to his subject and so maintain the unity of his essay. But in some situations—certainly in describing and narrating and also at times in arguing—he may simply supply details and impressions and leave it to the reader to recognize what the central idea is. If the writer has done his job well, the reader will come to the right conclusion.

3. Topic sentence, pointer statement, and thesis statement. If a reader asks what a paragraph adds up to, it probably needed a topic sentence. If he asks why he's suddenly in the middle of a new subject, it probably needed a pointer statement. If he asks what the purpose of the whole paper is—what it all adds up to—the writer should have formulated a thesis statement.

A topic sentence sums up what a paragraph or sequence of paragraphs *says*. A pointer statement tells what the paragraph or sequence of paragraphs will *do* (or, sometimes, what it has done). "There are three kinds of joggers" is a pointer, an organizational signpost indicating that each kind of jogger will now be described. "But what do we mean by *success?*" is an implied promise to discuss the term.

An expository or argumentative paper usually has several topic sentences and perhaps a pointer or two. By contrast, it has just one thesis statement, and that statement may or may not appear in the paper. Whether or not it does, it's the writer's expression of the controlling idea of the entire paper.

See **Outline form 2, Paragraph indention, Thesis statement, Unity 2.**

Transition

Make the transition between these sentences (or paragraphs or parts of your paper) clear and smooth.

Transitions are words or phrases or sentences that show the relationship between one statement and another, one paragraph and another, one part of a paper and another. When you write a sentence or paragraph as an isolated unit—as if nothing had preceded it and nothing is to follow it—your reader is bound to be puzzled. A lack of transition between one paragraph and another or one section of the paper and another is sometimes a sign of faulty organization and sometimes simply evidence that you've neglected to provide a signpost (a word, a phrase, a sentence, or even a paragraph) that shows readers where they've been and where they're going. A lack of transition between sentences usually indicates that you haven't thought through the relationship between consecutive ideas.

1. Transitions as signals. The most familiar of the markers that indicate relationships and knit a piece of writing together are conjunctions and adverbs— *and, but, still, yet, for, because, then, though, while, in order that, first, second, however, moreover, therefore,* and so on.

Some of the choices available to indicate the common logical relationships are these:

a. Addition. When you want to call attention to the fact that you're adding something, *and* is the usual connector. Others that indicate equivalent, coordinate, or similar ideas are *also, again, once again, too, likewise, moreover, furthermore, then, in addition, by the same token, similarly, analogously.* You can indicate restatements with such phrases as *that is, to clarify, more simply,* or by clauses like *what this means is.*

b. Contrast. When the relation is one of contrast—ranging from direct contradiction through various degrees of opposition, qualification, restriction, and concession—some of your choices are *but, yet, however, nevertheless, nonetheless, by contrast, at the same time, instead, in place of, conversely, actually, in fact, to be sure, at any rate, anyway, still, of course, on the contrary, on the other hand, provided that, in case.*

c. Alternatives. You can call attention to an alternative or option by using *or, nor, either, neither, alternatively, on the other hand* (often following *on the one hand*).

d. Causal relations. You can indicate a causal relationship with *for, because, since, then, as.* You can point to a result or consequence with various words and phrases, among them *so, then, therefore, thus, hence, accordingly, as a result, in consequence.*

e. Illustration. When what follows illustrates what has come before or particularizes it in some way, some of your choices are *for example, for instance, thus, to illustrate, in particular, namely.*

f. Sequence. When the relation is sequential, your transitions may indicate relationships of time or space in the subject itself, or they may point up the organization of the paper. Sample time indicators are *then, soon, after, now, earlier, later, ten years ago.* Sample space indicators are *here, there, on top, in the middle, below, on the left, on the right, beyond.* You can indicate sequence by transitions like *for one thing, for another; first, second, third; to begin with; in short, in brief; finally, to summarize, in conclusion, as we have seen.* Other transitions bring out the relative importance of points—*more important, less important, above and beyond.*

2. Transitions and style. A transition should give an accurate indication of the relationship you intend. Beyond that, the transition marker should be in keeping with the style and tone of your paper.

a. Accurate markers. *Actually* and *incidentally* are overworked as transitions. Since *actually* often introduces a correction and *incidentally* a digression, both may be signs that revision is needed. An unwarranted transition—for example, a *therefore* when what follows is not the result of what precedes—can be seriously misleading.

b. Apt markers. Though *first, second, third* are preferable to old-fashioned *firstly, secondly, thirdly,* they're appropriate only when the material demands emphatic division. Overuse of any of the heavier connectives *(however, nevertheless, consequently)* can clog your style. Often you can make a transition that's just as clear, less obtrusive, and stylistically more pleasing by dealing with the substance of your paper—by repeating a key word from sentence to sentence, by using a synonym or a pronoun to echo or pick up the key word, and by binding sentences or parts of sentences by means of parallel structures. Whether emphatic or subtle, transitions are your chief means of giving a piece of writing coherence.

Transitive and intransitive verbs

A transitive verb has a direct object; an intransitive verb does not: The janitor put *(transitive)* the books on the shelf, but they soon vanished *(intransitive).* Many verbs are transitive in one sense and intransitive in another: He grows corn; The corn grows well. See **lay, lie; set, sit.**

trite # Triteness

Replace the trite expression with one that is fresher.

The most troublesome trite expressions, or clichés, are worn-out figures of speech or phrases: picture of health, break of day, reign supreme, from the face of the earth, crack of dawn, acid test. What was once fresh and striking has become stale and boring from being used again and again with no sense of its figurativeness. But triteness is not a matter of age. Yesterday's vogue expression can be as boring to a reader as one that dates back generations. In fact, a young reader may be more familiar with a new cliché than with an old one. So if you find yourself writing down a phrase without even stopping to think about it, stop and think about it. Think twice. Trite expression is the natural vehicle for trite ideas.

This doesn't mean that you should mistrust everyday English. Often a well-established phrase, with its connotations, will express your meaning accurately and succinctly. Going out of your way to avoid an expression only because it's been used many times before may force you into awkwardness, incoherence, or absurdly "fine" writing. The important thing is to be aware of what you're putting on paper, to be conscious of your stylistic choices and rhetorical decisions.

See **Figures of speech, "Fine" writing, Formulas, Vogue words.**

try and

The standard idiom *try and*—"Neither Congress nor the Court itself seemed prepared to try and force him to resign" *(Newsweek)*—appears regularly in general and informal contexts, but formal stylists and many general stylists prefer *try to*.

-type

The use of *-type* in compound modifiers (Polaris-type missile, family-type programs) has spread in all varieties of usage but continues to irritate many readers. Most writers choose *type of* (Polaris type of missile) or, where possible, simply omit *type* (family programs). The practice of shortening *type of* and *make of* to *type* (this type letter) and *make* (that make car) is informal.

Underlining

Underlining in manuscripts is used to mark titles that aren't quoted, words used as words, foreign expressions that haven't been anglicized, and—sparingly— words or word groups that you want to emphasize. See **Italics.**

Understatement

Understating is one means of emphasizing: Eight o'clock classes are not universally popular. See **Figurative language, Figures of speech, Negatives and style.**

uninterested

To be uninterested is to lack interest; to be disinterested is to be neutral, which is not the same thing. But see **disinterested, uninterested.**

unique

In strict formal usage *unique* means "single," "sole," "unequaled" and consequently is not compared. In general usage *unique,* like many other words that once had an absolute meaning, has become an adjective of degree. As an emphatic "unusual," "rare," or "remarkable," it's often found compared with *more* or *most:* "The more unique his language, the more peculiarly his own will be the colouring of his language" (Otto Jespersen, *Mankind, Nation and Individual from a Linguistic Point of View*). Because of this varied usage, a reader may find unqualified *unique* ambiguous. The writer of the following sentence may have been guarding against that possibility: "It is a unique festival, and there is nothing like it in the world" (Harold C. Schonberg, *New York Times*). Though redundant by strict formal standards, the second clause is practical. See **Comparison of adjectives and adverbs.**

United States

Like many proper nouns, *United States* is often used as an attributive (that is, as an adjective preceding the word it modifies): "There are some who think that the United States attempt to overthrow the Castro government was an act of international immorality" (Richard H. Rovere, *New Yorker*). No apostrophe is needed. Since *United States* has no adjectival form, its use as an attributive often sounds awkward, unless it's abbreviated to *U.S.* In most contexts *American* is preferable. See **American.**

un Unity

Unify this passage.

A sentence, a paragraph, or a paper is unified when its parts fit together to make a consistent whole. You weaken the unity of what you write when you include material that stands outside—or seems to stand outside—the core of thought or feeling you want to communicate.

Your first obligation as a writer is to have a purpose in writing and a controlling idea to which everything you include in the paper contributes. Your second obligation is to build your sentences and paragraphs in such a way that your train of thought, and in the end your purpose, will be clear to your audience.

Failures in unity can be real, as when a writer introduces irrelevant material, or apparent, as when a writer doesn't make plain to his readers a relationship that's perfectly plain to him. The first is a failure in reasoning (see **Logical thinking**). The second is a failure in composition, especially in continuity (see **Coherence, Transition**). A sentence, a paragraph, or a paper may be coherent but not unified. It may also be unified but not coherent. Good writing is both coherent and unified.

Without the context—and here *context* means both your thinking about your subject and your expression of your thought—deciding whether a passage lacks unity or coherence is difficult. But some hints can be given about ways to strengthen passages that have been criticized for lacking unity.

1. Unity in sentences. For a sentence that lacks unity, there are three possible remedies:

a. Delete any phrase or clause that isn't related to the central thought. In the sentence "Parking space on the campus, which is one of the most beautiful in the state, has become completely inadequate, and recently the city council voted to increase bus fares again," delete the *which* clause.

b. Subordinate one statement to another to show the logical relationship. Even if readers of the sentence quoted in **a** can figure out a connection between the shortage of parking space and the cost of public transportation, the coordinating *and* obscures the writer's point. A possible revision: At a time when the shortage of parking space makes commuting to campus by car almost impossible, the city council has discouraged the use of public transportation by increasing bus fares once more.

c. Separate seemingly disconnected statements by making two sentences, and bring in material that will provide a logical link between them. Between a sentence about inadequate parking space and a sentence about increased bus fares, this sentence might be introduced: But the commuting student is not being encouraged to switch to public transportation. See **Coordination, Sentences, Subordination.**

2. Unity in paragraphs. As a general rule, a paragraph lacks unity when one or more of its sentences fail to contribute to its central idea. When that idea is expressed in a topic sentence, both writer and reader can see just where the discussion slides away from the main point. So it's wise to provide topic sentences when your subject is so complicated that a reader might need help in following your treatment of it. On the other hand, you can do without topic sentences if the logic of your thought, or the strength of your emotion, creates a unified topic *idea* that the paragraph gets across to your readers.

Sticking to a subject doesn't in itself guarantee unity. In a paragraph on Robert Frost, all the sentences may be about the poet, but if two of them deal with his current reputation, one with his last public appearance, one with his marriage, and three with his poem "After Apple-Picking," it's unlikely that the paragraph will have unity. Bringing together several loosely related subjects usually means that no one of them will be adequately developed and that the paragraph will have no central focus. See **Paragraph indention, Topic sentence.**

3. Unity in papers. Even when each paragraph is unified, the paper as a whole may not be. Each paragraph should bear on the writer's purpose (whether or not that purpose is expressed in a thesis statement), and the paragraphs should be in such an order and so linked that the reader sees the relation of each of them to the controlling idea. Arthur Schlesinger, Jr., uses careful linking in an article in *Foreign Affairs*. At one point, he writes: "Unilateralism breeds the arrogance of ignorance, and ignorance breeds bad policy." Six paragraphs later, he completes the linkage: "Unilateralism breeds something more than ignorance; it breeds illegality."

A useful way of testing a paper for unity is to outline it. Questions of relevance and relatedness can be more easily answered when you've seen through the surface of what you've written to the underlying structure. Reduce each paragraph to a heading. If your paper is brief—no more than four or five paragraphs, say—each paragraph may represent a main point; but in a longer paper the paragraphs should fall into logical groups or sequences, with each sequence developing a theme. Be on the lookout for a heading that doesn't logically follow the preceding heading or lead into the next one. If you find such a heading, reexamine your organization, and if there's no slot that the heading obviously fills, consider dropping the paragraph it stands for. If you find a sequence of paragraphs that strays from your central thesis, you need to do some rethinking and rewriting. See **Organization, Outline form, Thesis statement.**

until, till

Until and *till* (not *'til*) are interchangeable. See **till, until.**

Upside-down subordination

Subordination is said to be upside down when logically the dependent clause should be independent and the independent clause should be dependent. See **Subordination 3.**

Usage

The study of usage depends on wide observation of what people say and write in various situations. This observation serves as a basis for judging the standing of particular words, forms, and constructions. Works on usage include scholarly studies of the ways language is used, and has been used, in speech, in print, in letters, and so on; polls to determine attitudes toward particular usages; and guides to usage based in large part on the authors' personal taste. Both the polls and the guides focus on disputed usages—locutions accepted by some, rejected by others—and it is this area of usage study that has most interested the general public.

Students in particular should be aware of the influence of age on what readers accept and what they reject. All of us find it very easy to accept what we grew up with, but as we become older, accepting new words, new meanings, new forms of expression becomes increasingly difficult. One purpose of this book is to remind students that many of the usages they take for granted are offensive to some older readers. This doesn't mean that students should adopt the attitudes toward usage of the middle-aged—and certainly not of those who see the language in imminent danger of "destruction." It does mean that they should take into account the linguistic habits and tastes of their audiences whenever they write.

Researchers have built up a picture of what educated users of American English say and, more especially, write. But for many people who are interested in usage, what *is* is not nearly so important as what *should be*. Most of the popular guides to usage are conservative—that is, they restrict "correct" English to usages and constructions that this *Index* associates with formal styles.

The reaction to *Webster's Third New International Dictionary of the English Language* in 1961 revealed the intense concern about usage felt by an articulate minority of Americans. The publishers of the dictionary had decided to apply usage labels much more sparingly than in the past, on the grounds that the primary role of a dictionary was to record usage, not evaluate it, and that it was often impossible to label with any precision words taken out of context. Praised by many scholars, the decision was attacked in newspaper editorials and magazine articles as an abandonment of standards. Dictionaries published since then have been more prescriptive than *Webster's Third,* and until the publication of *Webster's Dictionary of English Usage* in 1989, few books of linguistic etiquette had been as liberal as *A Dictionary of Contemporary American Usage* by Bergen and Cornelia Evans, published in 1957.

The polling technique introduced into usage study in the 1930s has been adapted by commercial publishers of dictionaries and reference books on usage: panels of journalists, novelists, columnists, commentators, and others concerned in one way or another with verbal communication vote on the "acceptability" of items of usage presented to them by the editors, who select the panels and also the usage "problems" the panels consider. Majority opinion is almost invariably conservative. (Panel members are predominantly middle-aged and older.) Like the authors of the popular guides to "good English," panelists tend to express their opinions as vehemently and emotionally as do those ordinary citizens who write letters to newspapers and magazines deploring the corruption and decline of the language.

Such emotionalism reveals that while word watching can make anyone's reading more interesting and his writing both richer and more precise, it can also become an unfortunate obsession. It's bad enough when the watcher (and listener) insists on "correcting" the usage of others. It's much worse when he makes usage the criterion for judging not only their educational and social level but their intelligence and their character.

Like every user of the language, you must make your own choices. They should be intelligent choices, based on sound information. The best safeguard against avoidable bias is some principle of selection, and the principle proposed in this *Index* is appropriateness. There is also the intangible called taste. If, like most of us, you find some locutions too stuffy or too crude, you can simply not use them. No one can control the usage of others, but, with some effort, we can all learn to control our own.

utilize

Utilize, meaning "put to use for a purpose," is a rather formal verb.

verbal, oral

Though *verbal* is widely used to mean "spoken," many word watchers insist on *oral* for that meaning. See **oral, verbal.**

Verbals

The parts of a verb that function as nouns or adjectives are called verbals. For their various uses, see **Gerunds, Infinitives, Participles.**

Verbs

1. Forms. If we exclude *be* and the modal auxiliaries, all verbs can add to the base form *(ask, sing, tear)* the suffix *-ing (asking)*, the suffix *-s (asks)*, and the suffix *-ed (asked)* or use some other change in form as the equivalent of the *-ed: sing, sings, singing, sang, sung; tear, tears, tearing, tore, torn. Be* has eight forms *(be, am, is, are, was, were, being, been); can, may, must,* and other modal auxiliaries have only one or two forms. We recognize verbs by their form and their position in a sentence even when we don't know what they mean. In "I am sure that his words will coruscate," we recognize *am* and *will* as verbs because we've already learned their forms. Even if we've never seen or heard *coruscate,* we recognize it as a verb because it depends on *will.*

Verbs fall into two classes: a closed one (no new verbs are added) whose function is primarily grammatical, and an open one (new verbs are constantly added) in which the meaning of the words is important. In "He got hurt," *got* performs the grammatical function of showing past tense and passive voice, and *hurt* carries the lexical meaning. See **Auxiliaries, Gerunds, Infinitives, Participles, Principal parts of verbs, Tenses of verbs, Voice.**

2. Function. Verbs, with their modifiers and any objects or complements, form the predicates of clauses, which are combinations of subjects and predicates. See **Agreement, Clauses, Linking verbs, Objects, Predicates, Transitive and intransitive verbs.**

Verbs and style

The rhetorical function of a verb is usually to comment on the topic of a sentence. Generally speaking, the important action in a sentence should be in the main verb after the topic–subject has been stated. In the sentence "The possibility of a decision in regard to an investigation of reasons for student transfer exists," the one verb is *exists*. It states only that the very long and complicated topic–subject is there for the reader to consider. But the important action is not that a possibility exists; it's that someone may decide to investigate why students transfer: [The president?] may decide to investigate why students transfer. This sentence has two verbs—*decide* and *transfer*—and a verbal, the infinitive *to investigate*. The crucial actions in a sentence should be represented by verbs, not in the abstract nouns related to verbs. See **Absolute phrases, Conditional clauses, Nominalization, Passive voice, Subjunctive mood, Tense.**

Vernacular

Vernacular once meant "the local language as opposed to Latin." In England the word was used to refer to natural spoken English as opposed to formal literary English, and this usage gained social and political overtones in the United States. In the 1800s Mark Twain wrote stories and Walt Whitman wrote poems in styles adapted from ordinary speech. Since then it's been impossible to flatly oppose the literary language to the vernacular language, for the vernacular has been more important to American literature than the formal or academic. See **Colloquial English.**

very

1. As a qualifier. *Very* is used so often as a qualifier that some teachers and editors have tried to outlaw it. But as long as it's used sparingly, *very* is a better choice than overblown intensifiers like *incredibly, terribly, fantastically,* and so on.

2. With past participles. Some formal stylists condemn the use of *very* before past participles that are not established in adjectival function, on the grounds that *very* ("extremely") can't modify verbals. They insist that an adverb of degree, such as *greatly* or *much,* must stand between *very* and these participles—not "very disoriented" but "very much disoriented." In general practice some past participles regularly take *very* (very troubled), some *much* (much improved), some either (very pleased, much pleased), some neither (lighted). Usage is divided. Let your ear and your audience be your guides.

Vogue words

Particular words and expressions are constantly enjoying great popularity in one social or professional group or another, but a true vogue word is one that's moved into general usage and become a fad. Some begin in the slang of the black ghetto or the campus and find their way into the copy of advertising writers. Others start in the professions or the bureaucracy and become clichés through the efforts of journalists and commentators. A great many vogue expressions—"Have a nice day," "That's what [almost any large abstraction] is all about," "Make my day," "It's a whole new ball game," "Hang tough," "Go for it"—seldom appear in writing except in dialog. But countless vogue words and phrases clutter news stories and articles: *world-class, street smarts, power lunch, bottom line, state of the art, mode, glitz, sleaze, quality time, one-on-one.* Often the new expressions become clichés in a matter of weeks. Or words that have been around for years, like *tacky* and *scary,* achieve vogue status only to subside again.

Some vogue words and expressions have little specific meaning to begin with, in the contexts in which they appear. (For a time the word *like* was used in place of a grunt as a filler in conversation.) Through endless repetition other vogue words lose what force and meaning they had *(actually, basically, meaningful, relevant).* Still others take on so many meanings in so many different contexts as to become almost meaningless *(massive, concept, scenario).* Whether short and simple *(into* for ''involved with'') or long and fancy *(counterproductive),* all vogue words have one thing in common: they've become a bore. Writers should do their best to avoid using them.

See **Cliché, gobbledygook, Slang, Triteness.**

Voice

Voice is a term borrowed from the grammars of the classical languages, where it usually differentiates distinctive verb endings. In English, *passive voice* refers to constructions made with the past participle and some form of the verb *be* (was killed). All other verb forms are *active.*

	Active voice	Passive voice
Present:	he asks (is asking)	he is asked (is being asked)
Future:	he will ask	he will be asked
Perfect:	he has asked	he has been asked
Infinitives:	to ask, to have asked	to be asked, to have been asked
Participles:	asking, having asked	being asked, asked, having been asked

Get is also used for the passive, especially in informal English: If he should get elected, we'd be lost; Our house is getting painted. See **Passive voice.**

wake

English is oversupplied with verbs for waking from sleep (intransitive) and waking someone else from sleep (transitive). Most common is *wake (woke* or *waked; woke, waked,* or *woken),* to which *up* is frequently added in general English. *Awaken (awakened, awakened)* is almost as common but more formal. *Awake (awoke* or *awaked; awoke, awaked,* or *awoken)* is rather formal. *Waken (wakened, wakened)* is least used.

want

Except in the rather rare sense "have need" (They want for the bare necessities of life), *want* should not be followed by *for:* I want [for] you to go. Nor should it be followed by a *that* clause: I want that you should go.

Want for "ought," "had better" (You want to review all the notes if you're going to pass the exam) is informal.

Want in and *want out* (That dog wants out) occur in general and informal writing but not in formal.

way, ways

Way in the sense "far" is established in general writing, though not in formal: "It goes way back to his red-baiting days" (T.R.B., *New Republic*). *Ways* for "distance," as in "a little ways down the road," is folksy informal.

we

We is frequently used as an indefinite pronoun in expressions like "we find" and "we feel," to avoid passive and impersonal constructions. It's also used to mean "I and others," as in writing for a group or institution. In newspapers and magazines, editorial *we* may speak for the publication; in books it can mean "you readers and I," "all of us" (with *us* ranging from a limited group to the entire human race), or simply "I, the author." And there is the royal *we* of monarchs and popes, the corporate *we* of business letters, and, particularly since the growth of radio-television talk shows, the *we* that can only mean "I," as in an entertainer's "We always draw well in Vegas."

We for *I* has been taken up by some ordinary citizens, with no hint of publicity agents, teammates, or bureaucratic associates, on the peculiar grounds that it's more modest. It isn't.

See **I.**

well, good

Well is either an adjective (She looks well) or an adverb (He swam well). *Good* is usually an adjective (a good feeling). See **good, well.**

As an interjection in writing, *well* adds an informal note: "Once the cord is cut and the infant is put down on the warming table, it's, well, our baby" (Perri Klass, *Discover*).

what

When a predicate nominative connected to a *what* clause by a linking verb is singular, the verb is singular: What I want to discuss is the responsibility of students. When the predicate nominative is plural, usage is divided:

> What surprises and captures the reader is the hundreds of black-and-white photographs.—*Time*

> What he wanted were people who could stimulate.—Anthony Starr, *Esquire*

when, where

A *when* or *where* clause is probably the most common form for defining in informal usage and occurs often in general contexts: Welding is when (*or* where) two pieces of metal are heated and made into one. But there is strong prejudice against it. The grammatical argument is that an adverbial clause can't serve as the predicate complement of a noun, which requires as complement another noun or a noun phrase or clause: Welding is the process by which two pieces of metal are heated and made into one.

whether

Or not is required after *whether* when *whether* introduces a complete or elliptical adverbial clause: Whether [he is] right or not, he deserves a hearing. In noun clauses, *or not* may be used for emphasis; but it isn't necessary, and many writers prefer to omit it:

> Whether readers find him successful will depend on their patience.—Charles F. Mullet, *American Historical Review*

> If the child at home wonders whether he is loved, the pupil in school wonders whether he is a worthwhile person.—Robert Dreeben, *Harvard Educational Review*

When the alternatives are spelled out, *or not* is redundant: Whether [or not] the move is good or bad is debatable.

Repeating *whether* after *or* (Whether . . . or whether . . .) can be helpful to readers when the alternatives are long and complex, as in some formal or technical contexts.

See **Conditional clauses; if, whether.**

which

1. For broad reference. The use of *which* to refer to the whole idea of a preceding clause (They plan to tear it down, *which* is a pity) is well established, but objections are properly raised when the reference is so loose that, at first reading, the *which* seems to refer only to the preceding word: She liked the book, *which* was puzzling. Similarly, a reader shouldn't have to wrestle with two *which*'s, one of specific and one of broad reference, in a single short sentence: I worked Saturdays to earn money *which* was owed on the car, *which* pleased my parents.

2. In the possessive. *Whose* as the possessive of *which* is older and less cumbersome than *of which* and is preferred by most writers: "a pattern whose outlines are clearly visible" rather than "a pattern the outlines of which are . . ."

3. In parallel clauses. When parallel relative clauses with the same antecedent are connected by a coordinating conjunction, a writer sometimes omits the relative pronoun before the first clause and then uses it before the second: "It seems to hold as much promise for American politics as the second-hand legislative reforms [ ] Sinclair propounded in his novels, and which successive Democratic administrations enacted" (Andrew Kopkind, *New York Times Book Review*). In this example, the missing *which* should be inserted or the *which* after *and* dropped.

Sometimes a single adjective *which* clause is attached to a main clause by *and* or *but:* In elementary school I became interested in ballet, not a very popular art form where I lived, and which most of my classmates thought was silly. Omitting the *and* in this clumsy sentence only creates confusion, because without it the *which* doesn't seem to have any reference at all. The mixed construction can be turned into a balanced one by inserting *which was* before *not:* In elementary school I became interested in ballet, which was not a very popular art form . . . and which most of my classmates thought was silly. See **Subordination 2.**

4. *Which* or *that.* For the choice between *which* and *that* as relative pronouns, see **that.**

while

The central meaning of *while* is "during the time that": While the rest were playing cards, he was studying. In general English *while* is also used to mean "although" or "whereas" (While the cast is talented, the play is a bore) and to introduce the second of two clauses in place of *though* or *but* (The beagle was a thoroughbred, while the rest of the pack were mongrels). Because of the several senses, *while* can create ambiguity unless you use it with care. Among formal stylists there's some prejudice against *while* when no sense of time is involved.

who, whom

In all varieties of English, *who* is consistently used for subjects except when it is immediately followed by the subject of an interrupting clause. Then what *The New Yorker* used to call The Omnipotent Whom is common, as if the pronoun rather than its clause were the object of the interrupting clause: "children whom Taylor thinks can bend spoons by paranormal powers" (Martin Gardner, *New York Review of Books*). As subject, *who* is the right form in such constructions.

In formal styles *whom* is consistently used for objects, but informal and general styles often break the traditional rule. General usage permits *who* in questions like these:

And who was the hard sell aimed at?—Mary McCarthy, *New York Review of Books*

Who are they trying to impress?—Bruce Price, *Washington Post*

Educated writers sometimes accept *who* as object when they'd reject *I, we, he, she,* and *they,* because *who* is so often in subject territory, preceding the verb. When the pronoun functions as subject, function and position are in harmony, and *who* is the natural choice. When the pronoun functions as object, function and position are at odds. In formal contexts most writers ignore position and let function determine form. In casual conversation and casual writing, position is allowed to determine form. General usage usually favors the demands of function except when the pronoun introduces the whole sentence (Who can we turn to?). In college writing, subject *who* and object *whom* are usually the appropriate choices, unless *whom* sounds unnatural in the context.

See **one of those who.**

whose

Whose is often a better choice than *of which.* See **which 2.**

will, shall

Whether pointing to the future and expressing determination or simply indicating the future, *will* is more common than *shall* in all three persons. See **shall, will.**

-wise

Over a long period the suffix *-wise* was used to form a limited number of adverbs from nouns *(edgewise, lengthwise, slantwise).* Then it increased in faddish use, especially in an abstract rather than a special sense *(average-wise, budget-wise, weather-wise, tax-wise),* until new *-wise* words became a joke. Now both the overuse and the ridicule have died down, and some uses may be tongue-in-cheek: "an important plus elitism-wise" (Hendrik Hertzberg, *New Republic*).

When a noun has no established adjectival form, a *-wise* coinage may serve a need and save space. But often the *-wise* word lacks precision *(production-wise);* sometimes it saves no space *(economy-wise* versus *in economy);* and it may simply duplicate an existing word *(drama-wise* for *dramatically).* Besides, tacked-on *-wise* raises the blood pressure of some readers.

woman, lady, girl

An adult human female is a woman. Feminists oppose the use of *girl* for any human female who is no longer a child. *Lady* is used in a variety of formulas and set phrases—ladies and gentlemen, ladies' room, a real lady, ladylike— and in the names of a number of long-established women's organizations, like Ladies' Aid. As a social label, *lady* is applied to very different classes: daughters of dukes, marquesses, and earls in Great Britain, who bear the courtesy title *Lady,* and household and office "help" in the United States, the cleaning ladies.

As an adjective, *woman* is generally preferred (woman doctor, reporter, engineer, bartender) if an indication of sex is called for.

⌇ Wordiness

Replace the wordy expression with a more compact and exact one.

There are two cures for wordiness—surgery and treatment. Surgery means cutting out words. Treatment means revising or rewriting.

1. Cut out deadwood, the type of wordiness that contributes nothing but clutter:

> At [the age of] forty he was a handsome [looking] man.
> In [the case of] television commercials, stereotypes are everywhere.
> The writer is a member of a cultural minority because [of the fact that] he is a writer.
> The architecture [of the buildings] and the landscaping [of the grounds] speak of town pride.
> [It also happened that] we were the same age.
> He kept things moving in [the field of] basset breeding throughout [the entirety of] his career.

The most common deadwood consists of unnecessary phrases like "green *in color*," "seven *in number*," "rectangular *in shape*" and clichés like "in the business world" and "in the field of economics," which you may use without thinking. Good writing requires thought. When you revise a first draft, look closely at every phrase. Does "green in color" mean any more than "green"? Doesn't "in business" say everything that "in the world of business" says?

Sometimes a phrase that contributes nothing to the meaning of a sentence nevertheless fits its rhythm or has some other stylistic justification. Perhaps adding "in my life" to "for the first time" provides a desired emphasis. But often long-windedness seems to have its own appeal. The phrase "at this moment in time," used repeatedly by witnesses before the Watergate investigating committee in 1974, was widely ridiculed but also widely adopted. It survives today as living deadwood.

As a rule simply eliminating deadwood is a step toward a compact, direct, honest prose style.

2. Compress inflated passages. When deadwood is involved, no replacement is necessary, but loose, unfocused expression often demands rewriting:

> The reason that I'm telling all this is because I want to demonstrate in the clearest way possible that the cultural background of my family was of such a nature as to encourage my interest in the reading of books, magazines, etc.
>
> *Rewritten:* All this shows that my family background encouraged me to read.

Using unnecessary words produces flabby writing. You can often improve a first draft greatly by reducing long-winded phrases and other circumlocutions to single words that are more direct, more emphatic, and at least as clear:

Instead of	in this day and age	today
	at this point in time	now
	during the time that	while
	in the event that	if
	at the conclusion of	after

Combinations of adverbs and participles—common in technical and pseudo-technical writing—should be reduced whenever possible to adjectives alone: not "factually oriented" but "factual"; not "behaviorally related" but "behavioral."

wo Word order

Change the order of words or other elements to make the meaning clear or the phrasing more natural or more emphatic.

The placing of words and word groups in a sentence is the most important means of showing their grammatical relationships. Word order plays a major role in style, particularly in achieving emphasis.

1. Interrupted constructions. Keep your subjects close to your verbs. When a word or words interrupt a construction, the effect is usually clumsy unless the interrupter deserves special emphasis:

> ***Between subject and verb:*** Newspaper headlines *in these trying and confused times* are continually intensifying our fears.
>
> ***More natural:*** In these trying and confused times, newspaper headlines are . . .

2. Wandering modifiers. Keep your modifiers close to the words they modify. When modifiers are separated from their headwords, the result is frequently awkward, sometimes misleading:

> Bob recovered from exhaustion plus what apparently was a bug making the rounds following two days' bedrest.—Grace Lichtenstein, *New York Times*
> ***Better:*** Following two days' bedrest, Bob . . .
>
> Her uncle, King Leopold, was even unable to influence her.
> ***Better:*** Even her uncle . . .
>
> I decided that if I moved in the direction of the apple tree growing beside the fence calmly, I might make it before the bull charged.
> ***Better:*** . . . moved calmly in the direction . . .

3. Word order and emphasis. Don't change normal word order unless you have a reason for doing so. As a rule an element shifted from its usual position receives increased emphasis, as when the object is put before subject and verb:

Object first: I was surprised to find Salinger's novel on the list. *That book* I read when I was fourteen.

Predicate adjective first: Lucky are the ones who need no longer worry.

See **Ambiguity, Dangling modifiers.**

Wordplay

Some of the pleasure in writing and in reading comes from an unexpected variation of a familiar phrase. Here "everything going for it" is freshened:

> The stoat (also known as ermine or short-tailed weasel) seems to have everything going against it during the winter.—Mikael Sandell, *Natural History*

The same word used in different senses can give a witty turn to a sentence:

> Whoever is chosen to moderate [a debate] must not be unduly moderate.—Walter Goodman, *New York Times*

And the same sounds in different words can please as they inform:

> The author, dispassionate and compassionate . . .—Earl W. Count, *Key Reporter*

Wordplay has its hazards. When its main purpose is to show off the writer's versatility, the reader is likely to react negatively. Wordplay should reinforce meaning, not distract from it.

world

Inflated phrases with *world*—"the business world," "the fashion world," "the world of science" (or economics or politics or athletics)—can usually be collapsed: After graduation he went into [the world of] advertising. "Today's modern world" means "today." In other cases more specific language is preferable: This is especially true in the world of jazz [*better:* among jazz musicians]. *Area, field,* and *realm* are misused in the same way.

would, should

In indirect discourse, *shall* as well as *will* is likely to be reported as *would:* She said, "We shall see"; She said that we would see. See *should, would.*

would have

Would should not be joined to *have* in a conditional clause: If she *would have known* where he lived, she would not have asked for his address. In this case, the standard verb form is *had:* If she *had known* where he lived . . . Avoid piled-on conditionals. See **Conditional clauses.**

   Would of for *would have* is nonstandard.

ww   Wrong word

Replace the word marked with a word that says what you mean.

No word is right or wrong in itself. As a correction symbol, *ww* means that the word does not convey a meaning that makes sense in the context. In the sentence "What he said showed real comprehensibility of the problems of Asia," *comprehensibility* doesn't make sense; it's the wrong word. *Comprehension* (or *understanding*) would be the right word. In "Some people remain stagnant to the lessons of life," *stagnant* needs to be replaced—possibly by *oblivious.* In "I remember explicitly my first puff," *clearly* or *vividly* would be a good choice to replace *explicitly.* Errors like these occur when you use words without being sure of their meaning, when you confuse words of similar sound, or when you simply write too hurriedly and fail to proofread your work. Sometimes a spelling is so wide of the mark (*bonified* for *bona fide*) that a baffled corrector marks it *ww* or *mng.* See **Careless mistakes; Meaning; precedence, precedent.**

X

X   Correct the obvious error.

See **Careless mistakes.**

Xmas

X is the first letter in the Greek word for *Christ.* It's been used for centuries as an abbreviation in the word *Xmas,* pronounced exactly like *Christmas.* Today, however, *Xmas* is most likely to be pronounced *eks mus,* and for many its popularity with advertisers has given it unpleasant commercial connotations. Except for purposes of irony, *Xmas* is inappropriate in serious writing.

yet

Yet is both an adverb (The books haven't come yet) and a coordinating conjunction roughly equivalent to *but:* His speech was almost unintelligible, *yet* I found I enjoyed it. *But* is less formal and much more common.

you

In giving instructions, as in a how to paper, *you* is often a good stylistic choice: Then you glue your bottom strip *or* Then glue your bottom strip. It's better than repeated use of the passive: The bottom strip is then glued. As an impersonal pronoun, *you* is more common than *one* in general usage and not at all rare in formal:

> In a sense, Richard III, as Shakespeare sees him, is a little boy who has found out that God does not strike you dead when you tell a lie.—Arnold Edinborough, *Shakespeare Quarterly*

> There are at least three ways to treat any philosophical work: (1) You may inquire into its background. . . .—Frederick Sontag, *Journal of Religion*

Writers should avoid switching back and forth between *you* and *one* and should take care that their *you, your* is clearly indefinite, not personal. "Your parents place far too much emphasis on wealth and social status" might better begin "Our parents" or simply "Parents."
    See **one, they.**

youth

As a collective noun, *youth* meaning "young people in general" can be followed by either singular or plural verbs and pronouns. In American usage the singular construction is much more common: "Russian youth wants to avoid military conscription as sincerely as American youth does" (George Feifer, *New York Times Magazine*). But when *the* precedes *youth*, a plural verb is often desirable to make clear that more than a single person is meant: The increase in tuition made education too expensive for the youth (*better:* young people) who were most in need of it.
    Though the collective use includes both sexes, *a youth* ordinarily refers to a young man, and the usual plural is *youths.*
    Youth isn't a comfortable word for either a group or an individual. *Young people, adolescents, young men and women, girls and boys, boy(s),* or *young man* (or *men*) is often a better choice.
    See **kid.**

√ **A correction symbol indicating approval—"good idea," "well expressed," and so on.**

Correction Chart

To the student: When one of these correction symbols calls attention to a weakness in your writing, look up the *Index* entry that discusses the problem, and make the revision. The symbols in the chart are arranged alphabetically; page numbers for the entries follow the instructions.

ab Write out this word. Or use the standard abbreviation. 3

abst Make this word or passage more concrete or more specific. 6

adj Reconsider your choice of adjective, 10

adv Correct the form or change the position of the adverb. Or reconsider your choice of adverb. 12

agr Make the verb agree with its subject or the pronoun with its antecedent. 14

amb Make your meaning unmistakable. 20

apos ⌄ Insert an apostrophe. Or remove apostrophe. 26

beg Revise the beginning of your paper to make it lead more directly and smoothly into your subject or to stir your reader's interest. 33

cap Capitalize the word marked. 43

case Correct the mistake in case. 46

coh Make clear the relation between the parts of this sentence or between these sentences or paragraphs. 51

colon ⌃ Use a colon here. Or reconsider the use of this colon. 53

comma ⌃ Insert or remove comma here: C_1 between independent clauses, 56; C_2 with preceding and following elements, 57; C_3 with nonrestrictive modifiers, 58; C_4 with interrupting and parenthetical words and phrases, 58; C_5 in lists and series, 59; C_6 for clarity, 60; C_7 for emphasis,

60; C_8 between main sentence elements, 61; C_9 in conventional practice, 61; C_{10} with other marks of punctuation, 61

comp Correct the error in comparing this adjective or adverb. 64

conj Make this conjunction more accurate or more appropriate to the style of the passage. 69

coord Correct the faulty coordination. 75

cs Correct the comma splice. 62

d Replace this word with one that is more exact, more appropriate, or more effective. 89

dm Revise the sentence so that the expression marked is clearly related to the word it is intended to modify. 79

det Develop this passage more fully by giving pertinent details. 87

div Divide the word between syllables. 94

emph Strengthen the emphasis of this passage. 100

end Revise the ending of your paper to round out the discussion. 101

fig Replace this trite, inconsistent, or inappropriate figure of speech. 110

form Make this word or passage less formal, more appropriate to your style, subject, and audience. 114

frag Make this construction a grammatically complete sentence. Or join it to a neighboring sentence. 116

glos See this *Index* for an entry on the word marked.